On Interpretive Conflict

On Interpretive Conflict

JOHN FROW

The University of Chicago Press ❋ *Chicago and London*

The University of Chicago Press, Chicago 60637
The University of Chicago Press, Ltd., London
© 2019 by The University of Chicago
 For more information, contact the
University of Chicago Press, 1427 East 60th Street, Chicago, IL
60637.
Published 2019
Printed in the United States of America

28 27 26 25 24 23 22 21 20 19   1 2 3 4 5

ISBN-13: 978-0-226-61395-6 (cloth)
ISBN-13: 978-0-226-61400-7 (paper)
ISBN-13: 978-0-226-61414-4 (e-book)
DOI: https://doi.org/10.7208/chicago/9780226614144.001.0001

An earlier version of chapter 1 appeared in *New Literary History*
41, no. 1 (Winter 2016): 83–107. Copyright © 2016 Johns Hopkins
University Press.

Library of Congress Cataloging-in-Publication Data

Names: Frow, John, 1948– author.
Title: On interpretive conflict / John Frow.
Description: Chicago ; London : The University of Chicago
    Press, 2019. | Includes bibliographical references and index.
Identifiers: LCCN 2018060152 | ISBN 9780226613956 (cloth :
    alk. paper) | ISBN 9780226614007 (pbk. : alk. paper) |
    ISBN 9780226614144 (e-book)
Subjects: LCSH: Hermeneutics. | Criticism. | Gun control—
    United States. | Antisemitism. | Iconoclasm. | Climatic
    changes.
Classification: LCC BD241 .F769 2019 | DDC 303.3—dc23
LC record available at https://lccn.loc.gov/2018060152

♾ This paper meets the requirements of ANSI/NISO Z39.48-1992
(Permanence of Paper).

Contents

Acknowledgments

To the colleagues, friends, and loved ones who contributed, directly or indirectly, with intellectual and emotional support, to the making of this book.

Corrinne, Julie, Chris, Steven, and all the rest of you at the University of Alberta, where much of this book was delivered as a course of public lectures, for your smart feedback and your warm hospitality.

The two anonymous readers at the University of Chicago Press, for your constructive comments. Alan and Randy. Tamara, for your meticulous editing.

Georg, who knows the maths. Horst, who gets Kant.

Tony, Mark, Justin, Simon, Anne, Ken, Anna, Melissa, Nick, Ian, Kate, Steve, Meaghan, Stephen, Julian, Peter, Vanessa, Lesley.

My colleagues and students at the University of Sydney.

Toby, Naomi, Molly, Jimmy, Eleanor, Chris, Kai, Lotte, Clara, Alex, Samara, Bethany, Jonas, Matthew, Johanna.

Sandra.

In memoriam Ross Chambers: teacher and friend.

Introduction:
Institutions of Interpretation

In Franz Kafka's story "The Problem of Our Laws," the narrator outlines the paradox that the laws are a secret known only to the nobles who rule us. These laws have nevertheless been extensively interpreted; indeed, this interpretive tradition is so ancient that it has itself become a law, leaving almost no room for further interpretation. But in fact the laws may not even exist: all we have to go on is a tradition that says they exist and were entrusted to the nobility, but it is of the essence of the laws that they remain a secret. We can only guess at their existence from the hints written in old chronicles, and we can perhaps deduce certain principles from the conduct of the nobility. It is true that belief in the existence of the laws has done harm, but most people nevertheless believe that the remedy is to elaborate an even more extensive tradition of interpretation so that one day the laws will become clear, the law will belong to the people, and the nobility will disappear. We cannot reject belief both in the laws and in the nobility, because no one dares to reject our rulers: they are the only law we have.[1] Questions of being and questions of knowing come together in this story as functions of a class structure that generates endless interpretations of these laws that may not exist, that serve the interests only of the nobility, and that give the people a hope that they may escape the power that rules them through their belief in the laws. "The will to power interprets," wrote Nietzsche; "it defines limits, determines degrees, variations of power. . . . In fact, interpretation is itself a means of becoming master of something."[2]

The structure of interpretation represented in the story—restricted to an exclusive few (*nur einzelne*), endlessly speculative, and endowed with authority by its sheer age rather than by its grasp of a reality external to it—is something like the nightmare of an activity that feeds on itself, perpetuating an order of the world rather than changing it. Is all interpretation like this? Is all interpretation so subservient to power, so humbly paranoid, so bound to a hopeless faith that one day, when everything all at once becomes clear, the world will be transformed utterly?

This is a book about the act and the social organization of interpretation and about its relation to systems of social power. I argue that interpretation is never merely subservient to power because it is always conflictual and always overdetermined by social struggles: my examples have to do with gun control, anti-Semitism, the religious force of images, and climate change. But what could be more ridiculous than to write a book about inter-

1. Franz Kafka, "Zur Frage der Gesetze," in *Sämtliche Erzählungen*, ed. Paul Raabe (Frankfurt am Main: Fischer, 1970), 314–15; "The Problem of Our Laws," in *Franz Kafka: The Complete Short Stories*, ed. Nahum M. Glatzer (New York: Schocken, 1971), 437–38.
2. Friedrich Nietzsche, *The Will to Power*, ed. Walter Kaufman, trans. Walter Kaufman and R. J. Hollingdale (New York: Vintage, 1967), Book 3, §643. The German text reads: "Der Wille zur Macht *intepretirt* . . . er grenzt ab, bestimmt Grade, Machtverschiedenheiten . . . In Wahrheit ist Interpretation ein Mittel selbst, um Herr über Etwas zu werden." *Nietzsches Werke: Kritische Gesamtausgabe*, ed. Giorgio Colli, Mazzino Montinari, Wolfgang Müller-Lauter, and Karl Pestalozzi (Berlin: De Gruyter, 1996), Vol. VIII-1: *Nachgelassene Fragmente Herbst 1885 bis Herbst 1887*, 137, Aphorism 11027.

pretation? The term includes a multitude of the most esoteric and the most fundamental activities of human life, from the reading of the entrails of birds to the analysis of medical images to the million tiny ways in which we try to make sense of other people's actions (and our own) and of the complex wholes into which we fit them; from the scientific analysis of physical systems like the weather or cosmic or subatomic space to the rating of restaurants or television programs or the construction and construal of social data like unemployment figures or the bureaucratic evaluation of case files. Interpretation is endemic to the human condition, to our apprehension of otherness, our need to make sense of a world that exceeds and constantly frustrates our ability to predict it and control it. And it may even be delegated to nonhuman interpreters: web cookies, social media algorithms, recidivism algorithms used in sentencing prisoners, and programs that buy and sell shares on the stock exchange are all interpretive structures that sort meanings and values according to preestablished criteria.

So what do I mean by interpretation, and where do I draw its limits? Should it be restricted to textual exegesis and the discovery of hidden or implicit meanings—a matter of codes and keys—or broadened to include any act of making sense of something that's not immediately clear? A working definition, which I hope will be progressively clarified in the course of this introduction, might be that interpretation is a procedure that takes place within a formally or informally structured framework, and in a context of uncertainty or indeterminacy, for imputing intention or pattern to an object or an event or a set of data by placing it within an ordered series. The imputation may have an affective or an evaluative as well as a semantic form, or it may simply result in an action; it sorts what matters from what does not, and it engenders possible consequences.

As a matter of principle I want to work with an inclusive sense of interpretation, extending it beyond exegesis to the complex of knowing, interpreting, judging, valuing, feeling, and consequentially acting which works as an inseparable whole in every act of making sense of things. In practice, this book is largely restricted to rather traditional kinds of interpretation: the judicial reading of a constitutional amendment, the modeling of climate systems, theatrical interpretations of a play, and the judgments and emotions involved in iconoclasm and the placing of objects in an art museum. My argument is not about the *nature* or the *foundations* of interpretation and judgment, and it is not concerned with the traditional hermeneutic question of how to interpret *correctly*. It is about the frameworks that construct interpretable objects and enable and contain interpretation and the conflict of interpretations, and it is about the institutional and material machineries that sustain these frameworks and these conflicts.

II

The word Kafka uses for "interpretation" is *Auslegung*, which has the sense of an explication or exegesis, but more literally of a "laying out": that is, an analysis, a separation of something into discrete parts that are opened out to inspection; an unpacking of a condensed or folded meaning. He could also have used the word *Deutung*, as in Freud's *Die Traumdeutung*, or *The Interpretation of Dreams*. That word's etymology is obscure and contested; it may go back to ancient Germanic words for "a people" (with the sense of "vernacular meaning") or for "strength," but it also has a core bodily sense of "pointing [out] with a finger": showing where exactly something is located in relation to my own body.

Alternatively, Kafka could have used the word that German shares with English and the Romance languages: *Interpretation*. In English, the two most directly relevant senses of "interpretation" registered in the *Oxford English Dictionary* are "to expound the meaning of (something abstruse or mysterious); to render (words, writings, an author, etc.) clear or explicit; to elucidate; to explain" and "to make out the meaning of, explain to oneself." The Online Etymology Dictionary gives the sense "expound the meaning of, render clear or explicit." And Wiktionary defines the word more expansively as "to explain or tell the meaning of;

to translate orally into intelligible or familiar language or terms, applied especially to language, but also to dreams, signs, conduct, mysteries, etc."[3]

Etymologically, the word goes back through Middle English and Old French to the Latin *interpres*, "an agent, broker, explainer, interpreter, negotiator," made up of *inter-*, "between," and *-pres*, which is probably also the root of Latin *pretium*, "price." That Latin root is in turn referred by these three dictionaries to different points in the family of derivations from Proto-Indo-European (PIE): the Sanskrit *prath-*, "to spread abroad"; the hypothetical PIE root **per*, a preposition indicating motion away from the body of the speaker and toward the body of another, with a secondary sense of "to traffic in, sell"; and a connection with Ancient Greek *phrázein*, "to point out, show, explain, declare, speak," from which are derived *phradé* ("understanding") and *phrásis* ("speech"). The concept of interpretation is thus bound up with those of mediation, of selling or distributing, and of translation from one language to another. It indicates not just a gathering of sense toward me, a making clear to myself, but a sending forth, a distribution of sense.

The first citation for "interpretation" in the *Oxford English Dictionary* is Wycliffe, 1383, translating the book of Daniel: "I herde of thee, that thou mayst interprete derke thingis, and vnbynde bounden thingis." The words are taken from the story of Belshazzar's feast. In the fifth chapter of Daniel, the Babylonian king Belshazzar, holding a great celebration for his family, his retainers, and his subjects, is drinking from the golden vessels stolen from the temple in Jerusalem by his father (more accurately, his predecessor), Nebuchadnezzar, when he sees a disembodied hand writing on a wall; his counselors cannot understand the words and Daniel is brought to the king to interpret them. Belshazzar says:

3. See the Oxford English Dictionary (http://www.oed.com), the Online Etymology Dictionary (http://www.etymonline.com), and Wiktionary (http://www.wiktionary.org).

And now the wise men, the astrologers, have been brought in before me, that they should read this writing, and make known unto me the interpretation thereof: but they could not shew the interpretation of the thing:

And I have heard of thee, that thou canst make interpretations, and dissolve doubts: now if thou canst read the writing, and make known to me the interpretation thereof, thou shalt be clothed with scarlet, and have a chain of gold about thy neck, and shalt be the third ruler in the kingdom.

Then Daniel answered and said before the king, Let thy gifts be to thyself, and give thy rewards to another; yet I will read the writing unto the king, and make known to him the interpretation.

(Daniel 5:16–17 [KJV])

After describing the religious failings of both Nebuchadnezzar and Belshazzar, Daniel lists the words written and gives his interpretation of them:

And this is the writing that was written, MENE, MENE, TEKEL, UPHARSIN.

This is the interpretation of the thing: MENE; God hath numbered thy kingdom, and finished it.

TEKEL; Thou art weighed in the balances, and art found wanting.

PERES; Thy kingdom is divided, and given to the Medes and Persians.

(Daniel 5:25–28)

The words Daniel reads are in Aramaic and denote a sequence of weights that function as coinage values: the *minah*, which can also mean "counted" (*menāh*); the *tekel* or *shekel*, which can also mean "weighed" (*teqilta*); and the *peres*, of which *u-pharsin* or *parsin* is the plural form; it can mean "divided" (*perisāt*), or a half minah, and can also mean "Persia" (*Pārās*).[4] Daniel thus first gives a punning interpretation based on the names of the coins: numbered, numbered, weighed, divided; and then an expanded figurative interpretation: the days of your kingdom are num-

---

4. M. Clermont-Ganneau, "Mene, Mene, Tekel, Peres, and the Feast of Belshazzar," trans. Robert W. Rogers, *Hebraica* 3, no. 2 (1887), 88.

bered; you have been measured and found wanting; the kingdom will be divided between the Medes and Persians.

Daniel's authority for this interpretation is his ability to divine the intentions of God. This is a useful power for any prophet to have, since it cannot be challenged and since it allows him to silence those wise men and astrologers who cannot read the inscriptions on the wall; Belshazzar himself seems to be illiterate, since Daniel must first read the words to him before offering his interpretation. But Daniel's act of interpretation also turns out to be performative, for at the end of this book we read a terse description of what follows it:

> In that night was Belshazzar the king of the Chaldeans slain.
> And Darius the Median took the kingdom, being about threescore and two years old.
>
> (Daniel 5:30–31)

Reading the signs, divining a hidden order behind the inscrutable surface of things, is thus a source of power—in this case a power that is intimately bound up with the literacy of the scribe and with his ability to refuse the king's gifts.[5] The notion of an "interpretation" here designates the construal of a meaning that is concealed in plain sight. It is a central part of both the activities described in many religious texts (the activities of interpreters of dreams, oracles, sacred texts, or natural signs who have access to things hidden from ordinary men and women) and the way in which religious texts are treated in many cultures: as coded sources of a wisdom not available to ordinary men and women.

A venerable Enlightenment tradition has long since seen through this use of divination as a source of clerical power and replaced it with its own mythologies, of which the demystification of superstition (or the critique of ideology) is perhaps the most important. This sense of *interpretation* as critique is the currently prevalent understanding of the term, and it accounts for

---

5. Cf. Donald C. Polaski, "*Mene, Mene, Tekel, Parsin*: Writing and Resistance in Daniel 5 and 6," *Journal of Biblical Literature* 123, no. 4 (2004), 654–55.

much of the hostility with which the concept is viewed. The key formation here is the biblical criticism that, starting with Spinoza and accelerating with the historical philology of the early nineteenth century, begins to read the Bible not as the word of God but as a composite document reflecting the intentions and interests of men and the social groups to which they belong. The hermeneutic method that develops from this critical method then flows into the analysis of literary and historical texts as the disciplines of philology and history develop their increasingly sophisticated and reflexive methodologies in the course of the nineteenth and twentieth centuries, and it also informs the skeptical methodologies of sociology, anthropology, and the other social sciences.

The core sense of interpretation across these disciplines is the act of translation from the implicit to the explicit of a "meaning" that lies waiting to be unlocked from "texts and messages that already, if only darkly or evasively, seem gravid with utterance."[6] Occupying the gap within the text between its manifest and its implicate orders, the interpreter makes clear both what was obscure and the fact of its obscurity: he or she establishes the object retrospectively as having been in need of explication, and thereby ascribes to him- or herself (just as Daniel does in relation to the wise men and astrologers) an epistemological privilege vis-à-vis less expert readers. The task of the interpreter, reading between the lines and against the grain, is "to expose hidden truths and draw out unflattering and counterintuitive meanings that others fail to see."[7]

It is in order to reject that assumption of privileged insight that writers in the French poststructuralist tradition consistently refuse what they take to be the hermeneutic problematic of *explication de texte*—that Foucault, for example, will claim that "as far as possible I have tried to get rid of the principle of exegesis, of commentary; I have tried never to know the non-said which was

6. Stephen Connor, "Spelling Things Out," *New Literary History* 45, no. 2 (2014), 183.

7. Rita Felski, *The Limits of Critique* (Chicago: University of Chicago Press, 2015), 1.

present or absent in the texture of the text itself."[8] Luc Boltanski mounts a parallel argument against the assumption made by critical sociology that social actors perform under conditions of illusion (Bourdieu's *illusio*) and under the determinant influence of structures that can be unmasked, thus setting up an asymmetry between deceived social actors and the sociologist who has mastery of the truth of their situation.[9] And Bruno Latour argues that the tradition of viewing scientific "facts" through the lens of their linguistic and social conditions of possibility ("critique" in the Kantian sense) has played into the hands of conspiracy theorists—either naive or cynical—who have used it to undermine the "hard-won evidence" of climate change and other crucial "matters of concern."[10]

In contemporary literary studies, perhaps ever since Susan Sontag's polemical call to replace "a hermeneutics" with "an erotics of art,"[11] the critique of critique has become a central moment of methodological reflection. Critical reading, with its commitment to "the unbearable knowingness of skepticism"[12]—to "analytical detachment, critical vigilance, guarded suspicion,"[13] and pervasive irony—has come to look like the self-serving assertion of the expertise of an intellectual elite, as well as projecting a pseudo-politics which assumes that the close reading of a text can lay bare "its boldly subverting or cravenly sustaining the status quo." Literary texts are deciphered "as a symptom, mirror, index, or antithesis of some larger social structure—as if there

8. Michel Foucault, *Lectures on the Will to Know: Lectures at the Collège de France 1970/71*, ed. Daniel Defert, trans. Graham Burchell (New York: Palgrave Macmillan, 2013), 198.

9. Luc Boltanski, *On Critique: A Sociology of Emancipation*, trans. Gregory Elliott (Cambridge, UK: Polity Press, 2011), 20–21.

10. Bruno Latour, "Why Has Critique Run Out of Steam? From Matters of Fact to Matters of Concern," *Critical Inquiry* 30 (Winter 2004), 227.

11. Susan Sontag, *Against Interpretation, and Other Essays* (New York: Dell, 1969), 23.

12. Toril Moi, *Revolution of the Ordinary: Literary Studies after Wittgenstein, Austin, and Cavell* (Chicago: University of Chicago Press, 2017), 217; Moi contrasts "knowingness" with "a practice of acknowledgment" (216).

13. Rita Felski, *Uses of Literature* (Malden, MA: Blackwell, 2008), 2.

were an essential system of correspondences knotting a text into an overarching canopy of domination,"[14] and as if that act of decipherment were itself a kind of political activism, opening a conduit for the voices of the oppressed.

The archetypal interpreter, in this polemic, is the trained and disciplined reader who scrutinizes texts closely in order to penetrate their surface, to strip away their masks, to reveal a truth that must be won from them by the self-denying labor of hermeneutic suspicion. The metalanguages of Marxism and psychoanalysis, for example, work with a symptomatic model of interpretation that takes meaning to be "hidden, repressed, deep, and in need of detection and disclosure by an interpreter."[15] Against this complex of metaphors, alternative accounts of reading have proliferated: surface reading, distant reading, reparative reading, postcritical reading, reverential reading. . . . For example, Franco Moretti's influential development of forms of quantitative analysis that "share a clear preference for explanation over interpretation; or perhaps, better, for the explanation of general structures over the interpretation of individual texts,"[16] takes novelistic genres as given and then derives structures from large data sets organized around those genres in such a way that literary history can be conceived as an objective account of patterns and trends.

But of course the morphological categories that make quantitative analysis possible in the first place are never simply there to be observed and described; they are constituted in an interpretive

14. Felski, *The Limits of Critique*, 11.

15. Stephen Best and Sharon Marcus, "Surface Reading: An Introduction," *Representations* 108 (2009), 1. This characterization ignores Freud's account of the transferential construction of meaning (which, in the reciprocity of transference and countertransference, undermines the very possibility of a masterful "interpretation") and Marx's argument that ideologies are "forms of thought which are socially valid [*gültig*], and therefore objective, for the relations of production belonging to this historically determinate mode of social production" (a statement that undermines the very possibility of a masterful "ideology critique") (Karl Marx, *Capital: A Critique of Political Economy*, I, trans. Ben Fowkes [Harmondsworth, UK: Penguin, 1976], 169).

16. Franco Moretti, *Graphs, Maps, Trees: Abstract Models for a Literary History* (London: Verso, 2005), 91.

encounter and by means of an interpretive decision. In the same way, any attempt to create a "positive" knowledge of natural or historical events, processes, or systems must first frame them as such; as I argue in the final chapter of this book, even for the natural sciences and those social sciences that seek to emulate them, there is no knowledge that is not interpretive in some degree and in ways specific to the different disciplines.

Thus, as Rita Felski argues, these alternative models of reading (of which she herself espouses two, the postcritical and the reverential) remain, inescapably and indeed unproblematically, within the sphere of interpretation, and metaphors of depth or latency need not signify repression or occlusion:

> All texts teem with meanings that are covert or implied: the shadowy presence of other forms or genres, the traces and residues of their historical moment, the many-layered connotations of words and combinations of words. All texts mean more than they say, inspiring critics to elaborate on the elliptical, to expound on the implicit. Interpretation just is this act of drawing out the nonobvious.[17]

A stronger argument against interpretation is perhaps simply the fact that we live in a society of the open secret, in a world filled, on the one hand, with lies so blatant that they can be uttered without shame or any expectation that their exposure will matter, and, on the other, with an algorithmically composed electronic archive so vast that it holds details of every aspect of our lives and our activities and makes them available for corporations to sell us to advertisers and to agencies of the state for ubiquitous surveillance. Information interprets us. Everyone knows this. Our interpretations are seemingly without weight, and they contain no revelations.

Yet there is no escaping the imperative to interpret. Unless we are willing to abandon altogether the making of normative distinctions on the basis of field-specific judgments of truth or value, we have no choice but to engage in interpretive conflict

---

17. Felski, *The Limits of Critique*, 57.

and, as intellectuals, to explore the ramifications of interpretive systems. This book seeks to develop a descriptive account of the organization of information and of the modes and infrastructures of its interpretation, while recognizing that any such description always comes from somewhere, is always in some sense self-interested, and always derives from a will to power. If the problem of our laws is that they may not exist, it is nevertheless crucial to come to terms with the burning desire for their existence that is enacted in the tradition of interpretation and in our guesses at what, if anything, that tradition might entail.

III

Daniel can interpret the writing on the wall because he is able to divine an intention that lies behind and makes coherent sense of an apparently arbitrary inscription. The ascription of intention is the core strategy of all textual interpretation, but it is a problematic one because intention can only be imputed, never witnessed. In order to begin mapping out an account of the way the objects and methods of interpretation are systematically constructed and make possible specific kinds of interpretive conflict, I want to begin with two sets of arguments about intention elaborated through the conceptual and rhetorical apparatus of analytic philosophy, before moving on to explore the institutions of interpretation within and between which interpretive conflict takes place.

The first argument is that of the historian Quentin Skinner, in an early essay on methodology.[18] Skinner identifies two domi-

---

18. Quentin Skinner, "Meaning and Understanding in the History of Ideas," *History and Theory* 8, no. 1 (1969), 3–53; hereafter cited in the text. Skinner's later work shifts more explicitly—and in a Diltheyan formulation with deeply problematic underpinnings—away from *interpretation*, "if by that term we understand the process of analysing or deconstructing texts and passing judgement on their worth," towards *explanation*, "the attempt to determine why the works I am considering possess their distinctive characteristics"; Skinner, "Introduction," *Forensic Shakespeare* (Oxford: Oxford University Press, 2014), 2, and more generally in Skinner, *Visions of Politics*, vol. 1, *Regarding Method* (Cambridge: Cambridge University Press, 2002).

nant approaches to determining the meaning of historical texts: one textual, arguing for the autonomy of textual meaning, the other contextual, appealing to the role of "religious, political, and economic factors."[19] The dilemma for textualism is the impossibility of any clear separation between what a writer said and our own expectations of what he must have been saying. Our reading of past texts is unavoidably determined by what R. G. Collingwood called the "constellations of absolute presuppositions" by which the thought of any period is organized;[20] if we ignore the structured organization of our own expectations, we are liable to impute anachronistic patterns of thought to past writers, to hypostatize a doctrine by finding it immanent in texts where it is not actually enunciated, or to conceive of texts teleologically as premonitions or forerunners of later textual traditions. A writer who does not articulate a recognizable doctrine may be reproached for his failure to do so: Machiavelli, Hobbes, and Locke may be accused of not adequately formulating democratic doctrines, for example. Retrospective analysis may attribute a consistency to past bodies of thought which writes out their internal contradictions, hesitations, and incoherence. And texts may be read proleptically: Petrarch is said to initiate the Renaissance, Plato or Rousseau are cast as forerunners of twentieth-century totalitarianism.

The logically cogent argument against such temporal falsifications is, Skinner writes, the "special authority" that an agent has over his own intentions (28). In consequence,

19. These are, of course, traditional alternatives within the hermeneutic tradition: Spinoza, for example, insists, in chapter 7 of the *Tractatus*, that Scripture should be interpreted "by allowing no other principles or data for the interpretation of Scripture and study of its contents except those that can be gathered only from Scripture itself and from a historical study of Scripture"—except in cases of ambiguity or obscurity, in which case we may have recourse to linguistic usage, to the distinction between literal and metaphoric language, and to the historical circumstances and the "life, character and pursuits of the author of every book." Baruch Spinoza, *Theological-Political Treatise, Complete Works*, trans. Samuel Shirley (Indianapolis: Hackett, 2002), 457, 459.

20. R. G. Collingwood, *An Essay on Metaphysics* (Oxford: Clarendon Press, 1940), cited in Skinner, "Meaning and Understanding," 7, n. 18.

something else or yet

if a given statement or other action has been performed by an agent at will, and has a meaning for him, it follows that any plausible account of what the agent meant must necessarily fall under, and make use of, the range of descriptions which the agent himself could at least in principle have applied to describe and classify what he was doing. Otherwise the resulting account, however compelling, cannot be an account of *his* statement or action. (29)

Thus, accounts of the "anticipation" of a later thinker by an earlier one are strictly meaningless, because an anticipation cannot be intended. Further, a textualist methodology is incapable of understanding "the relations between what a given writer may have *said*, and what he may be said to have meant by saying what he said" (31): oblique strategies such as irony are not discoverable by inspection of the text itself.

If, rather than a text, the proper unit of analysis is taken to be the *idea*, there is the danger of conflating different meanings of a single word, or of ignoring that words may be used "with varying and quite incompatible intentions" (37). The study of ideas rests on a confusion of the distinction between meaning and use: that is, on "a failure to distinguish between the *occurrence* of the words (phrases or *sentences*) which denote the given idea, and the *use* of the relevant sentence by a particular agent on a particular occasion with a particular intention (*his* intention) to make a particular *statement*" (37).[21] The history of ideas has little time for agents making statements, which means we can't learn anything from such a history about the strategic purposes for which the statements were employed, nor, therefore, acquire any historical understanding of "what *point* a given expression might have had for the agents who used it, or what range of uses the expression itself could sustain" (38).

An alternative, contextual methodology would seek to avoid

21. The distinction between sentences and statements is drawn from P. F. Strawson, but it also recalls Foucault's parallel yet radically dissimilar distinction, *detaching* the statement from particular agents and intentions, in *The Archaeology of Knowledge*, published in the same year as Skinner's essay.

anachronism by understanding ideas as a response to circumstances, and thus by understanding all of the occasions and activities in which particular forms of words might have been used. But this approach leads either to circularity (ideas and context shape each other) or to a reduction of ideas to context. It is doubtful "whether a knowledge of the causes of an action is really equivalent to an understanding of the action itself" because, again, such an understanding requires that we get "the *point* of the action for the agent who performed it" (44). Every statement or action presupposes both an intention to have done it (a "cause") and "an intention in doing it, which cannot be a cause, but which must be grasped if the action itself is to be correctly characterized and so understood" (45). What Skinner means by the "point" of an action is its illocutionary force, the speaker's intention in producing it. This force is "co-ordinate with the meaning of the utterance itself, *and yet* essential to grasp in order to understand it" (46): it is not the same as the statement's meaning, then, but a prerequisite for identifying that meaning. A contextual study has no means of discovering illocutionary force. Skinner's example here is the question of whether Machiavelli's advice that a prince should learn not to be virtuous is a commonplace or a shocking novelty, sustaining or subverting a moral precept. Understanding its illocutionary force requires us to grasp "the intended force of the utterance in the mind of the agent who uttered it" (46); only one of these interpretations can be correct, and a correct interpretation cannot be reached either by study of the utterance itself (the meaning of which is quite clear) or by a study of the social context, which could yield both readings.

The object of study thus needs to be shifted away from either intellectual biographies or "histories of ideas tracing the morphology of a given concept over time": the proper understanding of historical texts should focus on what those texts "were intended to mean, and how this meaning was intended to be taken," that is, on an "intention to be understood, and the intention that this intention should be understood, which the text itself as an intended act of communication must at least have embodied" (48). This "complex intention on the part of the author" (49) takes place within a series of alternative possibilities of utterance, and its meaning is then realized within a linguistic context that gives guidance about which meanings it might have been possible to communicate.

Now, Skinner's argument seems to me to suffer from the weaknesses that have traditionally been associated with the intentionalist tradition.[22] Although he speaks of the realization of intentions within a linguistic and rhetorical context and has written at length about early-modern uses of classical rhetoric, he has little interest in the actual language and the cultural medium within which texts are shaped. Whereas key figures in the hermeneutic tradition such as Spinoza and Schleiermacher foreground the importance of an understanding of, respectively, the Hebrew and Koine Greek languages to their interpretations of the Old and New Testaments,[23] Skinner treats texts as the linguistically transparent medium through which authorial intention shines. The "constellations of absolute presuppositions" that he identifies as shaping *present* understanding are not so applied to the past, with the effect that texts are treated as the embodiment of a singular and recoverable authorial intention rather than as being layered with presuppositions embedded in the language and the culture. That intention (both an intention "to do" and an intention "in doing") is thought of as being prior to the medium in which it finds expression, as being knowable apart from that expression, and as controlling the form of the expression. Although the assertion of the authority of intention over its textual realization

22. For literary theory the locus classicus is W. K. Wimsatt, "The Intentional Fallacy," in *The Verbal Icon: Studies in the Meaning of Poetry* (Lexington: University of Kentucky Press, 1967), 3–18. For counter-arguments, cf. E. D. Hirsch, *The Aims of Interpretation* (Chicago: University of Chicago Press, 1976), and Stephen Knapp and Walter Benn Michaels, "Against Theory," *Critical Inquiry* 8, no. 4 (1982), 723–42.

23. Spinoza, *Theological-Political Treatise*, chapter 7. Friedrich Schleiermacher bases his claim that hermeneutics can "understand the author better than he does himself" on its philological focus on the author's language, where "much . . . is unconscious that must become conscious in us." Schleiermacher, *Hermeneutics and Criticism and Other Writings*, trans. Andrew Bowie (Cambridge: Cambridge University Press, 1998), 33.

is slightly qualified (psychoanalysis is adduced as claiming to be able to give "a fuller or more convincing account of the agent's behaviour than he could give himself" [28]), it is still no more than an assertion. The counterargument, and I think the more properly historical argument, would be that texts necessarily float free of intentions and of their first historical moment, that authorial interpretations of a text have no particular privilege, and that the *per*locutionary effects of any locutionary act (its uptake by a receiver) are multiple and cannot be derived from the act's illocutionary force. Grasping the "force" of a statement is equivalent to what Foucault calls understanding the statement's place within a series of statements, and that force is never singular.

These, too, are of course assertions, but I shall try to make the case for them in the course of this book, beginning with a rather different account of intention (one that still takes its bearings from the analytic tradition), that of the art historian Michael Baxandall in *Patterns of Intention.* The book is made up of four case studies—those of the construction of the Forth Bridge in Scotland, Picasso's *Portrait of Kahnweiler*, Chardin's *A Lady Taking Tea,* and Piero della Francesca's *Baptism of Christ*—but I shall confine myself largely to the first two.

Baxandall begins by asking what the art historian's object of analysis is. We do not explain pictures in their immediacy, he argues; we interpret them only under a verbal description which is already a kind of analysis. That is to say,

> every evolved explanation of a picture includes or implies an elaborate description of that picture. The explanation of the picture then in its turn becomes part of the larger description of the picture, a way of describing things about it that would be difficult to explain in another way.[24]

If we ask what this description describes, we realize that "what one offers in a description is a representation of thinking about

24. Michael Baxandall, *Patterns of Intention: On the Historical Explanation of Pictures* (New Haven: Yale University Press, 1985), 1; hereafter cited in the text.

a picture more than a representation of a picture" (5), and the thoughts that we represent are often indirect: metaphors, accounts of the effect the picture has on us, inferences about it, and an underlying assumption that pictures are willed products of human action. Describing a picture is a form of ekphrasis: descriptions are ostensive, which means that they are not separable from their objects (they "show" their objects) but also that there is necessarily a gap between the image and its verbal description. Our recourse to words has to do in part with the fact that words can generalize and that they therefore manifest not (just) an objective quality of the picture but "an aspect of its interest," a characterization (9); the description is a part of the object to be explained and "already embodies pre-emptively explanatory elements" (11).

Historical explanation can attend to either generalities or particulars; art historians are concerned with the deposits or traces of action, whereas the general historian attends to actions and only peripherally to traces. In seeking to explain an artifact, then, "we address a thing to which the maker's intention was attached, not a documentary by-product of activity" (14); and this means that our task is to reconstruct a problem to which the artifact is "a finished and concrete solution" and the circumstances in and from which the problem was formulated (15).

This leads Baxandall to his first case study, of the causal factors governing the structure of the Forth Bridge. If we ask why the bridge took this particular form (a long, elegantly cantilevered span), we will discover a constellation of causes. The first is the physical dimensions of the problem: the geography of the Firth of Forth, the need for the bridge to withstand strong side winds, the need for it to be high enough to allow ships to pass beneath it, and so on. Second, a constellation of "cultural" facts is brought to bear on the problem: the properties and the availability of steel, available models of bridge engineering in the 1880s, and questions of the aesthetics of bridges all have long prehistories and ramifications (the collapse of the Tay Bridge in 1879, for example). Finally, there are the qualities of the chief engineer,

Benjamin Baker: his skills, training, intellect, and philosophical outlook. If (setting aside the not unimportant fact that this was necessarily a team project) we seek Baker's intention in the construction of the bridge, it will take the form of a triangle comprising the bridge, an objective set of problems, and a set of culturally determined possibilities. Importantly, Baxandall makes clear that the concept of intention does not involve "a reconstruction of the maker's intentions" as a method for interpreting an artifact (vii); rather, it designates something like a reconstruction of the objective conditions and resources of which Baker made volitional use.

In the case of Picasso's *Portrait of Kahnweiler* we assume purposefulness, or "intentiveness" (42), both in the painter and in the historical object. Intention, the "forward-leaning look of things" (42), is a relation between the object and its circumstances, and it is not necessarily an act of conscious will:

> Some of the voluntary causes I adduce may have been implicit in institutions to which the actor unreflectively acquiesced: others may have been dispositions acquired through a history of behaviour in which reflection once but no longer had a part. Genres are often a case of the first and skills are often a case of the second. In either case I may well want to expand the "intention" to take in the rationality of the institution or of the behaviour that led to the disposition: this may not have been active in the man's mind at the time of making the particular object. (42)

What a painter does, by trade, is "make marks on a plane surface in such a way that their visual interest is directed to an end" (43), where "visual interest" is a primary specification for aesthetic objects—including those produced within a religious regime, such as icons—and a secondary one for such things as bridges. Picasso in 1910 set himself a "brief" consisting of three parts: the problem of representing three-dimensional objects in two dimensions; the relation of form to color (of accidental to intrinsic qualities); and the fiction of instantaneousness, as well as the problem of how to undo it by acknowledging the painter's sustained engagement with the work. This brief, which is more generally a position-taking toward past painting, corresponds to the set of problems and resources Baker faced and worked with in constructing the Forth Bridge.

There are also significant differences from the causal account of the construction of the bridge, however: the lack of a clear distinction between conception and execution, and the fact that there is no clearly defined "problem" for Picasso to address. One factor in this causal field is, necessarily, Picasso's volition; but importantly, Baxandall writes,

> The intention to which I am committed is not an actual, particular psychological state or even a historical set of mental events inside the heads of Benjamin Baker or Picasso, in the light of which—if I knew them—I would interpret the Forth Bridge or the *Portrait of Kahnweiler.* Rather, it is primarily a general condition of rational human action which I posit in the course of arranging my circumstantial facts or moving about the triangle of re-enactment. (41)

The choices Picasso makes in 1910 are responses to a set of formal problems that are "almost as impersonal as the structural properties of steel" (47); his formulation of his brief, by contrast, is intensely personal. Yet these choices are conditioned by particular social, economic, and cultural circumstances, for which Baxandall's metaphor is the form of barter-exchange called *troc* and which involve quite literal forms of market transactions. Within the available circumstances Picasso makes particular choices which in turn help modify the art market: he abstains from the unofficial "salons" where other painters exhibit; breaking with clients of his earlier work, he begins to use dealers; and he refuses group adherence ("cubism") in favor of marketing his own work. These strategies are an integral part of the "intention" of the work.

In his concluding essay on Piero, Baxandall explores the implications of his argument for dealing with pictures that are remote in time (and therefore in culture) from us. Our interest in the intention of pictures and painters is "a means to a sharper perception of the pictures, for us. It is the picture as covered by a description *in our terms* that we are attempting to explain" (109). There is thus a tension between the understandings of observers distant in time and of participants in a culture. While we attempt heuristically to imagine ourselves into past cultures, that attempt must be followed by a scrutiny and evaluation of the intuitions and explanations that this imagining generates. That second, distancing moment "must be in our terms and external to the mental universe of the object of study. If it were not, we ourselves would not have mental access to it for the purpose of scrutiny and criticism" (111). The picture offers the participant's knowledge, an insider's knowledge which is "complex, fluid and implicit." The observer's knowledge is, comparatively, "crude, over-explicit, and uninteriorized," and it is directed to aspects of the painter's world which to us seem striking or different but would not have occupied the foreground of Piero's attention (111). Like anthropologists, we may make use of concepts formulated by native informants, but to do so is to signal precisely an encounter with "an intentional mode in which we cannot ourselves operate" (116). These two forms of knowledge do not exist in isolation from each other: because our descriptions are not separable from their object, our reading of the picture "takes its meaning and precision from the reciprocal relation between the words we offer and the present work of art" (116).

IV

To impute an intention, then, is one part of making a description of an artifact or a text in the course of making sense of it. (In the case of the analysis of historical processes or of the natural world, what we posit is not an intention but a pattern: a meaningfully ordered configuration of the data.) A description is a framework of interpretation that specifies an interest. But interests are many; there are many, although not an unlimited number of, interpretive frameworks, and thus there are many different protocols for imputing intention or pattern. Moreover, such frameworks are multiple along both a vertical (diachronic) axis and a horizontal (synchronic) axis. The realization in time of the meaning of an artifact or text happens neither solely at a singular moment of origin, as Skinner's historicism would have it, nor solely in the interplay between that past and our present. The meaning of artifacts and texts changes constantly as they enter new cultural formations; indeed, a strong form of this argument would say that the artifact or text is not itself a material object but is, rather, the sum of that historical chain of interpretations that feeds into our present and helps shape it. I return to this argument in chapter 1, in a discussion of debates between those who wish to see the meaning of the US Constitution as fixed at a point in time and those who see it as an evolutionary process, and in chapter 2, where I examine successive conventions of performance of *The Merchant of Venice* as the figure of Shylock is reimagined in the light of successive encounters with his Jewishness.

Similarly, along the "horizontal" axis, interpretation is variable by the particular areas of knowledge to which it applies and by divergent interests within each area. The "constellations of absolute presuppositions" that Skinner, following Collingwood, takes as organizing the thought of any period are not homogeneously distributed across classes and genders and races and religions and educational and age cohorts but are layered: some presuppositions are so deeply ingrained that almost everyone shares them, but many are not. Interpretive cultures are conflicted and contested, reflecting but not reducible to conflicts of interest within and between social groups. In my own work since *Marxism and Literary History* I have used the concept of the *regime of reading* to understand this differentiation of interpretive cultures and how they organize practices. In later work I introduced the corollary concept of the *regime of value*, drawing in particular on Arjun Appadurai's formulation in his introductory essay to *The Social Life of Things*.

The concept of the regime is at one level a concept of the regulatory manifold of codes and values that govern the status and possible uses of texts by different social groups. It is a logical deduction from the fact that interpretation and valuation are not individual and idiosyncratic acts but are to some extent shared within groups: that there are regularities at a macro level which indicate the operation of common norms. These norms are not "real" and they are not determinative: they are the hypothesis we need in order to make sense of behavioral regularities, and as such they have explanatory but not predictive force. Regimes are an effect of reading and an extrapolation from reading, not a preexisting structure from which interpretations can be derived (it is for this reason that I do not attempt to enumerate a fixed set of possible or existing regimes), and no interpretation or valuation exhausts the possibilities given by the regime.

Produced by, rather than preceding, the act of interpretation, the categories of "text," "writer," and "reader" have the status, at another level of specificity, not of entities but of functions within a system that makes available a limited range of interpretive and evaluative strategies. Thus, text, writer, and reader are not the stable and independent origin and conclusion of the textual process, nor is their relationship that of a constant factor to an uncontrolled variable; they are moments of a particular regime, and they shift in value as texts move (in time or across cultures) from one textual system to another.

At a third level, finally, the concept of regime has to do with the material and institutional conditions (the sociotechnical assemblages) that facilitate and constrain the discourses of meaning and value that circulate within and between regimes. These assemblages include all of those inherited problems and resources—the material and cultural constraints—the working of which makes up what Baxandall defines as the intention informing any human artifact.

If, in one sense, the concept of regime seems to involve structural regularities and a certain semantic closure, my interest is in the *conflicts* of interpretation and valuation that occur both within regimes and between them: the ways in which the precarious moment of closure is constantly contested and continuously reconstituted. Regimes can best be examined at their edges, the points where they come into conflict with other regimes.

Appadurai's conception of the regime of value as a mechanism for "the commensuration of two intensities of demand"[25] requires no necessary depth of shared cultural knowledge between the participants to an exchange: in the case of transactions across cultural boundaries, the shared knowledge may be minimal; and in a certain sense, all negotiation of meaning and value takes place across cultural boundaries and at points of social tension. Moreover, even where transactions take place within secure cultural boundaries, positional disparities between the participants may entail quite disparate perceptions of the value of objects being exchanged. Regimes of reading and value never *fully* define the positions that may be occupied within them, nor do they ever fully contain them; in Michel Callon's phrase, every act of framing opens ambivalently both inward and outward, and every framing involves a greater or lesser degree of overflow.[26]

These principles seem to me to hold generally true of all interpretive or axiological judgments: what the "mid-level" concept of regime makes possible is a way of understanding how interpretations and valuations are arrived at, the "ordered series" that make them meaningful, the transactional and institutional dimensions of our dealings with texts (or, in the case of the natural sciences, with data), and the excess of our textual transactions over the frames that constrain and organize them. It seeks to come to terms with the problem of interpretive multiplicity and the relativity of value judgments without either imposing normative standards or excluding the position of the analyst from the account it offers. It does not imply an *absolute relativism*, such that no regime could be translated into the terms of another; on the contrary, the principle of relationality requires that we think

25. Arjun Appadurai, "Introduction: Commodities and the Politics of Value," in *The Social Life of Things: Commodities in Cultural Perspective*, ed. Arjun Appadurai (Cambridge: Cambridge University Press, 1986), 14.

26. Michel Callon, "An Essay on Framing and Overflowing: Economic Externalities Revisited by Sociology," in *The Laws of the Markets*, ed. Michel Callon (Oxford: Blackwell, 1998), 244–69.

in terms of a *relative relativism*, an articulation not of pure differences between fully self-identical formations but of partial, incomplete, and constantly contested differences between formations which are themselves internally differentiated and heterogeneous.[27] Since interpretation is always about contested value, and since the struggle over the value of a text or a thing is enacted across interwoven layers of time, I assume that every interpretive and axiological framework is the site of multiple temporalities. It is this principle that constitutes the ethicopolitical dimension of interpretation: it understands the past as a function of present interests, and the present, in turn, not as a homogeneous presence but as shot through with all the pasts that a text or a thing brings to it and all the futures through which it will pass.

V

An influential alternative account of the concept of regime has been elaborated by Jacques Rancière; let me briefly differentiate my account of the term from his. Rancière's concept of the regime of art seeks to explain the discontinuous frameworks of value that govern the way works of art are constituted and identi-

---

27. The concept of interpretive regime thus does not meet Donald Davidson's criterion for full conceptual relativism, namely, that "the failure of intertranslatability is a necessary condition for difference of conceptual schemes"; Donald Davidson, "On the Very Idea of a Conceptual Scheme," *Proceedings and Addresses of the American Philosophical Association* 47 (1973–1974), 12, 20. As a number of Davidson's critics point out, however, the possibility of translation between schemes does not rule out the radical incommensurability of particular conceptual clusters: any complex cultural concept may have no equivalent between one language and another and may need to be reconstructively glossed. D. K. Henderson gives the example of the Zande word *mangu* discussed by Evans-Pritchard, which denotes both a "witchcraft substance" found in the body and the witchcraft practices that emanate from it; the concept "is embedded in a web of 'theory', and *we do not antecedently have the relevant theory*"; D. K. Henderson, "Conceptual Schemes after Davidson," in *Language, Mind and Epistemology: On Donald Davidson's Philosophy*, ed. Gerhard Preyer, Frank Siebelt, and Alexander Ulfig (Dordrecht: Kluwer, 1994), 176. I discuss questions of relativism and commensuration at greater length in *Cultural Studies and Cultural Value* (Oxford: Clarendon Press, 1995), especially 151–54.

fied. Regimes have to do with the "sensible fabric of experience" within which the event of the work takes place, and that fabric is a function of

> entirely material conditions—performance and exhibition spaces, forms of circulation and reproduction—but also modes of perception and regimes of emotion, categories that identify them, thought patterns that categorize and interpret them. These conditions make it possible for words, shapes, movements and rhythms to be felt and thought as art.[28]

The assignment of an object to the category of art, and the mode of its assignment, will thus vary according to the regime in which it is apprehended. A statue of a goddess—the first-century Roman head of Juno Ludovisi, say—may be judged in terms of its intrinsic truth as a representation of a divinity, giving rise to questions about whether a god can be represented at all, whether this is a genuine divinity, and, if it is, whether the representation is adequate and appropriate. These are *ethical* rather than aesthetic questions, and Rancière refers to the regime that frames them as an ethical regime of art.

A second, *representative* regime of art, rather than questioning the validity of the divinity figured in the statue and the faithfulness of the representation, poses questions that have to do with imitation, understood not as "a normative principle stating that art must make copies resembling their models"[29] but, rather, as the relation between *poiēsis* and *mimēsis*, "making" and "resembling." Imposing a form on matter and bringing to bear a range of expressive conventions, the statue is

> the realization of a representation—the constitution of a plausible appearance that combines the imaginary traits of divinity with the archetypes of femininity, and the monumentality of the statue with

28. Jacques Rancière, *Aisthesis: Scenes from the Aesthetic Regime of Art*, trans. Zakir Paul (London: Verso, 2013), x.

29. Jacques Rancière, *The Politics of Aesthetics: The Distribution of the Sensible*, trans. Gabriel Rockhill (London: Continuum, 2004), 21.

the expressiveness of a particular goddess endowed with the traits of a specific character.[30]

The representative regime is thus characterized by a concern with rules of decorum and with the expressive potential of the different aesthetic genres.

Finally, in an *aesthetic* regime of art, the statue is defined neither by the truth or adequacy of its conception of the goddess, nor by its conformity to the canons of representation, but by a kind of self-sufficient and noninstrumental sensory apprehension: the artwork is a mode of freedom, an activity that has no end beyond itself, and which therefore "appears as the germ of a new humanity, of a new form of individual and collective life" (32). Art is thus freed "from any specific rule, from any hierarchy of the arts, subject matter, and genres," and in this freedom it fuses with the other dimensions of life in a promise of a universal and equal humanity, "one at last in tune with the fullness of its essence" (34–35); the aesthetic regime "simultaneously establishes the autonomy of art and the identity of its forms with the forms that life uses to shape itself."[31] The model here is Schiller's concept of aesthetic play—an important influence on the early Marx and on Marcuse's aesthetics—which prefigures the breaking down of the opposition between "intelligent form and sensible matter" and of the corresponding division of labor between brain and hand.[32]

The politics (or "metapolitics") at work here is at once utopian and nostalgic: the statue is the redemption of a full humanity that once existed (in what Marx called the "childhood of humanity") but has since been lost. But this is not a "politics" in the conventional sense: it is an intervention in what Rancière calls the "distribution of the sensible," that is, in the social order

---

30. Jacques Rancière, *Aesthetics and Its Discontents*, trans. Steven Corcoran (Cambridge, UK: Polity Press, 2009), 29; hereafter cited in the text.

31. Rancière, *The Politics of Aesthetics*, 23.

32. Rancière, *Aesthetics and Its Discontents*, 31.

that divides what is common to everyone and distributes access to it—specifying, for example, who counts as a participant in the civic order and who is not counted, who speaks and who must be silent. This is a distribution of bodies, and of the things that different kinds of embodied human beings may do. One word for this distribution is (*police*;) developed as an instrument of *raison d'Etat* in the absolutist state, the concept of police covers the senses of policy, of administration, and of enforcement. It has to do with technologies of distribution of power, and Rancière opposes it to the concept of *politics*, meaning "whatever disrupts the orderings of police." As Tony Bennett puts it, such a politics

> does not play a part in the distributional struggles about the alloca-
> tion of rights and rewards across the division of humanity into dif-
> ferent occupations. It intrudes into such orderings of the social . . .
> the assertion of the equality of speaking beings. It is an intervention
> produced by those who, previously of no account, lacking any politi-
> cal or civic status, assert their rights to be seen and to be heard, and
> thus to be taken into account.[33]

Politics in this sense is quite distinct from Hannah Arendt's notion of a specific and discrete political sphere, with roles distributed according to interests and competences; and it supposes a
marked—indeed, an absolute—dichotomy between those who
"have" and those who do not have power. The embodiment of
powerlessness is the demos, "the collection of those with no title
to dominate or be dominated,"[34] but the demos is not a concrete
class or collectivity. It is "an abstract separation of a population
from itself," a "process of subjectivation" which has the function of introducing discord and heterogeneity into the ordered
distribution of the common.[35] Its point of articulation, the pure,
voiceless one, is the proletarian, and in practice, for Rancière

---

33. Tony Bennett, "Guided Freedom: Aesthetics, Tutelage and the Interpretation of
Art," in *Making Culture, Changing Society* (Abingdon, UK: Routledge, 2013), 136.

34. Jacques Rancière, "Introducing Disagreement," trans. Steven Corcoran, *Angelaki:
Journal of the Theoretical Humanities* 9, no. 3 (2004), 6.

35. Rancière, "Introducing Disagreement," 6.

this means the figure of the artisan. Rancière's major work of historical analysis, *Proletarian Nights*, gives us the words of the working-class intellectuals and poets, the tailors and journeymen and cobblers whose struggle in the revolution of 1830 is as much an aesthetic one as it is that of an organized politics.[36] This group's absolute lack of power gives rise to the absolute universality which is the principle of politics, and since that principle is founded solely on the value of equality, other struggles that we may think of as political—religious or ethnic struggles, for example—do not qualify as "real" politics.[37]

The aesthetic is thus at once a particular historical regime and a universal category of emancipation realized in "a certain suspension of the normal conditions of social experience."[38] The plenitude that is promised by the aesthetic precludes hierarchy, and it is for this reason that sociological analyses of the artwork as a vehicle of social distinction, separating class from class on the basis of taste discriminations, are invalid, or at best are valid only for the "representative" regime. Hierarchies of knowledge and competence impose a social order, and "aesthetic experience eludes the sensible distribution of roles and competences which structures the hierarchical order."[39]

How useful, then, is Rancière's conception of the various regimes of art? Not very, I think: it comes encumbered with the baggage of a Kantian aesthetics grounded in a historically anomalous conception of the subject of democratic politics, and it rests on an eschatological notion of history as the site of a future, aesthetically grounded redemption of a full humanity. Rancière's regimes have a historical existence (the aesthetic regime, for example, comes into being at the beginning of the nineteenth

36. Jacques Rancière, *Proletarian Nights: The Workers' Dream in Nineteenth-Century France*, trans. John Drury (London: Verso, 2012).

37. Jacques Rancière, "The Thinking of Dissensus: Politics and Aesthetics," in *Reading Rancière*, ed. Paul Bowman and Richard Stamp (London: Continuum, 2011), 4.

38. Jacques Rancière, "Thinking between Disciplines: An Aesthetics of Knowledge," trans. Jon Roffe, *Parrhesia* 1 (2006), 2.

39. Rancière, "Thinking between Disciplines," 4.

century and is associated with the universalization of art that finds its expression and one of its enabling conditions in the collection and exhibition of visual art in the museum);[40] but, as Hal Foster notes, Rancière retains from his Althusserian moment a fascination with the sharp discontinuities between regimes (the epistemological break that marks off one regime from another),[41] together with a lack of precision about the relation between logical structure and historical process and a total indifference to non-Western regimes of art. The three regimes—ethical, representative, and aesthetic—each correspond to a philosophy of art: respectively, those of Plato, Aristotle, and Kant. But does this mean that the ethical is almost immediately displaced by the representative regime, which then lasts (with some overlap with the ethical regime) for several millennia? Is the entire history of Western religious art to be squeezed into a Platonic doctrine of the ethical and pedagogic function of art? And are the Kantian categories of aesthetic judgment—of disinterested spectatorship performing an inner freedom—adequate to the politicized or popular cultures of modernity? I develop an alternative conception of the grounding of the aesthetic regime of modernity in the institution of the museum in chapter 3.

VI

The conception of regime that I offer here is at once more modest and more specific in its application than Rancière's (it offers no overarching narrative of historical stages), and it is more immediately focused on interpretive conflict than on the promise of a future redemption. Let me offer three examples of fundamentally incommensurable regimes of knowledge and interpretation (the more precise word here than regimes of "reading").

The first is that of conflicting understandings of a single docu-

40. Rancière, *Aisthesis*, 30.

41. Hal Foster, "What's the Problem with Critical Art?," review of Jacques Rancière, *Aisthesis, London Review of Books*, October 10, 2013, 14–15.

ment, *Te Tiriti o Waitangi* (the Treaty of Waitangi), signed in February 1840 between representatives of the British Crown and forty-six Māori *rangatira*, or chiefs, from the North Island of Aotearoa/New Zealand, and later ratified by hundreds of other *rangatira*. The document, which purports to transfer sovereignty over New Zealand from Māori to the Crown, exists in the authoritative Māori version and a number of English versions; the conflict of interpretation has to do with the translation of several key concepts, in particular, the words *kāwanatanga, rangatiratanga,* and *taonga.*

In the English versions of the Treaty, the *rangatira* cede to the Queen of England "absolutely and without reservation all the rights and powers of sovereignty" over the territories that they control, and they in turn are guaranteed the "exclusive and undisturbed possession" of their lands and property. The word that "sovereignty" translates is *kāwanatanga,* a neologism based on a phonetic rendition of "governor," *kāwana*; the concept of sovereignty has no direct equivalent in Māori. An earlier treaty, the Declaration of Independence of New Zealand, signed at Waitangi in 1835 and reaffirmed by further signatures as late as July 1839, had used the word *mana,* a complex Polynesian concept which includes a meaning something like "spiritual authority," to guarantee that "all sovereign power and authority" (*Ko te Kingitanga ko te mana*) resided "entirely and exclusively in the hereditary chiefs and heads of tribes in their collective capacity."[42] The distinction between sovereignty and the continuing rule of the chiefs (*rangatiratanga*) is not meaningful within the Māori cosmos; nor is the possibility of the alienation of land and "possessions" (*taonga,* which are spiritually tied to their owners), although that was precisely what the British envisioned: a peaceful, commercially based transfer of land to European settlers, based in the preemptive rights of the Crown.

42. Cited in D. F. McKenzie, *Oral Culture, Literacy and Print in Early New Zealand: The Treaty of Waitangi* (Wellington: Victoria University Press, 1985), 41; hereafter cited in the text.

As Donald McKenzie argues, however, the more fundamental conflict is between the interpretive regimes of a literate and an oral culture and the different ways of embedding truth in language that they embody. The preparation of a written treaty is grounded in the implausible belief that the twenty-five years of European settlement and missionary activity in New Zealand had been sufficient to establish a literate culture with radically novel understandings of the role of memory and historical time and a readiness on the part of Māori "to accept a signature as a sign of full comprehension and legal commitment, [and] to surrender the relativities of time, place and person in the oral culture to the presumed fixities of the written or printed word" (10). It entirely contradicted an oral mode of decision-making for which a written document would have been at most a component of a larger process of discussion and eventual consensus, where the written text had no overriding authority. In signing the treaty, many of the *rangatira* (of whom even those who could form a signature were functionally illiterate) "would have made complementary oral conditions which were more important than (and certainly in their own way modified) the words on the page. For the non-literate, the document and its implications were meaningless; for the barely literate, the ability to sign one's name was a trap" (40). Finally, rather than superseding the Declaration of Independence of New Zealand, the *Tiriti o Waitangi* would have been seen by Māori as continuing its guarantees of *mana* and *rangatiratanga.* But those oral discussions and understandings that constitute the full "text" of the treaty have disappeared without trace, and only the written text survives to carry its limited and contested versions of a consensus to later times.

My second example is Michael Warner's account of the universalization of the norm of "critical reading," a universalization that assumes that this Western, university-based regime, in relation to which all other modes of reading would count as "pretheoretically uncritical," is the only possible way to tie our dealings with texts to reflexive reason and a "normative discipline of subjectivity."[43] In fact, this "pious labour" (36) of critical reading has a specific history and produces specific ethical effects: as Ian Hunter long ago demonstrated, it was most fully developed within and for the late-nineteenth-century pedagogical institution of "English" and works to construct a certain kind of ethical persona, detached from the immediacy of judgment and deploying textual analysis as a form of cultivated self-scrutiny.[44]

Warner locates the intellectual origins of the regime of critical reading in the holistic biblical analysis of Locke and Spinoza, and he contrasts it with a religious regime exemplified by a reading of the scriptures by Mary Rowlandson, who was held captive by Indigenous Americans in 1676 and who took certain passages in Jeremiah to refer directly to the promise of salvation from her own captivity. Rowlandson is precisely the sort of reader against whom Locke's analytic schema was directed: uninterested in the philological resources of "analytic collation, linguistic comparison, contextual framing, or any other effort at detachment from the rhetoric of address" (31), she reads the biblical text on the assumption that it "is everywhere uniformly addressed by God, in the vernacular, to the believer" (31). She takes alighting on passages by chance to be a form of providential direction, but this is not a passive mode of reading; to the contrary, "it requires repetition, incorporation, and affective regulation" (31), and it is supported by an extensive theological apparatus and extensive instruction in devotional manuals on the correct application of scripture. Mary Rowlandson is a highly trained reader: the regime that shapes her reading, with its focus on "the elemental dyad of God and the soul as the situation of address" (31), is a rival framework to that of critical reading: not pretheoretical, strongly reflexive in its own way, but directed to different ends

43. Michael Warner, "Uncritical Reading," in *Polemic: Critical or Uncritical*, ed. Jane Gallop (New York: Routledge, 2004), 16; hereafter cited in the text.

44. Ian Hunter, *Culture and Government: The Emergence of Literary Education* (London: Macmillan, 1988).

and with a quite different understanding of how a text addresses a reader and of how intention is to be imputed to it.

My third example is drawn from Michèle Lamont's study of the mediation of evaluative criteria from different academic disciplines in the work of interdisciplinary panels. Reviewers of funding applications on such panels are required to reach a consensus on the basis of their own disciplinary criteria but also by accommodation of the criteria specific to other disciplines. In practice, they tend to develop shared rules of deliberation, which include respecting the autonomy of individual disciplines and deferring to the expertise of colleagues from other disciplines, as well as "promoting methodological pluralism and cognitive contextualization (that is, the use of discipline-relevant criteria of evaluation)."[45] Every academic discipline—it's perhaps a tautology to say it—has its own evaluative culture, its own preferred objects of analysis, and its own sense of how those objects are best to be understood. It works with implicit or explicit claims to authority and with conventions about the role of empirical data, the way in which theory frames those data, the kinds of methodological reduction that are permissible, and so on. Each, similarly, has a preferred epistemological style, which Lamont categorizes as "comprehensive" (based in *Verstehen*, attention to details, and contextual specificity), "constructivist" (attending reflexively to the locus of enunciation), "positivist," or "utilitarian." A key divide running through the humanities and social sciences has to do with the distinction between fields that acknowledge the role of interpretation in shaping the terms of analysis and fields that do not, with the key variable being perceived proximity to or distance from the natural sciences. Another divide exists between nomothetic and idiographic fields: those that seek to establish general laws and those that seek to understand particulars.

The snapshots Lamont gives of the particular disciplines are slightly caricatural, yet instantly recognizable: philosophy takes

---

45. Michèle Lamont, *How Professors Think: Inside the Curious World of Academic Judgment* (Cambridge, MA: Harvard University Press, 2009), 6; hereafter cited in the text.

an exceptionalist view of its access to truth; literary studies has undergone a crisis of legitimation, undermining its traditional object and thus its own disciplinary coherence; history, by contrast, is built on a strong agreement that what underpins good historical craftsmanship is close, patient archival work; cultural anthropology, like literary studies, has forsaken its traditional object, "primitive societies," and undergone an identity crisis, engaging in reparative boundary work and reflecting extensively on its own status as writing; political science has been dominated by the rise of rational-choice theory and by a stark division between quantitative and qualitative methodologies; and economics has built a strong consensus around the necessity of mathematical formalism. The evaluative clashes to which these methodological and epistemological differences give rise cannot be reconciled by appeal to some metatheoretical principle such as falsifiability, because any such principle is itself open to interpretation and contestation; and it is only the review panels' recognition of the incommensurability of evaluative criteria, in a process that combines in equal parts mutual respect and mutual contempt, that allows for the "universality" of a consensual decision-making.

Distinct regimes of interpretation thus embody distinct cosmological and epistemological understandings; distinct forms of wisdom, legality, and power inherent in the printed or the spoken word (or in any other medium); and distinct modalities of truth embedded in the authority of the laboratory, or of fieldwork, or of the representative sample and the double-blind experiment, or of the careful scrutiny of texts, or of the wisdom of the elders. They deploy distinct protocols of evidence and proof for generating those truths,[46] and their forms of demonstration and argumentation are well formed in quite different ways. As a precognitive

---

46. "Both judges and historians invoke the notions of evidence and proof, but their respective regulative ideals of justice and truth decisively contribute to the understanding of what is to count as a piece of evidence, what is to count as a proof." Arnold I. Davidson, "Carlo Ginzburg and the Renewal of Historiography," in *Questions of Evidence: Proof, Practice, and Persuasion Across the Disciplines*, ed. James Chandler, Arnold I. Davidson, and Harry Harootunian (Chicago: University of Chicago Press, 1994), 307.

frame, the regime posits an object that exists "not in the abstract void of theoretical reflection, but in time, space, aspect."[47] And regimes of interpretation mobilize distinct forms of participation in the analytic or aesthetic situation and correspondingly distinct effects of subjectivity; they form distinct types of ethical (knowledgeable, scrupulous, wise, pious) persona.

An act of interpretation need not be expressed in propositional form. It may take the form of an act of choice, a decision, an attitude, an emotion. Mary Rowlandson demonstrates her understanding of scripture by weeping and rejoicing in the Lord. More generally, regimes of interpretation are never distinct from regimes of valuation: every statement of truth or wisdom, every interpretive act, however expressed, simultaneously enunciates a set of values, together with a greater or lesser degree of affective force. Every regime of interpretation thus appeals to an implicit or explicit metadiscourse which justifies its actions and ends. A legal discourse may appeal to an explicitly articulated doctrine of originalism in the interpretation of a constitutional text; a performance of *The Merchant of Venice* may rely for its positive interpretation of the character of Shylock upon an implicit sense of a common humanity that transcends race; acts of iconoclasm may draw upon both biblical injunctions against the worship of idols and a deep-rooted apprehension of the presence of the demonic in the figural image; and the modeling of climate change takes place in the context of a sense of a shared project conducted by a vast and almost anonymous community of scrupulous and self-critical researchers devoted to the impersonal ends of science.

Because these metadiscourses are at once methodological and value-laden, they are also forms of justification, in the sense that Luc Boltanski and Laurent Thévenot use the term to describe the orders of rationality and worth that they take to organize the social universe. These six discrete orders correspond to different models of justice, and clashes between them are negotiated

47. Mieke Bal, *Travelling Concepts in the Humanities: A Rough Guide* (Toronto: University of Toronto Press, 2002), 137.

either by the imposition of the values of one order on another (an imposition that Boltanski and Thévenot call "critique") or by attempts to specify a compromise through appeals to a higher or hybrid common good. *Justice* is not only an ethical and legal term but also has its French sense (*juste*) of "what is right and fit"; Boltanski and Thévenot attend to "differences in the way the sense of fitness or rightness is expressed, by recognizing a number of different forms of generality, each of which is a form of worth that can be used to justify an action."[48] "Orders of worth" are thus ways of thinking about the social universe and of providing a rationale for how one behaves in it. They are the orders of generality to which people appeal in order to justify an argument, a position, a take on the world, grounded in models of good social order; and such appeals claim universality. The core work of the conduct of daily life is that of shifting between different orders of worth, without foreclosing any one of them. The kind of compromise that averts such foreclosure requires suspending a clash between worlds by recognizing the presence of "beings that matter in different worlds" (277) and not subjecting them to a test that works only in one world (since each world employs specific kinds of critique against other worlds). But compromises are fragile, and tests must be constantly repeated; new hybrid objects and new principles of equivalence continually evolve, in ways that favor "the clarification of the common good that is being sought" (283).

Regimes of interpretation are not substantive orders of being in the way that Boltanski and Thévenot envisage the orders of worth (and they have even less in common with Bruno Latour's distressingly metaphysical conception of the "modes of existence" of social being),[49] but they share a reliance upon a metadiscourse of justification and value. Since the principles of justice and worth

48. Luc Boltanski and Laurent Thévenot, *On Justification: Economies of Worth*, trans. Catherine Porter (Princeton: Princeton University Press, 2006), 14.

49. Bruno Latour, *An Inquiry into Modes of Existence: An Anthropology of the Moderns*, trans. Catherine Porter (Cambridge, MA: Harvard University Press, 2013).

invoked are not immediately compatible with those of other orders or other regimes, social action thus constantly confronts uncertainty, the clash of guiding principles and evaluations, and even "the very identification of the beings that matter and those that do not" (224). Interpretive agreement is always possible, but it takes place by means of translation or negotiation or struggle across porous borders, and it is never guaranteed in advance.

VII

"The laws are very ancient; their interpretation has been the work of centuries, and has itself doubtless acquired the status of law [*auch diese Auslegung ist schon wohl Gesetz geworden*]; and though there is still a possible freedom of interpretation left, it has now become very restricted."[50] What does it mean for a tradition of interpretation to acquire the status of law, and just how restricted is the freedom that it allows? My final argument about the social organization of interpretation has to do with its institutional dimension and with the relation between institution and interpretive conflict.

Kafka's narrator accepts a monolithic view of this institution that has grown up around the laws; his is an understanding of "institution" as a completed state rather than a continuously active process of instituting, consolidating, achieving an appearance of finality through constant interpretive struggle. The notion of institution, Samuel Weber writes, "is one in which *instituted* organization and *instituting* process are joined in the ambivalent relation of every determinate structure to that which it excludes, and yet which, qua excluded, allows that structure to *set itself apart*":[51] it brings itself into being by bringing into being both its object ("the laws," for example) and whatever stands outside it (the question of the existence of the laws; alternative ways of

---

50. Kafka, "The Problem of Our Laws," 437; "Zur Frage der Gesetze," 314.

51. Samuel Weber, *Institution and Interpretation*, Theory and History of Literature 31 (Minneapolis: University of Minnesota Press, 1987), xv.

interpreting the laws). It thus has the task, in Boltanski's words, "of stating the whatness of what is," and therefore "of saying and confirming what matters": that is, of *"fixing reference,* especially when it bears on objects whose value is important and whose predicates must be stabilized by definitions."[52]

We can say then that the formation of an interpretive institution requires

> the establishment of types, which must be fixed and memorized in one way or another (memory of elders, written legal codes, narratives, tales, examples, images, rituals, etc.) and often stored in definitions, so as to be available, when the need arises, to qualify, in a situation of uncertainty, states of affairs that are the object of ambiguous or contradictory usages and interpretations. In particular, institutions must sort out what is to be *respected* from what cannot be . . . . That is why the phenomenology of institutions attributes to them as an essential property their capacity to establish enduring or even, in a sense, eternal entities. Unlike the individual bodies of those who give them a voice, serve them, or simply live and die in spheres of reality that they help to cohere and to last, they seem removed from the corruption of time.[53]

To put this in the language of actor network theory: Institutions are chains formed by the recruitment and consolidation of material and immaterial allies; the longer the chain, the more durable the institution and the entities it puts into circulation. The solidity of an interpretive institution like medicine, for example, is built around a material infrastructure of hospitals and clinics and laboratories; state-sanctioned structures of training and certification; a knowledge base that rests upon a taxonomy of normal and pathological conditions of the body, including entities such as "diseases" together with their etiology, and of proper and improper, licit and illicit knowledges; an interpretive craft that takes the form, in modernity, of the clinical gaze, with a dispersed and networked subject (general practitioners, specialists, technicians,

52. Boltanski, *On Critique,* 75–76.
53. Boltanski, *On Critique,* 75.

nurses, paramedicals, etc.) and which is technologically mediated by instruments ranging from the stethoscope to various forms of computer-assisted imaging; the forms of authority and prestige that (very differently in different social orders) accompany that craft; a range of possible actions including pharmacological, surgical, and psychological treatment, each of these having its own regulatory infrastructure; a set of financial conditions of possibility; and so on.

The ontological heterogeneity of these interlocking components of the medical institution means that the concept of infrastructure, with its suggestion of a material base supporting a superstructure of immaterial practices, doesn't quite work. A more precise (because less bounded) way of representing that heterogeneity is perhaps Foucault's model of the *dispositif*, which is designed specifically as a rejection of such dichotomous conceptions of being: discursive practices, he argues, "are not purely and simply modes of fabricating discourse. They take shape in technical ensembles, institutions, schemas of behavior, types of transmission and circulation, and in pedagogical forms which both impose and maintain them,"[54] and they are subject to specific modes of transformation, linked to modifications taking place outside them (in production, social relations, political institutions), inside them (new techniques of knowing), or alongside them (other discursive practices).

Crucially, interpretive institutions are not the stable counterpart of interpretive conflict but are, rather, the ongoing and always provisional *outcome* of conflict. Science remains a strong and authoritative knowledge system because, and only to the extent that, its every knowledge claim is subject to attack and demolition *within the rules of its own game*; its stability is predicated on a state of constant, systematic, controlled insecurity.

The major institutions of knowledge and interpretation (which

54. Michel Foucault, "Course Summary," *Lectures on the Will to Know: Lectures at the Collège de France 1970/71*, ed. Daniel Defert, trans. Graham Burchell (New York: Palgrave Macmillan, 2013), 225.

I take to be broader in scope than the various regimes they encompass)[55] facilitate and constrain interpretive conflict and are in turn shaped by it. They allow the facts and the truths particular to each interpretive regime to be established and promulgated in accordance with protocols of evidence and proof that are always local; they allow those protocols to be contested and reshaped within each regime; and they allow truths to be contested and translated across regimes. For the formally acquired knowledges, disciplinary training tends to work as a kind of categorical absolute, without possibility of transcendence except in the terms set by the discipline itself. To emphasize the relativity of truths across regimes is not to say that all truths are equally valid, but the question of validity is itself one to be argued for and validated within and across the metadiscourses of each regime. The truths of climate science are real, but I cannot prove this absolutely. The truths of creationist science are unreal, but I cannot prove this absolutely. Nor do I seek to; the most I can do is try to describe, as precisely as possible, the ways in which truths are interpretively produced and sustained and contested within each area of social life.

VIII

We tend to think of interpretation as being a reflection upon an already given reality, but the force of my argument about interpretive regimes is that they are at the same time and in the same movement *institutive* regimes: they establish an object, bring it into being as an object of knowledge and understanding and value, and generate ways of reflecting upon it. My focus in this book is thus both upon interpretive conflicts and upon the institutions that productively sustain them.

The chapters that follow explore in different ways the tension,

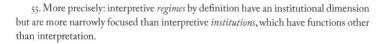

55. More precisely: interpretive *regimes* by definition have an institutional dimension but are more narrowly focused than interpretive *institutions*, which have functions other than interpretation.

but also the ambiguity, between conflict and institution. I do this by way of a series of four case studies, which are meant to be neither exemplary nor comprehensive. They do, however, raise in a variety of ways those problems of interpretive conflict and interpretive institutions that I find of central interest for this project.

Chapter 1, "Reading with Guns: *District of Columbia v. Heller*," explores a 2008 US Supreme Court case that brings into play two starkly contrasted readings of the Second Amendment to the United States Constitution: a textualist, or "originalist," reading written for the majority by Justice Antonin Scalia, and a "contextualist" reading written by two of the dissenting justices. There is, as well, a plethora of interpretive commentary on the case, illuminating both the methodological principles applied by the judges and the range of possible ways of understanding a constitutional text with major social implications (in this case, for the continuing disastrous consequences of the deregulation of gun ownership in the United States).

The detailed readings of the obscure one-sentence text that constitutes the Second Amendment analyze in great depth its semantic and syntactic structures, the range of relevant precedents, and the issue of the relevance of its drafting history and the intentions of its legislators. These readings raise the crucial question of whether the meaning of a constitutional text can be restricted to the moment of its origin; Scalia's originalist principles constitute an extreme version of historicism, locating the authority of the Constitution entirely in an originary act of popular sovereignty that privileges it over all later legal acts resting on democratic representation. These principles contrast with those of common-law interpretation which understand the law as an evolving body of doctrine that changes to meet new social circumstances, new social norms, and the need constantly to adapt the general principles enunciated by the Constitution to contemporary understandings.

Heller raises crucial questions about the principles of textual interpretation, but it also has its own interpretive context in controversies over gun control, and in particular in the ideological and legislative power wielded by the National Rifle Association. The court's discovery of a previously unarticulated constitutional right (the right of private citizens to carry guns for self-defense) is firmly rooted in the libertarian principles of the US gun lobby. Yet its judgment in this case is made as though it were entirely free of any such context: the court endows the text of the Constitution with an absolute authority and envisages its own decision-making processes as taking place within an apparently timeless and transcendental institution. That interpretive institution is neither timeless nor transcendental but rather a field of self-reinforcing authority which enables and contains dissenting views and is composed of quite heterogeneous materials: a multiplicity of legal domains, a network of material and immaterial orderings, and disparate forms of discourse and the prejudgments and tacit understandings that underpin them.

Chapter 2, "Contract, Custom, and the Multiple Historicities of *The Merchant of Venice*," tries to come to terms with what looks to many today like an anti-Semitic caricature: since the Holocaust, the figure of Shylock has made Shakespeare's play almost unreadable. I first try to make sense of the play's generic and structural anomalies (the fact that its three interwoven plots conclude, respectively, in acts 3, 4, and 5) by showing how the semantic associations clustered around the themes of usury, mercantilism, and the gift are threaded through these three plots. Whereas most readings of the play contrast the worlds of Venice and Belmont as orders of contract and the gift, of law and grace, of the Old and New Testaments, I trace some of the legal transformations occurring in sixteenth-century England in order to argue the opposite: that Shylock is the representative of an older, customary economy and Portia and the world of Belmont of a new order of contractual relations which assumes the intentionality of behavior and self-consciousness about motives. Shylock, on this reading, is a figure from an archaic and customary past.

But this reading is still grounded in a singular historical time, and it does what all "interpretation" (all exegesis) does: it offers the criteria for a single reading of the play that best fits the textual and contextual evidence. Such a reading imposes itself by reducing the text to its historical moment of origin and by refusing the ongoing history of interpretations and uses of the text; it thereby fails to come to terms, in particular, with the ways in which *The Merchant of Venice* contributes to the history of symbolic struggles over anti-Semitism. I take the history of changing performances of the play as a metonym of changing interpretations over three centuries and as one of the ways in which the figures of Jewishness and usury have functioned as condensed and overdetermined moments of social tension. Our own reading of the play is necessarily a moment of that tension and the interpretive institution of the theater has played a central role in shaping it.

Chapter 3, "Icon, Iconoclasm, Presence," explores the entanglement of two institutionally grounded regimes which endow a work of art with a particular ontological status, a particular affective force, and a particular modality of judgment: the aesthetic regime of religion, which constitutes the image or sculpture as an icon charged with the powerful presence of the god or saint, and the aesthetic regime of the art museum, which transforms that charged image into an object of detached contemplation. Both regimes are paradoxically shaped by an iconoclastic impulse: the image of the god or saint may come to be perceived as idolatrous or demonic, and figural representation is displaced by the abstract artwork, a pure aesthetic form that is destined for a timeless existence in the art museum. Iconoclasm, which I investigate in some depth through its two major appearances in the history of Western art—those of Byzantium and the Protestant Reformation—seeks to destroy the aura of the work of art; but that aura survives and thrives in every representation of the human figure, in the iconoclastic refusal of presence by the sacralized work of art, and in the mass media systems of the star, the celebrity, and the selfie.

The final section of chapter 3 is a meditation upon the work of an Australian Indigenous artist, Dorothy Napangardi, which is deeply informed by the Jukurrpa, or Dreaming, of which she is a custodian: a complex of story, ritual, dance, body decoration, song, and a temporal structure that is at once ancestral and present, transcendental and yet immanent in daily life, which she seeks to represent through paintings of great formal complexity and apparently pure abstraction from figural content. At the same time, her paintings are ordered by an economy that orders relations between the sacred, the commercial, and the aesthetic in a way that renders them fully at home within the institutions of Western art. I suggest some of the ways in which Napangardi's work can be read in relation to the sacred, and some of the tensions between such a reading and the fact that it can only (if at all) be made accessible by way of that institutional order.

Finally, chapter 4, "Construing Climate Change," begins with the problem of the dissonance between the strong agreement among climate scientists about the prospect and indeed the actuality of increasingly catastrophic climate change, and the ambivalence or indifference of the lay population. I map out the roles played by the denialist counterinstitutions of knowledge and the media, and particularly the way those institutions, funded by the fossil-fuel industries and engaged in culture wars directed against a supposedly elite knowledge class, have helped reduce the science of climate change to a proxy in broader economic and political struggles.

One of the charges frequently made by denialists is that climate science is not grounded in a correspondence with the observed data; a central argument of this chapter concerns the relation between scientific models and a "reality" that is only indirectly available to them and that is configured in a form that is amenable to analysis. I begin making this argument by appealing to the extreme but informative analogy of experimental high-energy particle physics, which seeks to analyze the infinitesimally small and transient traces of the debris of particles shattered in collisions, registered only in detectors and then reconstructed in an interpretable shape. Climate simulation modeling works by converting the continuous differential equations that express the rates of change of dynamic phenomena over infinitesimal intervals into algebraic difference equations that express rates of change in terms of discrete and discontinuous intervals and which can be computationally solved. These models use heuristic assumptions which may not be "true," such as the supposition that the atmosphere is composed of discrete layers, and they subject their analyses of interactions between the major climate subsystems to a series of counterfactual variations in order to understand the causal role of greenhouse gases in climate change.

Simulation models cannot be measured against "the data" because there are no data independent of the models that shape them; higher-level models can be compared only with another model—data sets that have been constructed over long periods, reanalyzed to correct for numerous systemic sources of error, and then further corrected by comparison with simulation models that extrapolate from empirical observations to generate globally consistent results. Climate modeling thus works with data that have been "smoothed" and "tuned." It also uses parameterizations, mathematical functions that build in assumptions about chaotic phenomena that can't be modeled directly. The epistemic solidity of the craft of modeling thus cannot be derived from its access to and reflection of a field of independently given data but is, rather, a function of a rigorous craft knowledge (*technē*, "practical wisdom");[56] of the convergence of many different models on an explanation of climate change that directly implicates greenhouse gases; and, more generally, of the resources and constraints of the institution of science, which I understand both as a normative apparatus and as deeply entangled with the imperatives of capitalism.

The institution of climate-change science is publicly represented by the Intergovernmental Panel on Climate Change (IPCC), which brings together in a fraught synthesis the interpretive institution of science and the interests of policy analysts and policy makers. It tries to incorporate, but is in many ways

---

56. Aristotle, *Nicomachean Ethics*, book VI, chap. 4, § 1140a, in *The Basic Works of Aristotle*, ed. Richard McKeon (New York: Random House, 1941), 1026.

directly in conflict with, the alternative interpretive model of economics, which has as its primary task to put a price on the benefits and costs of present action and future consequences. Both economic analysis and climate simulation models are structured to minimize the representation of catastrophic events with a relatively low probability; it may be the case that the IPCC's assessments downplay the significance of tipping points, sudden nonlinear moments of change from one state to another, the risk of which becomes significant with warming anywhere over 1°C. It looks increasingly probable that in this century, Arctic sea ice and the Greenland ice sheet will be entirely lost, which will in turn contribute exponentially to increased warming.

I conclude chapter 4 with a brief discussion of the reasons for the relative reliability of the interpretive institution of science and the relative unreliability of the counterinstitutions of denial, and I discuss the kinds of and the limits to knowledge that science is able to produce.

IX

These four analyses seek to describe interpretive formations which institute realities and conflicts over those realities. The book is— inevitably—haunted by Marx's injunction in the eleventh thesis on Feuerbach that "the philosophers have only *interpreted* the world in various ways; the point, however, is to *change* it";[57] it is haunted by a dread of the endlessness of interpretation. Yet Marx's dichotomy of *interpreting* and *changing* is problematic, grounded as I think it is in the desire for an immediacy that would bypass reflection and that would draw its strength from

---

57. "Die Philosophen haben die Welt nur verschieden *interpretirt*, es kömmt drauf an, sie zu *verändern*." Karl Marx, "Theses on Feuerbach," in Karl Marx and Frederick Engels, *Collected Works*, vol. 5 (London: Lawrence and Wishart, 1976), 8; "ad Feuerbach," in Karl Marx and Friedrich Engels, *Gesamtausgabe* IV: 3 (Berlin: Akademie Verlag, 1998), 21.

an interpretation that is not "various" but singular. There is no politics that is not variously interpretive, and no interpretation that does not suggest a pathway beyond the given order of things.

As I noted earlier, "any . . . description always comes from somewhere, is always in some sense self-interested, always derives from a will to power": it is in that sense that my descriptions are political and that they engage with the political consequences of interpretation. This is not the sweeping emancipatory politics to which Rancière, for example, aspires: I share the suspicion of any large political claims made for intellectual work. The politics I envisage here is the ordinary philological politics of understanding strange languages and their creation of real and contested worlds. And, of course, "the point" is to engage in that contest, and to change those worlds.

Reading with Guns:
District of Columbia v. Heller

All new laws . . . are considered as more or less obscure and equivocal, until their meaning be liquidated and ascertained by a series of particular discussions and adjudications.

«JAMES MADISON[1]»

I am not so naïve (nor do I think our forebears were) as to be unaware that judges in a real sense "make" law. But they make it *as judges make it,* which is to say *as though* they were "finding" it.

«ANTONIN SCALIA[2]»

If Kafka writes so intensively about the Law it is because the law, bureaucracy, and theology are the intertwined figures of a hierarchical social order built on the necessity and the impossibility of interpretation. My first case study is of an American judgment that sets in play an interpretive conflict that is resolved with the performative construction of a right and the reality it brings into being.[3]

1. James Madison ("Publius"), *The Federalist* 37 (January 1788), 269.

2. Scalia, J., concurring in *James B. Beam Distilling Co. v. Georgia,* 501 U.S. 529, 549 (1991).

3. Here and in chapter 4 I write predominantly about the United States of America because, while it seems to talk only to itself, and however specific its culture, through

The case of *District of Columbia v. Heller*,[4] decided by a 5–4 split in June 2008, is remarkable for two reasons: It was the first time that the United States Supreme Court had engaged with the full implications of the Second Amendment to the US Constitution, holding that the amendment articulated the right of private citizens to possess firearms for such purposes as self-defense; and the decision, written by the late Justice Antonin Scalia, was self-consciously and explicitly "originalist,"[5] seeking to determine the "original public meaning" of the text of the amendment without regard to the intentions of those who framed and ratified it, using the text itself as the primary evidence for its meaning at the moment of its enunciation, and confining its legal force to that historically delimited meaning. The decision invalidated the District of Columbia's comprehensive gun-control legislation but left the way open to more restricted laws controlling the possession of firearms in the United States.

The way in which the decision was reached has implications for the practice of textual interpretation more broadly. First, it raises questions about how texts migrate from the past and are incorporated into each successive present. Against the historicism that constitutes the unexamined norm of originalist interpretation (and this includes both the "textualist" originalism of Scalia's ruling and "contextualist" forms of historical analysis) I argue that texts have no privileged "original meaning" but change their meanings (differently at different levels of determinacy) as they acquire new purposes and uses. Second, I seek to specify the institutional dimensions of the regime of interpretation that effects the translation of past texts into present structures of inter-

---

its movies and television, through its trade agreements and its arms industry, through its carbon emissions and its carbon politics, America talks hard to the rest of the world.

4. *District of Columbia, et al., Petitioners v. Dick Anthony Heller*, Supreme Court of the United States, 554 U.S. 570, March 18 2008, Argued; June 26, 2008, Decided (LexisNexis) (also: 128 S. Ct. 2783).

5. Cass R. Sunstein, "Second Amendment Minimalism: *Heller* as *Griswold*," *Harvard Law Review* 122 (2008), 246: *District of Columbia v. Heller* "is the most explicitly and self-consciously originalist opinion in the history of the Supreme Court."

est. In the broad sense in which I define it here, the interpretive regime is not just a matter of the rules of a discursive game but is effected by a mix of material, political, and disciplinary infrastructures (the interpretive *institution* of the Law) that make those rules binding upon a particular interpretive community. Finally, I examine the play of blindness and insight that constitutes, in this case and more generally, the rhetorical condition of possibility for the establishment of a truth which then defines and enacts a reality.

I

The text of the Second Amendment, ratified in December 1791 as one of the ten amendments to the Constitution which make up the Bill of Rights, reads as follows:

> A well regulated Militia, being necessary to the security of a free State, the right of the people to keep and bear Arms, shall not be infringed.[6]

This enigmatic document—a "manifestly puzzling text,"[7] "perhaps one of the worst drafted" of all of the Constitution's provisions,[8] and syntactically nonsensical unless one disregards its idiosyncratic punctuation[9]—has given rise to an enormous interpretive literature, most immediately in the clash between Scalia's majority opinion and the two dissenting opinions written by Justices Stevens and Breyer. These two sides craft diametrically opposed interpretations:

---

6. A later version of the amendment as ratified by the states reads: "A well regulated militia being necessary to the security of a free state, the right of the people to keep and bear arms shall not be infringed."

7. Nelson Lund, "The Second Amendment, *Heller*, and Originalist Jurisprudence," *UCLA Law Review* 56 (2009), 1344.

8. Sanford Levinson, "The Embarrassing Second Amendment," *Yale Law Journal* 99 (1989), 644.

9. The best discussion is David S. Yellin, "The Elements of Constitutional Style: A Comprehensive Analysis of Punctuation in the Constitution," *Tennessee Law Review* 79, no. 3 (2012), 687–756, especially 688–89, n. 5.

Emphasizing different parts of the historical record, they draw different historical conclusions. They diverge on the significance to be attached to the extant judicial precedent. And they urge different readings of the sparse language of the amendment, the dissent emphasizing and the majority opinion minimizing the significance of the introductory language.[10]

We should start, then, with the syntax of this single sentence composed of a main clause and an absolute clause that qualifies it. Here the interpretive crux has to do with the politically charged distinction between a "prefatory" and an "operative" clause,[11] and with the nature of the qualification: does the initial absolute clause ("A well regulated Militia, being necessary to the security of a free State") merely explain the right to keep and bear arms ("*because* a militia is necessary . . ."), or does it limit it ("*because and to the extent that* a militia is necessary . . .")? In Scalia's view, the function of the prefatory clause is to announce a purpose or justification but not to limit the operative clause grammatically;[12] although there is a logical link between the two, the operative clause ("the right of the people to keep and bear Arms, shall not be infringed") is relatively autonomous, and indeed Scalia treats it first and foremost as a self-contained unit before going on to discuss the prefatory clause. Stevens criticizes that reversal of the order of the clauses, with its consequent hierarchical ordering, and he treats the initial clause as a restrictive enunciation of the amendment's purpose: not to protect civilian uses of firearms, which are nowhere mentioned, but solely to preserve the

10. Robert W. Bennett, "Originalism and the Living American Constitution," in *Constitutional Originalism: A Debate,* ed. Lawrence B. Solum and Robert W. Bennett (Ithaca: Cornell University Press, 2011), 132.

11. "Nelson Lund . . . helped shift the focus of Second Amendment interpretation by characterizing its first clause as 'prefatory' and its second clause as 'operative'—and received a Second Amendment chair funded by the NRA for his work." Reva B. Siegel, "Dead or Alive: Originalism as Popular Constitutionalism in *Heller,*" in *The Second Amendment on Trial: Critical Essays on District of Columbia v. Heller,* ed. Saul Cornell and Nathan Kozuskanich (Amherst: University of Massachusetts Press, 2013), 112.

12. Justice Antonin Scalia, "Opinion," *District of Columbia v. Heller,* 2789.

institution of the militia.[13] What is more generally at issue here, however, is the divergent uses made of eighteenth-century conventions of statutory interpretation of prefatory materials. For Scalia, the key text is an English case from 1716 which declares that a preamble cannot restrict the effect of words used in the "purview";[14] Stevens cites the greater weight that Blackstone allows to contextual materials when words are "ambiguous, equivocal, or intricate," in which case "the proeme, or preamble, is often called in to help the construction of an act of parliament."[15] "In light of the Court's invocation of Blackstone as 'the preeminent authority on English law for the founding generation,'" Stevens writes, "its disregard for his guidance on matters of interpretation is striking."[16]

A second area of contention concerns the semantics of key terms such as "keep and bear arms," "well regulated," "Militia," and "the people." For "keep and bear arms" there is solid evidence from linguists and professional historians that the phrase "bear arms" had, at the time, an almost exclusively military meaning. Kozuskanich documents this through statistical analysis of digitally archived documents from the time of the Constitution's framing,[17] and the amicus brief submitted by a group of linguistics professors notes that the term only changes its idiomatic military meaning when additional modifying language (such as "for self-defense") is attached to it.[18] "To bear arms" is the equivalent of *arma ferre*, and as Wills wryly comments, "one does not bear

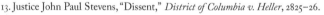

13. Justice John Paul Stevens, "Dissent," *District of Columbia v. Heller*, 2825–26.

14. *Copeman v. Gallant*, 1 P. Wms. 314, 24 Eng. Rep. 404 (1716); Scalia, "Opinion," 2789, n. 3.

15. William Blackstone, *Commentaries on the Laws of England* (Oxford: Clarendon Press, 1765), 59–60, cited in Stevens, "Dissent," 2838.

16. Stevens, "Dissent," 2838–39.

17. Nathan Kozuskanich, "Originalism in a Digital Age: An Inquiry into the Right to Bear Arms," in *The Second Amendment on Trial*, ed. Cornell and Kozuskanich, 290.

18. Dennis E. Baron, Richard W. Bailey, and Jeffery P. Kaplan, Brief for Professors of Linguistics and English as Amicus Curiae, *District of Columbia v. Heller*, http://www .scotusblog.com/wp-content/uploads/2008/01/07-290_amicus_linguists1.pdf.

arms against a rabbit":[19] *arma* are, etymologically, war equipment, and the word has no singular form. "Keep and bear" is a single phrase, having to do with the rights of a militia: "To keep-and-bear arms was the distinguishing note of the militia's permanent readiness, as opposed to the army's duty of taking up and laying down . . . their arms in specific wars. The militia was maintained on a continuing basis, its arsenal kept up, its readiness expressed in the complex process specified by 'keep-and-bear.'"[20]

For Scalia, however, that military application of the phrase is only unequivocal when "bear arms" is coupled with "against." His strategy is to break the phrase into its component parts, which allows him to find that the word "arms" includes weapons that are not used for military purposes (2791),[21] that "keeping" arms doesn't have an exclusively military sense (2792), and that the word "bear" means "carry" and, when used with "arms," refers to carrying for confrontation and "in no way connotes participation in a structured military organization" (2793). The argument made by the linguistics professors that the military sense of "bear arms" can be modified if a particular purpose expressly qualifies it (such as "for the purpose of killing game") is summarily dismissed:

> That analysis is faulty. A purposive qualifying phrase that contradicts the word or phrase it modifies is unknown this side of the looking glass (except, apparently, in some courses on linguistics). . . . If "bear arms" means, as the petitioners and the dissent think, the carrying of arms only for military purposes, one cannot simply add "for the purpose of killing game." The right "to carry arms in the militia for the purpose of killing game" is worthy of the Mad Hatter. (2795–96)

Stevens's rejoinder to this, arguing that the purposive phrase changes the meaning from an idiomatic military sense to a literal

---

19. Garry Wills, "To Keep and Bear Arms," *New York Review of Books*, Sept. 21, 1995, http://www.nybooks.com/articles/archives/1995/sep/21/to-keep-and-bear-arms.

20. Wills, "To Keep and Bear Arms."

21. And that, just as the First Amendment protects "speech" in modern media of communication, so the Second Amendment is not restricted to the forms of weaponry available and even conceivable in the eighteenth century.

sense, relies on a notion of the "most natural meaning" of "bear arms" in the absence of a qualifier, a natural meaning that can be confirmed by reference to the preamble. But such a reference is precisely what Scalia discounts by means of the privilege he allows to the "operative" clause: the prefatory reference to the militia is incidental to the right enunciated in the second clause, since that right is not restricted to the narrow purposes of maintaining the state militias.

In order to define the right in this expansive manner, it must be tied to "the people" as a whole, and this whole is then either equated with or exceeds the militia, broadly conceived. Scalia thus contrasts the rights-bearing people, as the entirety of the citizenry, with the subset of able-bodied males within a certain age range which makes up the militia (2791), and he thereby refuses to read the "militia" of the initial clause as synonymous with the "people" of the second. As Amar notes, this makes the link to the preamble textually irrelevant; it is the people, not the militia, who bear the right.[22]

If we assume that the reference in the prefatory clause to the militia is in some way integral to the amendment's structure, however, then the question becomes one of the kind of right that is established and the way in which it is related to the importance of a "well regulated Militia." Scalia reads the amendment as the codification of a common-law right to bear arms for self-defense and as an incorporation and universalization of the separate English statutory right enunciated in the 1689 Declaration of Rights, which allowed "the Subjects which are Protestants" to have arms for their personal defense; the facilitation of the militia is no more than a secondary effect of these personal rights. Scalia's historical evidence is drawn largely from English constitutional jurisprudence and from anti-Federalist arguments made during the ratification period. It assumes a continuity with "a body of writings absorbed by Americans prior to 1776," with-

---

22. Akhil Reed Amar, "*Heller, HLR*, and Holistic Legal Reasoning," *Harvard Law Review* 122 (2008), 166.

out accounting for the ways in which the revolution transformed popular thinking about the militia.[23] The amicus brief submitted by a group of academic historians, by contrast, points to the broader context of debate and to the paucity of contemporaneous references to the private keeping of firearms: the fact that the modern controversy over the Second Amendment "has been forced to squeeze so much modern interpretive blood from so few evidentiary turnips . . . is itself an indicator of how minor a question this was at the time."[24] This is to say, rather than either a personal or a collective right, the Second Amendment articulates a civic right, which is closely tied to a duty of military service. Saul Cornell recalls that the amendment

> was drafted and ratified by a generation of Americans who feared standing armies and had witnessed a systematic policy to disarm their militias. With these concerns in mind, America's first constitutions explicitly protected the right of citizens to keep and bear those arms necessary to meet their militia obligation.[25]

That civic right is complicated, however, by the struggles between Federalists and proponents of states' rights that came to dominate debates over the framing and ratification of the Bill of Rights. Specifically, at issue was whether power over the militia would be centralized in Congress or whether the amendment would leave a residual military power with the states, which could be used as a check on federal power.

Here the question of the drafting history becomes crucial. Scalia gives it short shrift: investigating the history aims to establish legislative intent, but intent is neither unitary nor, in most cases, able to be objectively reconstructed. Since there is rarely any awareness on the part of legislators that a particular word-

23. Jack N. Rakove, "The Second Amendment: The Highest Stage of Originalism," *Chicago-Kent Law Review* 76 (2000), 151–52.

24. Jack N. Rakove, et al., "Brief of Amici Curiae," in *The Second Amendment on Trial*, ed. Cornell and Kozuskanich, 55.

25. Saul Cornell, *A Well-Regulated Militia: The Founding Fathers and the Origins of Gun Control in America* (New York: Oxford University Press, 2006), x.

ing is likely to give rise to problems of interpretation, for nearly all "issues of construction" there is, effectively, no "intent."[26] For Stevens and for the academic historians, however, examination of the drafting history gives a clear indication of the relevant purpose of the amendment, and that purpose serves to anchor interpretation in its historical context.

At the First Federal Congress in 1789, James Madison was given the task of sorting and assembling proposals from the states for amendments to the Constitution and shepherding them through the drafting process. (He wrote to a correspondent that year of the need to placate the states, which had agreed to ratify the Constitution only on a "tacit compact" of later amendments to do with the militia.)[27] His initial formulation of what was to become the Second Amendment read as follows:

> The right of the people to keep and bear arms shall not be infringed; a well armed, and well regulated militia being the best security of a free country; but no person religiously scrupulous of bearing arms, shall be compelled to render military service in person.[28]

As Stevens points out, this text is striking for its omission of civilian uses of firearms (something that the Virginia Ratifying Convention, for example, had proposed), and Madison's inclusion of an exemption for conscientious objectors "confirms an intent to describe a duty as well as a right, and it unequivocally identifies the military character of both."[29] That focus on the exemption of religiously scrupulous persons from military service in person was at the heart of debates in the House of Representatives, but the third clause was withdrawn when the amendment reached the Senate because of fears that it could be used

---

26. Antonin Scalia, "Common-Law Courts in a Civil-Law System: The Role of United States Federal Courts in Interpreting the Constitution and Laws," in Antonin Scalia, *A Matter of Interpretation: Federal Courts and the Law. With Commentary by Amy Gutmann, Gordon S. Wood, Laurence H. Tribe, Mary Ann Glendon, and Ronald Dworkin* (Princeton: Princeton University Press, 1997), 32.

27. Cited in Stevens, "Dissent," 2835, n. 23.

28. Cited in Rakove, "The Second Amendment," 120.

29. Stevens, "Dissent," 2835.

oppressively to refuse military service to particular groups, and thus to disarm "the people."[30] In the House committee to which Madison's draft was referred, two changes were made: the first two clauses were transposed and separated by a comma, not a semicolon, "an editorial decision," Cornell argues, "that linked the clauses containing the militia and the right of the people more closely";[31] and a more specific definition of the militia was offered ("composed of the body of the people"), which was in turn eliminated by the Senate in order to leave to Congress the power of determining the composition of the militia. The Senate also rejected a motion to insert the phrase "for the common defence" after "arms."[32]

The overall effect of these ideological struggles was to qualify more strongly the power given to Congress by Article I, Section 8 of the Constitution, namely:

> To provide for organizing, arming, and disciplining, the Militia, and for governing such Part of them as may be employed in the Service of the United States, reserving to the States respectively, the Appointment of the Officers, and the Authority of training the Militia according to the discipline prescribed by Congress.

That clause is already a carefully worded compromise; the Second Amendment further qualifies federal power by insisting on the right of the militia to be properly supplied with arms. Although in its historical context the amendment offers little of relevance to an individual-right interpretation, its ambiguous phrasing nevertheless gave rise to at least two conflicting understandings of its force: on the one hand, a civic right to bear arms in the organized, armed, and disciplined state militia; on the other, a "revolutionary" understanding "assigning to the state militias the awesome power to resist federal authority by force of arms."[33]

From Shays's Rebellion in 1786 to the Oklahoma bombing by

---

30. Rakove, "The Second Amendment," 127.

31. Cornell, *A Well-Regulated Militia*, 60.

32. Rakove, "The Second Amendment," 122.

33. Cornell, *A Well-Regulated Militia*, 5.

Timothy McVeigh, a strand of American thought has conceived not the "well regulated" but the "popular" militia as the key vehicle of resistance to governmental tyranny. This conviction runs counter to that other constitutional clause which empowers the Congress to call forth the militia "to execute the Laws of the Union, suppress Insurrections and repel Invasions,"[34] and it lays bare a deep paradox in the notion that citizens of a democratic state might "carry out a right of revolution against the government while at the same time claiming protections within it."[35] The notion of popular resistance to tyranny must insist upon "its pre-, extra-, and even anticonstitutional functions . . . to the point of revolution."[36] Yet it is precisely this antigovernmental right that Scalia invokes in his privileging of "the right of the people" against a militia-related right. If the right is only to keep and bear arms as a member of an organized militia, he says, this is no safeguard against tyranny, since Congress has plenary authority to organize and equip the militia, and the amendment would therefore guarantee no more than "a select militia of the sort the Stuart kings found useful, but not the people's militia that was the concern of the founding generation."[37] Only the people armed can defend its liberty against government.

This libertarian conviction that popular sovereignty takes precedence over the sovereign state runs through much of the academic writing that argues for an individual right to possess firearms. The proclaimer of the so-called Standard Model of interpretation of the Second Amendment, Glenn Harlan Reynolds, contends that the present-day National Guard cannot be the militia to which the amendment refers because members of the guard are "armed, paid, and trained by the federal government" and "are required to swear an oath of loyalty to the United

---

34. Constitution of the United States of America, Article I, Section 8.

35. Robert J. Spitzer, "Lost and Found: Researching the Second Amendment," *Chicago-Kent Law Review* 76 (2000), 361.

36. Rakove, "The Second Amendment," 109.

37. Scalia, "Opinion," 2802.

States government, as well as to their states";[38] whereas the function of the citizens' militia is, by implication, "to train itself for action (against) the government."[39] Sanford Levinson makes a similar argument by citing Max Weber's definition of the state as "the repository of a monopoly of the legitimate means of violence"; this, he writes,

> is a profoundly statist definition, the product of a specifically German tradition of the (strong) state rather than of a strikingly different American political tradition that is fundamentally mistrustful of state power and vigilant about maintaining ultimate power, including the power of arms, in the populace.[40]

That American tradition generates a republican politics in which ordinary citizens should "participate in the process of law enforcement and defense of liberty rather than rely on professionalized peacekeepers, whether we call them standing armies or police" (650–51). The strongest version of this republican politics "would hold it to be a 'privilege and immunity of United States citizenship'—of membership in a liberty-enhancing political order—to keep arms that could be taken up against tyranny wherever found, including, obviously, state government" (651). This, as Spitzer puts it, is "a bona fide constitutional argument proposing that vigilantism and citizen violence, including armed insurrection against the government, are legal, proper, and even beneficial activities within the Second Amendment umbrella,"[41] and it perhaps confirms Wendy Brown's contention that the amendment "is ambiguous about whether it grants citizens the right to bear arms for protection *of* the state, *against* the state, or *against one another*."[42]

38. Glenn Harlan Reynolds, "A Critical Guide to the Second Amendment," *Tennessee Law Review* 62 (1995), 476–77.

39. Wills, "To Keep and Bear Arms."

40. Levinson, "The Embarrassing Second Amendment," 650; hereafter cited in the text.

41. Spitzer, "Lost and Found," 362.

42. Wendy Brown, "Guns, Cowboys, Philadelphia Mayors, and Civic Republicanism: On Sanford Levinson's *The Embarrassing Second Amendment*," *Yale Law Journal* 99 (1989), 662.

II

To isolate the historical moment of the Second Amendment's "original public meaning" or of the purposes and intentions of its framers is arguably an impossibility, and the attempt to do so raises methodological questions about the relation between a constitutional provision; the chain of judicial decisions stretching over several hundred years which, in Madison's words, "liquidate and ascertain" its meaning; and the politically charged present into which this chain flows and from which we read both the provision and its continuing life. That chain of decisions constitutes at once a set of precedents and, in principle and as a consequence, the coherence of a body of established and evolving law. We usually view it through the model of common law, but how does the common law relate to the interpretation of statutes and, therefore, to constitutional construction?

This is a question to which Scalia has given considerable thought. His answer is that they are radically different modes of interpretation. Citing Dwarris on statutes to the effect that "an act of Parliament cannot alter by reason of time; but the common law may, since *cessante ratione cessat lex*" (that is, when conditions change, the law changes), he goes on to say that "this remains (however much it may sometimes be evaded) the formally enunciated rule for statutory construction: statutes do not change," nor, a fortiori, does the Constitution. Its rationale is perpetual: the whole purpose of a written constitution "is to prevent change—to embed certain rights in such a manner that future generations cannot readily take them away."[43]

Scalia's target here is an alternative interpretive tradition of "living constitutionalism" which affirms the existence of "a body of law that (unlike normal statutes) grows and changes from age to age, in order to meet the needs of a changing society" (38) and which therefore discovers certain implied rights in the Constitu-

---

43. Scalia, "Common-Law Courts in a Civil-Law System," 40; hereafter cited in the text.

tion, such as the inadmissibility of unlawfully obtained evidence of guilt, or evolving standards of what constitutes "cruel and unusual punishment." For such an evolutionary understanding of the Constitution, every question remains open: the death penalty may, for example, be found unconstitutional, even though its use is explicitly contemplated at a number of points in the Constitution. And that openness to change gives rise, according to Scalia, to two problems: it begs the question of the principles according to which the Constitution may be thought to evolve, and it thereby undermines the liberties that have been inscribed in the written text and which it is the duty of the jurist to preserve (44, 46). A particularly stark example of what it means to read the purpose of the Constitution as the preservation of unchanging liberties arises in a 1990 case involving the Sixth Amendment, which provides for the right of an accused person to be confronted with the witnesses against him or her. The case involved a young child,[44] and the Supreme Court allowed her to "confront" the person accused of sexually abusing her by way of closed-circuit television; Scalia dissented from that decision because the word "confront" implies "face-to-face," with all the pressure on the witness that confrontation may imply. Little children were just as liable to be upset by such pressure in 1791 as they are today; all that has changed, he writes, is "the society's sensitivity to so-called psychic trauma" and its assessment of the proper balance of protection; the Supreme Court's decision, therefore, eliminated a liberty.[45]

One possible objection to Scalia's position is that his practice as a judge requires him to align his decisions with precedents established by earlier holdings, in accordance with the doctrine of *stare decisis*. This is implicitly a common-law approach, and indeed it is arguably true that "in any common-law system statutory construction seems bound to take on many of the characteristics of common-law interpretation."[46] Scalia's response to

44. *Maryland v. Craig*, 497 U.S. 836 (1990).
45. Scalia, "Common-Law Courts in a Civil-Law System," 43–44.
46. Gordon S. Wood, "Comment," in Scalia, *A Matter of Interpretation*, 59.

this is to argue that *stare decisis* is not a part of but an exception to his originalist philosophy, a compromise that he is pragmatically bound to respect but for which he holds little respect: "The whole function of the doctrine," he writes, "is to make us say that what is false under proper analysis must nevertheless be held to be true, all in the interest of stability."[47] What might make this compromise less obviously hypocritical is the fact that, as Mark Tushnet puts it,

> in a legal system with a relatively extensive body of precedent and with well-developed techniques of legal reasoning, it will always be possible to show how today's decision is consistent with the relevant past decisions. Conversely, however, it will also always be possible to show how today's decision is inconsistent with the precedents.[48]

Precedents can always be distinguished because every case is different from every other and because it is always difficult to isolate a single principle for which a precedent stands. The distinguishing of precedents is what Scalia does with great agility in *District of Columbia v. Heller,* where the few important forerunners in the Supreme Court had failed to discover in the Second Amendment the individual right to bear arms for self-defense that Scalia and his four colleagues found there in 2008.

The key earlier decisions were *Cruikshank,*[49] *Presser,*[50] and *Miller.*[51] Each made somewhat abstruse and tangential rulings on the right to bear arms. *Miller* is the major precedent, and it turned on the question of the kind of weapon that could be banned: in this case, sawn-off shotguns were held not to be arms that "have some reasonable relationship to the preservation or efficiency of a well regulated militia," not to be part of "the ordinary military equipment," and not to be able to contribute to

---

47. Antonin Scalia, "Response," in Scalia, *A Matter of Interpretation,* 139.

48. Mark V. Tushnet, "Following the Rules Laid Down: A Critique of Interpretivism and Neutral Principles," *Harvard Law Review* 96, no. 4 (1983), 818.

49. *United States v. Cruikshank,* 92 U.S. 542 (1875).

50. *Presser v. Illinois,* 116 U.S. 252 (1886).

51. *United States v. Miller,* 307 U.S. 174 (1939).

"the common defense."[52] *Miller,* that is to say, takes seriously the view that the right articulated in the Second Amendment relates exclusively to militia-related uses, and hundreds of subsequent lower-court decisions have relied on this view.[53] Scalia, however, finds that *Miller* is "not only consistent with, but positively suggests, that the Second Amendment confers an individual right to keep and bear arms."[54] It is true that, "read in isolation, *Miller*'s phrase 'part of ordinary equipment' could mean that only those weapons useful in warfare are protected": "M-16 rifles and the like," for example. But such a reading would be perverse, and instead "we . . . read *Miller* to say only that the Second Amendment does not protect those weapons not typically possessed by law-abiding citizens for lawful purposes, such as short-barreled shotguns" (2815–16). But in any case, however supportive it may be of the current ruling, *Miller* can be distinguished by the fact that only the government offered a submission in the hearing, and the court discussed none of the history of the Second Amendment; the reliance of lower courts on "an uncontested and virtually unreasoned case" is thus, to Scalia, "erroneous" and is in any case outweighed by "the reliance of millions of Americans . . . upon the true meaning of the right to keep and bear arms" (2815, n. 24) (even if, as Stevens caustically points out, that true meaning had never been articulated by the courts).[55]

Yet the question of the kind of arms that the people may keep and bear is not solved either by ruling out "dangerous and unusual weapons" or by making handguns the prototype of permitted weapons on the grounds that they are the type most commonly used for self-defense. *Miller* could well be taken to support an argument "that the individual citizen has a right to keep and bear bazookas, rocket launchers, and other armaments that are

52. *Miller,* 178.

53. Stevens, "Dissent," 2823, with citations in n. 2; Sunstein, "Second Amendment Minimalism," 252.

54. Scalia, "Opinion," 2814; hereafter cited in the text.

55. Stevens, "Dissent," 2845.

clearly relevant to modern warfare, including, of course, assault weapons."[56] Scalia, who once parenthetically mused, "The 'right to bear arms,' I suspect, is limited to musketry in the National Guard,"[57] seems aware of the contradictions:

> It may well be true today that a militia, to be as effective as militias in the 18th century, would require sophisticated arms that are highly unusual in society at large. Indeed, it may be true that no amount of small arms could be useful against modern-day bombers and tanks. But the fact that modern developments have limited the degree of fit between the prefatory clause and the protected right cannot change our interpretation of the right.[58]

Rather than accept that the amendment might simply be obsolete, however, the majority refuses those extreme implications by enumerating a series of exceptions to the right to own guns: in addition to ruling out "dangerous and unusual weapons," it recognizes prohibitions on possession by felons and the mentally ill, laws forbidding the carrying of firearms in schools or government buildings, and laws imposing conditions on the sale of arms. These exceptions are pure assertions,[59] what Justice Breyer calls "judicial *ipse dixit*";[60] they certainly have no grounding in the text of the amendment, and they leave open the many questions of what will count as acceptable gun-control policy.

III

The notion that the US Constitution might in some respects be obsolete is by definition unthinkable within an originalist framework. Because the supremacy of the Constitution as a source of law is derived from "a direct expression of popular sovereignty,

56. Levinson, "The Embarrassing Second Amendment," 654–55.

57. Scalia, "Response," in Scalia, *A Matter of Interpretation*, 136.

58. Scalia, "Opinion," 2817.

59. Carlton F. W. Larson, "Four Exceptions in Search of a Theory: *District of Columbia v. Heller* and Judicial *Ipse Dixit*," *Hastings Law Journal* 60 (June 2009), 1372.

60. Justice Stephen Breyer, "Dissent," *District of Columbia v. Heller*, 2870.

superior in authority to all subsequent legal acts resting only on the weaker foundations of representation,"[61] the Constitution must then exercise its legal force, without modification, over all subsequent periods of time.[62]

Originalism as a methodology of statutory interpretation is associated with the backlash against what was perceived to be the judicial activism of the Warren and Burger courts (1953–1969 and 1969–1986),[63] and its intellectual warriors include many key figures of the Nixon and Reagan administrations: Robert Bork, Edwin Meese, William Rehnquist, and others. Originalism is probably best understood as a family of related theories, including claims that the meaning of the Constitution is "fixed" (in the linguistic sense) at the time of framing and ratification; that good interpretation requires recovery of an original public meaning but not necessarily of the intentions of the framers or ratifiers; that original public meaning as embodied in the text of the Constitution has binding or constraining force; and, more controversially, that we can distinguish constitutional interpretation (the determination of linguistic meaning) and constitutional construction (the construal of the legal effect of the text, which enables it to be applied).[64]

In Scalia's hands, originalism is turned decisively away from questions of intention, on the grounds that looking beyond the text to an unexpressed meaning gives judges license to read their

61. Jack N. Rakove, *Original Meanings: Politics and Ideas in the Making of the Constitution* (New York: Vintage Books, 1996), 9.

62. Originalism in this sense is directly descended from a post-Reformation theology of scriptural exegesis which "fundamentally prohibits addition to or subtraction from a single sacred text. Such a textual culture demands . . . exact replication of the text, regardless of history's passage, regardless of tradition. Tradition, indeed, is precisely the mark of all that is fallen, since tradition is by definition a disfiguring accretion upon the single pure text, a single source of legitimate authority." James Simpson, *Under the Hammer: Iconoclasm in the Anglo-American Tradition* (New York: Oxford University Press, 2010), 111.

63. Burger was a conservative, but his court continued many of the doctrinal trends of the Warren court.

64. Cf. Lawrence B. Solum, "We Are All Originalists Now," in Solum and Bennett, *Constitutional Originalism: A Debate*, 2–3.

own values into the text. "Intentions" may be heterogeneous, or inconsistent, or simply unknowable, and it is undemocratic "to have the meaning of a law determined by what the lawgiver meant, rather than by what the lawgiver promulgated. . . . It is the law that governs, not the intention of the lawgiver."[65] His own preferred term for his philosophy of interpretation is "textualism," a method of fidelity to the constitutional text that differs from strict constructionism in acknowledging that words may have a range of meanings rather than a single literal meaning, but restricting interpretation to that delimited range. The First Amendment guarantee of freedom of speech, for example, may be read as a synecdoche for communication in general, including technological forms not foreseen at the time of drafting; but the moral principles enunciated in the Constitution are immutable. If the text forbids "cruel and unusual" punishments but envisages the application of the death penalty, then this is "conclusive evidence that the death penalty is not (in the moral view of the Constitution) cruel."[66]

Assisting in the restriction of possible interpretations of a text is a set of interpretive rules known as "canons of construction"; they include such maxims as *expressio unius est exclusio alterius* (the explicit mention of one thing implies the exclusion of another; for example, if a sign says that children under twelve enter free, then there is an implicit exclusion of thirteen-year-olds from that free entry), *noscitur a sociis* (a word is given its meaning by the words around it), and *ejusdem generis* (a general term in a list of specific things implicitly includes only things of that same kind). Scalia and Bryan Garner have compiled a summary of fifty-seven such "valid canons," on the premise that applying them consistently will make statutory interpretation more predictable and more constrained.[67] As William Eskridge argues

65. Scalia, "Common-Law Courts in a Civil-Law System," 17.

66. Scalia, "Response," in Scalia, *A Matter of Interpretation*, 146.

67. Antonin Scalia and Bryan A. Garner, *Reading Law: The Interpretation of Legal Texts* (St. Paul: West, 2012).

in an extended critique, however, "For any difficult case, there will be as many as twelve to fifteen relevant 'valid canons' cutting in different directions, leaving considerable room for judicial cherry-picking."[68] Moreover, their canon of "valid canons" is selective, omitting, for example, the canon of *stare decisis*; and it either assumes the validity of canons which are not normally applied in the drafting of legislation or, conversely, disregards canons (such as those which suppose that committee reports can be used "to resolve technical ambiguities or to confirm statutory plain meanings") which are in fact routinely applied.[69]

A different kind of criticism, made by Richard Posner, is that the canons of construction Scalia seeks to apply are anachronistic, since they differ from the "loose," Blackstonian doctrine of interpretation that was predominant in the eighteenth century.[70] Blackstone summarizes the general principles of the doctrine as follows:

> The fairest and most rational method to interpret the will of the legislator, is by exploring his intentions at the time when the law was made, by signs the most natural and probable. And these signs are either the words, the context, the subject-matter, the effects and consequence, or the spirit and reason of the law.[71]

The words must be interpreted "in their usual and most known signification; not so much regarding the propriety of grammar, as their general and popular use"; but when they are ambiguous, the other dimensions of interpretation come into play. Of these, "the most universal and effectual way of discovering the true meaning of a law, when the words are dubious, is by considering the reason and spirit of it; or the cause which moved the legislator

---

68. William N. Eskridge Jr., "Review: The New Textualism and Normative Canons," *Columbia Law Review* 113, no. 2 (March 2013), 531.

69. Eskridge, "Review," 543.

70. Richard A. Posner, "In Defense of Looseness: The Supreme Court and Gun Control," *The New Republic* August 27, 2008, 33.

71. Blackstone, *Commentaries on the Laws of England*, sec. 2, "Of the Nature of Laws in General."

to enact it." From this arises equity, defined by Grotius as "the correction of that, wherein the law (by reason of its universality) is deficient": that is, equity underpins the discretion of the judge to determine the fair and reasonable application of a general law to the particular circumstances of a case.

Both of these criticisms—the difficulty of establishing a consistent list of "valid canons" and their anachronistic dissonance with the canons of interpretation prevalent at the time the Constitution was drafted—may be taken as instances of a more general problem that any attempt to constrain interpretation will, as Stanley Fish puts it, "turn out upon further examination to have been the product of interpretation."[72] Yet there is certainly an argument to be made for judicial constraint.

In one sense, the point of applying an originalist methodology to the US Constitution is clear. Many of its provisions, such as the terms of office of the president and of members of Congress, are concrete, specific, and not open to dispute. Some of its language has changed its meaning since the eighteenth century. It would be inappropriate to read "domestic violence" in Article IV, Section 4, for example, in its current sense of assault within a household rather than in its earlier sense of riots or disturbances within a state, or to read the guarantee in the same clause of "Republican government" as referring to the political party of that name, since that would mean that the import of the term would have changed arbitrarily. Accepting that the original meaning of words in the text of the Constitution should be preserved "serves important rule-of-law values: predictability, fairness, nonretroactivity, coordination, and the restraint of arbitrary power."[73]

In another way, however, the extension of this argument beyond a few rather simple instances in which literal interpretation

72. Stanley Fish, "Force," in *Doing What Comes Naturally: Change, Rhetoric, and the Practice of Theory in Literary and Legal Studies* (Durham: Duke University Press, 1989), 512.

73. Jack M. Balkin, *Living Originalism* (Cambridge, MA: Harvard University Press, 2011), 39.

is feasible would rely upon a positivistic detachment of meaning from interpretation. Fish again:

> Meanings only become perspicuous against a background of interpretive assumptions in the absence of which reading and understanding would be impossible. A meaning that seems to leap off the page, propelled by its own self-sufficiency, is a meaning that flows from interpretive assumptions so deeply embedded that they have become invisible.[74]

Phrases such as "due process of law" or "equal protection" are, on their face, by no means self-evident; they require that process of "liquidation and ascertainment" that Madison saw as integral to the judicial "making" of law. This is in part a matter of historical contextualization and in part a matter of application of a general principle to specific circumstances.

Questions of historical context are of central concern to the historians who engage with Scalia's textualist methodology. For Jack Rakove, proper historical method

> assumes that the meaning of a provision cannot be ascertained by staring at it long enough or juxtaposing it with other relevant clauses, but must instead be derived from usage or elaborated in terms of some contemporary context of thought and debate, thus requiring the intrepid interpreter to initiate an inquiry into sources extrinsic to the text.[75]

For Saul Cornell, neither Scalia's amateur or "law-office" history nor Stevens's historicizing dissent can be counted as "historical contextualism," the methodology employed by most historians; indeed, most historians "are militantly anti-originalist."[76] Gordon Wood, for example, writes, "It may be a necessary fiction for lawyers and jurists to believe in a 'correct' or 'true' interpretation of the Constitution in order to carry on their business, but we

74. Stanley Fish, "Still Wrong After All These Years," in *Doing What Comes Naturally*, 358.

75. Rakove, "The Second Amendment," 113.

76. Saul Cornell, "Originalism on Trial: The Use and Abuse of History in *District of Columbia v. Heller*," *Ohio State Law Journal* 69 (2008), 626.

historians have different obligations and aims."[77] Seeking such a singular and "correct" interpretation, Scalia uses the historical evidence selectively, ignores the available detailed and systematic accounts of the force of the phrase "keep and bear arms" in favor of anachronistic sources and atomistic analysis, and discounts the climate of anxiety about placing state militias under federal control in which the Second Amendment was drafted. His argument that there existed "a general consensus on the meaning of the Second Amendment that supports an individual right with no connection to the militia," Cornell writes, "is simply gun rights propaganda passing as scholarship."[78]

Any such argument to historical context, however, no matter how telling its critique of the amateur historiography of judges, still supposes that the legal force of the Constitution is to be located in that single historical moment of its enunciation. Yet this supposition is clearly untenable. Let me return to the Eighth Amendment's prohibition on "cruel and unusual punishment." Scalia's originalist position on this is apparently clear: the prohibition must be restricted to those punishments that would have been seen as cruel and unusual in 1791. Yet he himself has drawn the line at the practice of flogging, which was nevertheless acceptable at that time.[79] Scalia seems somewhat abashed at this inconsistency (he calls what he's doing "faint-hearted originalism," as though he really should have been harder of heart), but arguably it's not an inconsistency at all.

What changes from one historical context to another is not the literal meaning of the words "cruel and unusual," but rather the class of punishments that would be described by those words. Jack Balkin explains this distinction as one between the "original meaning" of the words and "a more limited interpretive prin-

77. Gordon Wood, "Ideology and the Origins of Liberal America," *William and Mary Quarterly* 44 (1987), 632–33; cited in Cornell, "Originalism on Trial," 627.

78. Cornell, "Originalism on Trial," 629.

79. Antonin Scalia, "Originalism: The Lesser Evil," *Cincinnati Law Review* 57 (1989), 861.

ciple, *original expected application*":[80] the kinds of things people in 1791 would have thought to be included in the class. Ronald Dworkin similarly distinguishes between what one intends to say and what one intends to be the consequence of saying.[81] Our fidelity should be to what the text says but not to the originally expected consequences; values change, technologies change, the very structure of the constitutional order changes; the delegitimation of slavery, the extension of full citizenship to women, and the massive expansion of the powers of the federal government to regulate the economy that arose from the New Deal settlement are most likely inconsistent with the expectations of the founding generation, but they are not aberrations, and they have come about in part through a process that Balkin calls a "building out" of the Constitution by way of constitutional construction.[82] If we define a constitutional regime as consisting on the one hand of a set of "basic principles and assumptions about constitutional rights, duties, and powers and the proper role of government" and on the other of "the institutions and practices that grow up around these principles and assumptions," then the current regime would include such things as Social Security, labor and consumer protection standards, environmental protection, a federal bureaucracy regulating these things, centralized monetary and fiscal policies, a massive defense establishment, the Voting Act, and equal rights for women and black people; very few of the elements of this regime would have been ideologically palatable to the framers of the Constitution, and most of them "arose from state-building constructions that were ratified or supported by the judiciary."[83]

The distinction between original meaning and original expected application turns in part on the question of the level of generality at which the Constitution is pitched. Scalia reads its

80. Balkin, *Living Originalism*, 7.
81. Ronald Dworkin, "Comment," in Scalia, *A Matter of Interpretation*, 116.
82. Balkin, *Living Originalism*, 11.
83. Balkin, *Living Originalism*, 109.

language as uniform, specific, and prescriptive. "It would be most peculiar," he writes, "for aspirational provisions to be interspersed randomly among the very concrete and hence obviously non-aspirational prescriptions that the Bill of Rights contains. . . . It is more reasonable to think that the provisions are all of a sort." Not all constitutional language is concrete and particular, of course, but even the abstract and general terms refer "to *extant* rights and freedoms possessed under the then-current regime."[84] If, however, the more abstract provisions of the Constitution are read as a statement of general moral principles, then working out their application to changing historical circumstances would be the core business of judges and a matter of respecting the Constitution's intrinsic demands.[85] Dworkin accordingly marks a distinction between a (general) *concept*—for example, of a right—and a specific *conception.* If I appeal to a concept of equality or cruelty, I pose a moral issue, and my own view of the matter has no particular standing; if I lay down a conception of these things, I seek to respond to that moral issue with a particular understanding.[86] Deciding that flogging and the death penalty are, in the present time, cruel and unusual forms of punishment would effectively respond to the concept of cruelty laid down in the Constitution, but not to any historically specific conception of it. And this is not a matter of changing the Constitution, since "in fact the Court can enforce what the Constitution says only by making up its own mind about what is cruel."[87]

The central problem of constitutional interpretation is that of determining the degree of determinacy or indeterminacy to be ascribed to its various provisions. Many key terms—"due process," "equal protection," "unreasonable searches and seizures,"

84. Scalia, "Response," in Scalia, *A Matter of Interpretation*, 135.

85. The locus classicus is Chief Justice Marshall's opinion in *McCullough v. Maryland* (17 U.S. 316 [1819]), arguing that the generic form of the constitution requires it to deal in general outlines rather than prolix detail.

86. Ronald Dworkin, *Taking Rights Seriously* (Cambridge, MA: Harvard University Press, 1978), 135.

87. Dworkin, *Taking Rights Seriously*, 136.

and so on—seem to be open-ended invocations of principle; and principles, as Balkin puts it, are norms that "do not determine the scope of their own extension."[88] Balkin would argue that the tradition of successive constructions of the text of the Constitution are what endow it with its legitimacy; it is not just "an instrument for settlement and minimization of costs" but "a promise to be redeemed," "a set of principles that must be restored or fulfilled" (56); it contains "commitments that We the People have only partially lived up to, promises that have yet to be fulfilled"; and "interpretive fidelity requires faith in the redeemability of an imperfect Constitution over time" (75, 79). David Strauss's argument that the real, unwritten Constitution is that of judicial and nonjudicial precedents cuts through this kind of religious piety, seeing constructions of the Constitution just as historically evolving constructions, not as restorations of or a return to an original compact with the American people. Notions of fidelity to the Constitution's text cannot account for the interpretive shifts that have reread the Sixth Amendment as imposing an obligation on government to provide counsel, rather than just requiring it not to deny the right to counsel, or that have read the Warrant Clause as requiring warrants, "although it says nothing of the kind."[89] Rather, such interpretive shifts must be explained as the application of common-law principles to constitutional construction.

On a common-law reading, then, the Constitution consists of more than the document drafted in 1787 together with its subsequent amendments:

> There are settled principles of constitutional law that are difficult to square with the language of the document, and many other settled principles that are plainly inconsistent with the original understandings. More important, when people interpret the Constitu-

88. Balkin, *Living Originalism*, 44; hereafter cited in the text.

89. David A. Strauss, "Common Law Constitutional Interpretation," *University of Chicago Law Review* 63, no. 3 (1996), 921.

tion, they rely not just on the text but also on the elaborate body of law that has developed, mostly through judicial decisions, over the years.[90]

The text of the Constitution plays only a nominal role in such decisions, which are largely made "by reference to 'doctrine'—an elaborate structure of precedents built up over time by the courts—and to considerations of morality and public policy."[91] First Amendment doctrine on protection of speech, for instance, with its test of "clear and present danger" first formulated by Justice Holmes in a 1919 dissent, its emergent distinction between "high-value" (political) and "low-value" (for example, obscene or commercially misleading) speech, and its slow and uneven working out of protection for speech that advocates force or the breaking of the law,

> developed over time, fitfully, by a process in which principles and standards were tried and sometimes eventually accepted, sometimes abandoned, sometimes modified, in light of experience and an ongoing, explicit assessment of whether they were sound as a matter of policy.[92]

Respect for the text is certainly one of the ground rules by which the legal game is played, but it has no privileged status as the equivalent of the "command of a sovereign"; "the text and the original understanding of the First Amendment are essentially irrelevant to the American system of freedom of expression as it exists today."[93] It is originalism that seeks to enforce that privileging of a transcendental textual authority.

90. Strauss, "Common Law Constitutional Interpretation," 877; cf. Mark Tushnet, *The Constitution of the United States of America: A Contextual Analysis* (Portland: Hart, 2009), 1: "The 'efficient' constitution of the United States . . . can be found in various written forms, but the document called the US Constitution is only one, and not the most important, of them."

91. Strauss, "Common Law Constitutional Interpretation," 883.

92. David Strauss, *The Living Constitution* (New York: Oxford University Press, 2010), 76.

93. Strauss, *The Living Constitution*, 55.

IV

All of this, however, treats interpretation as a matter of philosophical and methodological choice, abstracted from social interests and from the interests that are specific to the institution of the law. Yet, far from being merely an interpretive response to the letter of the text, to the context of 1791, or to the tradition of judicial precedent, *Heller* has its own interpretive context in the controversies over gun control and gun rights that have wracked American society over the last half century and that have both drawn on and helped to promulgate a fantasy of the gun as "a central icon of American liberty."[94]

By the end of the twentieth century and under the influence of a powerful gun lobby, the American public, and particularly American politicians, had largely abandoned the pursuit of meaningful gun control. A libertarian movement for gun rights emerged in the 1970s, and the Reagan counterrevolution set in place a series of institutional strategies that sought to transform the received meaning of the Second Amendment. These included the appointment of key judges, such as Scalia, and key policy bureaucrats, such as Stephen Markman, who headed the Office of Legal Policy.[95] As chief counsel for Orrin Hatch's Subcommittee on the Constitution, Markman had helped produce *The Right to Keep and Bear Arms*, which found a "long-lost proof" that the amendment expressed an individual right. Under his guidance, the office produced various publications, including an *Original Meaning Jurisprudence* sourcebook, which sought to institutionalize his views about the proper method of interpreting the Constitution, identifying "favored and disfavored lines of cases that tracked 'social issues' of the New Right (for example, the rights of criminal defendants, school prayer, and contracep-

---

94. William D. Merkel, "*The District of Columbia v. Heller* and Antonin Scalia's Perverse Sense of Originalism," *Lewis and Clark Law Review* 13, no. 2 (2009), 355.

95. Siegel, "Dead or Alive: Originalism as Popular Constitutionalism in *Heller*," in Cornell and Kozuskanich, *The Second Amendment on Trial*, 100.

tion and abortion)."[96] In 1993 and 1994, under the Clinton administration, Congress passed moderate gun-control legislation requiring background checks and banning assault weapons. This provoked a backlash from the National Rifle Association (NRA) which helped bring about a Republican victory in House and Senate races in 1994. Over the same two decades, a group of "gun rights advocates, single-topic academics, and contrarian and clever constitutional theorists"[97] helped make an individual-right reading of the Second Amendment respectable; their work was picked up by "a shadow realm of ideological think tanks that nurtured and supported much of the revisionist scholarship used by the *Heller* majority."[98]

Heller is a product, then, of thirty years of organized culture wars; there is a direct line of connection between the libertarian, law-and-order reading that came out of decades of mobilization inside and outside the academy and the "original public meaning" of the Second Amendment that the decision in *Heller* proposes.[99] The case translates the concerns of a "powerful and aggressive social movement,"[100] deeply embedded in the state itself and obsessed with the gun as a fantasy object in the national imaginary, into settled judicial doctrine. On one view, its reading is a rationalization of a focused set of economic and political interests represented by the NRA;[101] on another, it is a form of popular constitutionalism, responding, whether knowingly or not, to a broad shift in public sentiment. In either case, its reading is firmly rooted in the present, and its discovery of a previously unarticulated right is fully within the tradition of common-law jurisprudence.

96. Siegel, "Dead or Alive," 100–101.

97. Merkel, "*The District of Columbia v. Heller* and Antonin Scalia's Perverse Sense of Originalism," 350.

98. Saul Cornell and Nathan Kozuskanich, "Introduction: The D.C. Gun Case," in Cornell and Kozuskanich, *The Second Amendment on Trial*, 9.

99. Siegel, "Dead or Alive," 112.

100. Sunstein, "Second Amendment Minimalism," 252.

101. Cf. Scott Melzer, *Gun Crusaders: The NRA's Culture War* (New York: NYU Press, 2009); Adam Winkler, *Gunfight: The Battle over the Right to Bear Arms* (New York: W. W. Norton, 2013).

The interesting question, I think, is not whether *Heller* or any other decision translates a set of political interests into judicial doctrine but, rather, by what means that act of translation into specifically legal terms is carried out. To ask this question engages some of the central tenets of legal hermeneutics: the mediation of multiple temporalities and multiple structures of interest in the engagement with a text endowed with absolute authority, and the constitution of that authority by means of specific legal protocols of truth and a specific institutional apparatus.

The court that decides in *Heller* is an apparently timeless and transcendental entity. Time and again Scalia refers to a judgment made, for example, in 1833 as "our decision,"[102] as though all the generations of dead justices were standing by his side, united, despite all their manifest disagreements, by the coherence of the doctrine that they have collectively elaborated. Bruno Latour writes similarly of the Conseil d'Etat as a kind of Platonic form:

> The sovereign body to whom commissioners address themselves is . . . composed of two hundred years of phantom counsellors, aggregated by the sheer power of the address in one unique and majestic body of thought that is *ne varietur*, but which nevertheless is endowed with an obscure and stuttering voice which, like that of Pythia, has to be ceaselessly interpreted, assessed, clarified and even rectified.[103]

What does this invocation of an immortal body mean? No doubt, it signifies the majesty and the seamless continuity of the Law; but we can perhaps also take this fiction as a representation of the institutional order of the law, perduring and untouched by the accidents of mortal fallibility. This is the order of the regime of interpretation that endows the text of the Constitution (or, in the case of the Conseil d'Etat, the body of French administrative law) with its privileged status as an object of understanding that specifies the authoritative framework of norms and conventions

---

102. Scalia, "Opinion," 2806, n. 20.

103. Bruno Latour, *The Making of Law: An Ethnography of the Conseil d'Etat*, trans. Marina Britman and Alain Pottage (Cambridge, UK: Polity Press, 2010), 15.

by which it may properly be understood. Both science and the law, Latour writes, have their origins in

> the ancestral learning that still constitutes the basic apprenticeship of scientists and lawyers, namely, the manipulation of texts, or of inscriptions in general, which are accumulated in a closed space before being subjected to a subtle exegesis which seeks to classify them, to criticize them and to establish their weight and hierarchy, and which for both kinds of practitioner replace the external world, which is in itself unintelligible. . . . With scientists, as with judges, we find ourselves already in a textual universe which has the double peculiarity of being so closely linked to reality that it can take its place, yet unintelligible without an ongoing work of interpretation.[104]

That work of interpretation supposes and depends upon a text that its very activity creates as an interpretable object. It both "solicits the question of its object" and at the same time "predicates that object, not in the abstract void of theoretical reflection, but in time, space, aspect."[105] Animated by a frame of attention and by specific rules of recognition,[106] the text of the Constitution becomes something like a sacred object, a sovereign source of knowledge which is at once obscure and mysterious and yet pregnant with an unspoken significance: it promises to reveal a truth—the unchanging truth of the people's right to keep and bear arms, for example—which must be wrested from it by a difficult interpretive labor.

Luc Boltanski and Laurent Thévenot have argued that the sociocultural universe is organized by a number of *orders of worth*—the civic, the industrial, the domestic, and those of fame, of inspiration, and of the market—which are at once modes of justification and modes of rationality. These orders overlap in everyday life and give rise to conflicting and sometimes contra-

104. Latour, *The Making of Law,* 223.

105. Mieke Bal, *Travelling Concepts in the Humanities: A Rough Guide* (Toronto: University of Toronto Press, 2002), 137.

106. Cf. Matthew D. Adler and Kenneth Eimar Himma, eds., *The Rule of Recognition and the U.S. Constitution* (New York: Oxford University Press, 2009).

dictory appeals to guiding principles and evaluations.[107] The six orders they identify do not include a legal order, although the concept of justice is central to Boltanski and Thévenot's account of how each order works. Yet legal interpretation depends upon a specifically legal order of justification, the specific form of legal reasoning for which Latour says the French equivalent is the *moyen*, the legal "means" or argument. Legal reason is that way of thinking that conforms to the protocols of truth and of sound reasoning that are central to the craft of the law—such things as attention to the letter of the law, the application of appropriate standards of scrutiny, and deference to and distinguishing of precedents. An order of legal reason is a way of generating knowledges, truths, and authority from a set of assembled materials by means of those established protocols; it projects and schematizes a bounded world and provides its practitioners with detailed instructions for handling it.[108]

Jack Balkin illustrates a similar concept, that of the legal culture, which has "its own assumptions about which texts are authoritative and what are the permissible and impermissible argumentative moves and operations on authoritative texts," by invoking a counterexample from rabbinical interpretation: the technique of *gematria*, used to discover hidden meanings in the Torah and other parts of the Hebrew Bible. Gematria is an Assyro-Babylonian numerological code, later adopted into Jewish thought, which counts up the numbers assigned to Hebrew or Aramaic letters in a word or phrase, compares them with other words or phrases, and draws the appropriate interpretive conclusions. "Arguments using Gematria," Balkin writes, "are bona fide textual arguments in a particular religious culture; one of

107. Luc Boltanski and Laurent Thévenot, *On Justification: Economies of Worth*, trans. Catherine Porter (Princeton: Princeton University Press, 2006).

108. Steven Mailloux would call this order a *rhetorical hermeneutics*; cf. Steven Mailloux, "From Segregated Schools to Dimpled Chads: Rhetorical Hermeneutics and the Suasive Work of Theory," in *Rhetoric's Pragmatism: Essays in Rhetorical Hermeneutics* (University Park: Pennsylvania State University Press, 2017), 13–22.

the reasons why they are valid moves is that the religious culture assumes that God has placed certain coded meanings in divinely ordained texts for later interpreters to discover."[109] But the use of gematria would be inappropriate in, for example, American constitutional interpretation, where the guiding conventions and background assumptions are quite different.

Those conventions and assumptions derive not from the Constitution itself but from a field of "interpretive pre-understanding"[110]—what Gadamer calls *Vorurteil*, prejudgment or "prejudice"[111]—that governs the rules of legal disputation. Scalia, Stevens, and Breyer disagree bitterly about the assessment of linguistic and historical evidence and the binding force of the precedents in *Heller*; but they can do so because their disagreement is contained and enabled by an underlying agreement about their interpretive responsibility and the general form of legal reasoning that should carry it. The "rules" that they follow emerge from a judicial institution that "constrains the concept of rule-guidedness"[112] and their understanding of what counts as applying a legal rule; but rules, as Fish argues, are not available independent of interpretation:

> Rules, in law or anywhere else, do not stand in an independent relationship to a field of action on which they can simply be imposed; rather, rules have a circular or mutually interdependent relationship to the field of action in that they make sense only in reference to the very regularities they are thought to bring about.[113]

The legal regime is thus a self-reinforcing machinery, the authority of which is continually confirmed in the application of its tacit constraints.

109. Balkin, *Living Originalism*, 353, n. 16.

110. Stanley Fish, "Fish v. Fiss," in *Doing What Comes Naturally*, 125.

111. Hans-Georg Gadamer, *Truth and Method*, 2nd ed., trans. Joel Weinsheimer and Donald G. Marshall (New York: Continuum, 1998 [1960]), 270.

112. Tushnet, "Following the Rules Laid Down," 822.

113. Fish, "Fish v. Fiss," in *Doing What Comes Naturally*, 123.

Yet although one of the functions, or at least one of the effects, of the legal order is to contain and to reconcile political and interpretive differences, the unity of its ideal Platonic form is illusory: it is neither self-contained nor homogeneous, and like all institutions, which persist and survive "through repetition—through the citation of rules and the performance of practices"—it is "never present as such."[114] We can consider its heterogeneity along three different dimensions. The first concerns the multiplicity of legal domains: torts, taxation law, criminal law, corporate law, constitutional law, administrative law, maritime law, and international law all have quite distinct and irreducible objects and goals and regulate distinct spheres of life according to distinct but overlapping structures of normativity. Second, the legal order does not work solely at the level of a "pure" discursive mode: the regime of legal interpretation is made up not just of rules and conventions and precedents but of a whole network of orderings: a constitutional order, with its judicial hierarchies and their relation to other arms of government, but also robes and chambers and microphones and files, attendants and clerks and guards, systems of registration and certification, transcripts and enforceable orders and academic commentaries, legal and paralegal education systems, prisons and warders, and police forces and armies, which are the ultimate support of the order of the law. Finally, the law is constituted by quite heterogeneous discourses, including that of the legislative statute (black letter law), legal argument and advocacy, judicial decision, elaborated doctrine (both casuistic and academic), commentary, paraphrase, summary, index, newspaper reports, expert and lay testimony, bureaucratic documents, forms of pleading, contracts, and the everyday gossip through which the categories of the law are translated into "experience."

This complex and cumbersome apparatus nevertheless works ceaselessly to produce the imaginary unity of doctrine out of the raw materials of statutes and precedents and social interests:

114. Caroline Levine, *Forms: Whole, Rhythm, Hierarchy, Network* (Princeton: Princeton University Press, 2015), 62.

Explicitly, continuously, obsessively, law seeks to pave the way for the effective mobilization of the totality in the specific case. Procedure, hierarchy of norms, judgement, file and even the wonderful word "moyens" . . . : all of the terms speak of this movement of totalization and mobilization, of controlling and reinforcing, of steering and connecting.[115]

The order of legal interpretation is a vast piece of machinery for the sublimation of disparate social interests into a discourse of universality.

V

The originalist methodology that Scalia espouses in *Heller* should probably have produced the opposite result, that is, the limitation of the right to keep and bear arms to the archaic institution of the militia.[116] Such a finding would have brought with it a series of difficult questions: What is the contemporary equivalent of the militia? Which weapons should members of the militia be allowed to keep and bear—muskets? assault rifles? rocket launchers? What would constitute a good regulation of the militia? And above all, why should "fears rooted in the historical memories of the eighteenth century" still exercise power over the very different social conditions of the present?[117]

These are all good reasons (apart from the intrinsic philosophical problems of historicism) to be critical of Scalia's originalist methodology. Saul Cornell comments that "rather than grounding his claims in a dubious originalist argument based on a tortured and intellectually dishonest reading of the evidence, he might have simply argued that the Second Amendment gradually evolved into an individual right over the course of American history."[118] Arguably, however, Scalia has misunderstood his own

115. Latour, *The Making of Law*, 260.
116. Posner, "In Defense of Looseness," 32.
117. Rakove, "The Second Amendment," 165.
118. Cornell, "Originalism on Trial," 639.

methodology and produced a reading that, *within the scope of the common-law traditions of constitutional interpretation,* is a "correct" one. Regardless of the context of origin, the Second Amendment can indeed be construed as enunciating a right which is valid beyond its original expected application—just as the First and Fourteenth Amendments pronounce general rights which have evolved with unforeseen and unforeseeable consequences.

It's difficult to acknowledge this possibility both because Scalia's reading treats the available evidence tendentiously and in violation of his own interpretive principles, and because the decision has significantly contributed to the ongoing catastrophe of American firearms regulation.[119] But in "liquidating and ascertaining" at least one defensible meaning of this "obscure and equivocal" law, Scalia has, for better or worse and within the limits of the particular interpretive game in which he plays, made law precisely *"as judges make it,* which is to say *as though"* he was, in fact, "'finding' it." And the place in which he finds it is not the text of the Constitution but the repertoire of prejudgments, of *Vorurteil,* always invisible in plain sight, that are assembled by the legal apparatus in all its ontological complexity and that constitute the conditions of possibility and validity of legal interpretation.

---

119. "Unlimited gun violence is the natural and probable—and in that sense intended—consequence of a deregulated regime with unlimited access to guns. . . . Out on the legal horizon, the forecast remains essentially unchanged—as far as the eye can see. This inaction is itself an action, a deliberate choice, an affirmation and embrace of the awful, terrible, but easily foreseeable consequences of legal inaction. . . . I conclude that substantive gun control measures are—in the context of American cultural history—not merely improbable but essentially impossible." Charles W. Collier, "The Death of Gun Control: An American Tragedy," *Critical Inquiry* 41, no. 1 (Autumn 2014), 124, 105.

2

Contract, Custom, and the Multiple Historicities of *The Merchant of Venice*

A Daniel come to judgement; yea, a Daniel!

«SHYLOCK, in *The Merchant of Venice*»

The Merchant of Venice is "a profoundly and crudely anti-Semitic play";[1] it "is inextricably implicated in the prejudice and hypocrisy with which it works and on which it depends. . . . It prompts unsavory responses from some in the audience and allows and even induces pleasure for those who are entertained by Shylock's abuse";[2] it is "an unavoidably offensive play"; "there is no doubt that Shakespeare's Jew is based on a stereotype, a vicious caricature of a little understood and much maligned race";[3] and "it

---

1. Derek Cohen, "Shylock and the Idea of the Jew," in *The Merchant of Venice*, ed. Leah S. Marcus (New York: Norton, 2006), 193.

2. Steven Mullaney, *The Reformation of Emotions in the Age of Shakespeare* (Chicago: University of Chicago Press, 2015), 92.

3. Jonathan Miller, *Subsequent Performances* (New York: Viking Penguin, 1986), 155; cited in Gayle Gaskill, "Making *The Merchant Of Venice* Palatable for U.S. Audiences," in *The Merchant of Venice: New Critical Essays*, ed. John W. Mahon and Ellen Macleod Mahon (New York: Routledge, 2002), 375.

would have been better for the last four centuries of the Jewish people had Shakespeare never written this play."[4]

The Merchant of Venice belongs, rightly or wrongly, to the history of anti-Semitism, and without an immense labor of remediation, the values with which the figure of Shylock is invested make the play painful to read and difficult to stage. It raises problems about the discrepancy between what we assume to be Elizabethan values and what we take to be our own historical perspective. As I detail later, the ascription of anti-Semitism to the play is contested (in part because it may be anachronistic), and there is a long history of recuperative interpretation of the character of Shylock; later in this chapter I examine the play's interpretive history, taking the theater as an evolving institution of interpretation—and it is of course very much a play about interpretation and judgment, from the choice that must be made between the three caskets to Shylock's trial and his praise of Portia/ Balthazar as "a Daniel come to judgement." But *The Merchant of Venice* poses other interpretive problems which frame the status of Shylock in the structure of the play, and I begin my reading with some of those questions.

I

The first problem I address concerns the play's generic framework. The external textual evidence for the play's assignment to a genre is given by the title page and the running head in the first Quarto text, which is the basis of most later editions. The full title is "The most excellent Historie of the *Merchant of Venice*. With the extreame crueltie of *Shylocke* the Iewe towards the sayd Merchant, in cutting a iust pound of his fleshe and the obtaining of *Portia* by the choyce of three chests";[5] the running head is "The

4. Harold Bloom, *Shakespeare: The Invention of the Human* (New York: Riverhead, 1998), 190–91; cited in Gaskill, "Making *The Merchant Of Venice* Palatable," 375.

5. William Shakespeare, *The Merchant of Venice*, ed. John Drakakis, Arden Shakespeare Third Series (London: Bloomsbury, 2010), 9; citations of the play in the text are to this edition.

Comical History of the Merchant of Venice," which supplies the usual modern abbreviated title, *The Merchant of Venice.* "Historie" means "story" and is barely a generic term; "comical history" is the closest we get to a generic description, and it corresponds to most analysts' sense that the play's dominant mode is that of the romantic comedy.

That sense is complicated, however, by the way the story of the merchant and the Jew fails to fit neatly into that generic pattern. Shylock can of course be read as the grasping *senex,* the symbol of an obstructive patriarchal power that must be overcome by the young lovers in the model of comic structure that derives from the Hellenistic and Roman New Comedy. The full title's foregrounding of "the extreame crueltie of *Shylocke* the Iewe" and of the conflict between Shylock and Antonio, however, together with the fact that the character of Shylock has historically come to loom much larger than his apparently secondary role in the play would warrant, seem to indicate that its generic structure can't be contained within a single category.[6] The play was entered in the stationer's register in 1598 as "a book of the Merchant of Venice, or otherwise called the Jew of Venice,"[7] and that ambivalence reinforces the sense many readers have of a structural oscillation between these two. "Which is the merchant here, and which the Jew?" asks Portia, entering the trial in the character of the lawyer Balthazar (4.1.170).

We can approach the ambivalence at the heart of the play from a different direction by noticing that its "three delicately interconnected episodes"[8]—the story of the three caskets, the

---

6. Thus already in 1709 Nicholas Rowe wrote, in his introduction to the life and works of Shakespeare, "Tho' we have seen that Play Receiv'd and Acted as a Comedy, and the Part of the *Jew* perform'd by an Excellent Comedian, yet I cannot but think it was design'd Tragically by the Author. There appears in it such a deadly Spirit of Revenge, such a savage Fierceness and Fellness, and such a bloody designation of Cruelty and Mischief, as cannot agree either with the Stile or Characters of Comedy." Cited in *Shakespeare, The Merchant of Venice: A Casebook,* ed. John Wilders (London: Macmillan, 1969), 25.

7. C. L. Barber, *Shakespeare's Festive Comedy: A Study of Dramatic Form and Its Relation to Social Custom* (1959; repr., Cleveland: Meridian Books, 1963), 167.

8. Lawrence Danson, *The Harmonies of* The Merchant of Venice (New Haven: Yale University Press, 1978), 20.

story of the bond given by Antonio to Shylock, and the story of the wedding rings given away by Bassanio and Gratiano to Portia and Nerissa, who are disguised as a lawyer and his clerk—are resolved, respectively, in acts 3, 4, and 5. The core romantic-comedy plot, that is to say, is completed just over halfway through the play; the story of "the extreame crueltie of *Shylocke* the Iewe" is completed in the next act; and act 5 is left to deal with the less-than-comic aftermath of the romantic-comedy plot (or, we might alternatively say, with the less "romantic" dimensions of its working out). Lawrence Danson reads this structure as "a series of dramatic paradoxes, in each of which an apparently irresolvable dilemma is revealed at last to be no dilemma at all, as the opposing ends join in a circle of harmony";[9] but each of these resolutions can be read more darkly. Graham Midgley is, I think, more insightful about the structural problems caused by the imbalance or tension between the bond plot centered on Shylock and the other two plots: if we take the import of act 5 to be the continued dominance of the romantic comedy, then

> Shylock has been allowed to become far too imposing a figure in the previous four acts of the play (where he should have been little more than the equivalent of such characters as Don John or Malvolio in the other love comedies), and this fifth act is a desperate attempt to redress a lost balance. If, on the other hand, we accept Shylock as the central point of interest, the play collapses beautifully but irrelevantly in a finely-written act given over to a secondary theme.[10]

Midgley's suggested solution, however, which privileges the conflict between Antonio and Shylock over the world of love and marriage, is problematic because it depends upon excluding Portia and Belmont from any central role in the play.

---

9. Danson, *The Harmonies of* The Merchant of Venice, 20.

10. Graham Midgley, "*The Merchant of Venice*: A Reconsideration," *Essays in Criticism* 10, no. 2 (1960), 121. A. C. Bradley has a similar concern that the tragic character of Shylock is "a figure with which the destined pleasant ending will not harmonise." A. C. Bradley, *Shakespearean Tragedy: Lectures on Hamlet, Othello, King Lear, Macbeth* (1904; repr., London: Macmillan, 1962), 14.

Another way to understand the play's structure is to read it in terms of a movement from one triangular relationship, between Antonio, Bassanio, and Shylock (in which Bassanio has "engaged myself to a dear friend, / Engaged my friend to his mere enemy") (3.2.260–61) to another, between Antonio, Bassanio, and Portia.[11] Here the romantic comedy succeeds the bond plot because it is conceived more broadly (and I think more adequately) as including in the comedy both the play's titular hero, the merchant Antonio, and the ring plot. The advantage of this reading is that it brings to the fore the tension between the homosocial relationship between Antonio and Bassanio and the heterosexual comedy, and it makes better structural sense of the enmeshing of the play's three plots.

In the first of those triangles, Antonio and Shylock are paired as antagonists who are nevertheless not each other's diametrical opposites (see figure 1). Antonio enters the play in a state of unexplained sadness and leaves it an isolated figure, excluded from the marriages being celebrated and consummated around him in the poetry-saturated world of Belmont. What Jan Hinely calls "the peculiar meanness of his hatred of Shylock"[12] masks the continuity between his own trade as a merchant and Shylock's as a moneylender, and perhaps "the strain that the play's narrative is under to align Antonio's mercantilist practice with the theologically legitimized principles that govern commercial exchange."[13] I discuss later the significant differences between mercantilist and fiscal capitalism, but for now we can note merely that the "mercy" shown by Antonio toward Shylock at the conclusion of the trial scene is a matter of Antonio's accepting "the other half [of Shylock's wealth] in use," to be held in trust for "the gentleman / That lately stole his [Shylock's] daughter" (4.1.379–81), together

---

11. Cf. Leonard Tennenhouse, "The Counterfeit Order of *The Merchant of Venice*," in *Representing Shakespeare: New Psychoanalytic Essays*, ed. Murray M. Schwartz and Coppélia Kahn (Baltimore: Johns Hopkins University Press, 1980), 60.

12. Jan Lawson Hinely, "Bond Priorities in *The Merchant of Venice*," *Studies in English Literature, 1500–1900* 20 (1980), 222–23.

13. John Drakakis, "Introduction," in Drakakis, *The Merchant of Venice*, 111.

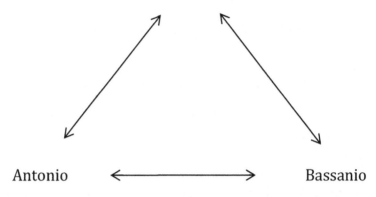

FIGURE I

with the Duke's stipulation that Shylock convert to Christianity and that he "record a gift / . . . of all he dies possessed / Unto his son Lorenzo and his daughter" (4.1.384–86). What this means is that "Antonio, who can have no way of knowing that his ships are not truly lost, has neatly recouped his losses and gained new capital to put *in use* (an apparent gaining of Shylock's vocabulary, along with his money)."[14] Furthermore, Shylock's conversion will entail the loss of the right to practice his trade as a moneylender, and the "deed of gift" he is forced to sign (5.1.292) is a travesty of the free giving that the play so extensively valorizes.[15]

The second triangle constructs Antonio as Portia's rival for the love of Bassanio and explores the dynamics of that rivalry (see figure 2). The social inequality between the merchant Antonio and the "most noble" lord Bassanio (1.1.57) is balanced by Bassanio's indebtedness to the merchant, and even more by the

14. Hinely, "Bond Priorities in *The Merchant of Venice*," 228.

15. Ronald A. Sharp, "Gift Exchange and the Economies of Spirit in *The Merchant of Venice*," *Modern Philology* 83, no. 3 (1986), 252: these gifts "clearly violate something in the spirit of gift."

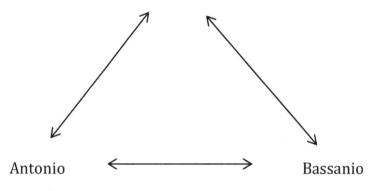

FIGURE 2

coercive generosity with which Antonio releases him from any feeling of indebtedness in order to allow Bassanio the means to pursue his suit with Portia. "Be assured," Antonio proclaims, "My purse, my person, my extremest means / Lie all unlocked to your occasions" (1.1.137–39). As it turns out, his purse is rather empty and he offers a greater gift, binding himself to the usurer as surety in what turns out to be a potentially fatal contract; as Portia puts it to Bassanio in act 5, "You should in all sense be much bound to him, / For, as I hear, he was much bound to you" (5.1.136–37). That bond (the pun on the two senses of this word is one of the play's major semantic hinges) will be cashed later—first, when Antonio writes a letter to Bassanio that sets his sacrifice against Bassanio's love for him in a nearly explicit piece of emotional blackmail:

> Sweet Bassanio, my ships have all miscarried, my creditors grow cruel, my estate is very low, my bond to the Jew is forfeit, and, since, in paying it, it is impossible I should live, all debts are cleared between you and I if I might but see you at my death. Notwithstanding, use your pleasure; if your love do not persuade you to come, let not my letter. (3.2.314–20)

Then, in act 4, Antonio asks Bassanio to give his (Bassanio's) wedding ring to the lawyer "Balthazar" in an act that would recognize the higher claim of Antonio's love over Portia's:

> My lord Bassanio, let him have the ring.
> Let his deservings and my love withal
> Be valued 'gainst your wife's commandement.

(4.1.445–47)

Yet in this same moment Portia, masquerading as Balthazar, "not only has the delicious opportunity to refuse her own money [from Antonio]; she also has Antonio's precious testimony that the balance of erotic credit is now hers":[16]

> ANTONIO: [We] stand indebted, over and above,
>   In love and service to you evermore.

(4.1.409–10)

It is this commitment that Portia will later enforce when she requires Antonio to pledge himself to her (this time with an even higher forfeit) just as he had previously pledged himself to Shylock:

> ANTONIO: I dare be bound again:
>   My soul upon the forfeit, that your lord
>   Will never more break faith advisedly.
> PORTIA: Then you shall be his surety. Give him this. . . .

(5.1.251–54)

Making Antonio the intermediary in the transfer of the ring reverses the ring's previous circulation away from Portia: she weds herself anew to Bassanio by way of her defeated rival. Antonio is a thwarted and almost, but not quite, tragic figure. As Hinely puts it:

> Inasmuch as Antonio experiences the discovery made so painfully in the sonnets, that love bestows the right to give but offers no assur-

---

16. Lars Engle, "'Thrift is Blessing': Exchange and Explanation in *The Merchant of Venice*," *Shakespeare Quarterly* 37, no. 1 (1986), 36.

ance that the gift will be returned, or even valued at its true worth, he holds our sympathy. But Antonio misunderstands the bond between himself and Bassanio, and his efforts to secure for himself first place in Bassanio's love are as disruptive, in their own way, of the comic harmony the play moves toward as are Shylock's efforts to turn money into flesh.[17]

If one dimension of this comic harmony involves Portia's assertion of her erotic credit against the homosocial bond between Antonio and Bassanio, the other dimension that is worked out in the fifth act has to do with the bare containment of female sexuality. For all the lyricism of Lorenzo and Jessica's duet at the beginning of the act ("In such a night as this . . . In such a night . . ."), it ends with the invocation of a series of faithless and betrayed lovers: Troilus and Cressida, Thisbe, Dido, Medea (5.1.1ff). And the play ends with Gratiano's obscene puns on penises and vaginas: ("Well, while I live, I'll fear no other thing / So sore as keeping safe Nerissa's ring") (5.1.306–7). Portia's taunting of Bassanio about his giving away the wedding ring, and symbolically her chastity—"that doctor" (that is, herself in the role of Balthazar) now "hath got the jewel that I loved" (5.1.223–24)—is closely followed, first, by the threat of adultery:

I will become as liberal as you;
I'll not deny him anything I have,
No, not my body, nor my husband's bed,

(5.1.226–28)

and then by an assertion that it has already happened: "For by this ring the doctor lay with me" (5.1.259). Portia's repossession of the ring, Leonard Tennenhouse writes, "not only signals that the betrothal vows have been violated, but it also implies, as the joking in the last act makes clear, that she has just cuckolded her husband, even as he has betrayed her."[18] The union of the lovers

17. Hinely, "Bond Priorities in *The Merchant of Venice*," 238.
18. Tennenhouse, "The Counterfeit Order of *The Merchant of Venice*," 59.

at the play's end, the core motif of romantic comedy, is built on the humiliation of Antonio and on these strong undercurrents of sexual threat.

II

A second interpretive move would look at the semantic associations clustered around the different forms of economy explored in the play: usury, mercantilism, and the gift. Let me start with the story of Jacob and Laban, told in Genesis 30, that Shylock recounts in act I to justify his activity as a usurer and in response to Antonio's self-righteous proclamation that "I neither lend nor borrow / By taking nor by giving of excess. . . . I do never use it" (1.3.57–58, 67). Shylock's story illustrates a taking of profit by sly dealing which is nevertheless "not . . . 'interest,' not as you would say / Directly 'interest'" (1.3.72–73): Jacob, promised by his uncle Laban "all the eanlings [newborn lambs] which were streaked and pied," peeled the bark from a number of branches, so that they were a mixture of light and dark colors, and "stuck up" these "wands" before the "rank" and "fulsome" ewes when they were engaged "in the doing of the deed of kind," with the effect that the lambs born "in eaning time" turned out "parti-coloured" and thus fell to him (1.3.75–85). "This," says Shylock, "was a way to thrive, and he was blest: / And thrift is blessing, if men steal it not" (1.3.85–86). "Thrift" is another of the play's centrally ambiguous terms: here it means material "thriving" or flourishing, the same kind of "thrift" that Bassanio foresees from his wooing of Portia (1.1.175); this thriving is associated with processes of natural increase, like the "work of generation" (1.3.78) that brings forth the lambs, or more generally the noncommercial economy of landowning that underlies Belmont. But "thrift" can also mean something rather different: its modern, capitalist sense of "thriftiness," being careful rather than prodigal with one's means; thus Shylock's servant Lancelet is an "unthrifty knave" (1.3.172), a wastrel; and Shylock cites the puritanical maxim "'Fast bind, fast find.' / A proverb never stale in thrifty mind"

(2.5.52–53). Between these two senses is a third: Shylock's daughter Jessica "with an unthrift love did run from Venice" and "steal from the wealthy Jew" (5.1.15–16): unthriftiness as prodigality, at once a generosity and a wastefulness that is equated with theft. Shylock's contention that "thrift is blessing, if men steal it not" distinguishes usury as a kind of thriving (he speaks a little earlier of "my well-won thrift, / Which he calls 'interest'" [1.3.46–47]) from its unthrifty opposite.

In response to this story, Antonio caustically replies:

> This was a venture, sir, that Jacob served for,
> A thing not in his power to bring to pass,
> But swayed and fashioned by the hand of heaven.
> Was this inserted to make interest good?
> Or is your gold and silver ewes and rams?
>
> (1.3.87–91)

Jacob, he is saying, does not control this outcome but is the mere servant of God; Shylock is rationalizing an event that is purely natural, as though his money generated more money by breeding. Shylock makes a joke of this in his reply: "I cannot tell, I make it breed as fast" [as ewes and rams] (1.3.92). This is what Antonio later describes as taking "a breed for barren metal" (1.3.129): perverting natural processes to unnatural ends, a concept that is close to a direct invocation of Aristotle's distinction between necessary and unnecessary ways of acquiring wealth and his condemnation of usury as a parody of generation.[19] The most hated sort of exchange, Aristotle writes in the *Politics*,

> is usury, which makes a gain out of money itself, and not from the natural object of it. For money was intended to be used in exchange,

19. Michael Ferber notes, "The ideology of comedy celebrates marriage and fertility, and Aristotle denounces the unnatural fertility of usury. So there are two reasons that Shylock, who makes his metal breed, loses his daughter and his wedding ring . . . and that the contestants in the casket game must swear, if they choose wrong, 'Never to speak to lady afterward/In way of marriage' (2.1.41–2): if they choose a breeding metal, they shall become sterile themselves." Michael Ferber, "The Ideology of *The Merchant of Venice*," *English Literary Renaissance* 20 (1990), 442–43.

but not to increase at interest. And this term interest, which means the birth of money from money, is applied to the breeding of money because the offspring resembles the parent. Wherefore of all modes of getting wealth this is the most unnatural.[20]

Just as unthriftiness is at once prodigality and waste or theft, so is thrift at once a thriving based in natural processes and a calculation of gain that perverts them. But those "natural" processes are themselves not unambiguous: in Shylock's telling of it, the story of Jacob's genetic modification of the lambs takes on overtones of sexual disquiet that are missing from the account in Genesis. Whereas the Geneva Bible refers to Jacob laying the "rods" in "the gutters and watering troughs, when they came to drink, before the sheep," Shylock's "He stuck them up before the fulsome ewes" sounds almost like a penetration. The "rankness" and "fulsomeness" of the ewes, the insistence on "the work of generation," "the act," "the doing of the deed of kind" (1.3.76–82) all bring a language of sexuality and perhaps of sexual disgust to this story about the breeding of money and to the self-loathing pun on "ewes" and "iewes" that runs through it.

Yet Antonio's distinction of his own mercantile practice from usury is less than convincing. The words "This was a venture, sir" recall the language with which both Antonio and those around him describe his business practice in act 1, scene 1: to have argosies ventured forth upon the seas is to deal with chance rather than certainty. This is precisely the opposition Francis Bacon draws in contrasting merchants with usurers: "For the usurer being at certainties, and others at uncertainties, at the end of the game most of the money will be in the box."[21] Yet Bacon also makes it clear that mercantile trade is dependent upon the flow of capital that usury makes possible. Antonio accepts the deal with Shylock because "Within these two months . . . I do expect return / Of thrice three times the value of this bond" (1.3.153–55);

20. Aristotle, *Politics*, I: 10, §1258b, trans. Benjamin Jowett, in *The Basic Works of Aristotle*, ed. Richard McKeon (New York: Random House, 1941), 1141.

21. Francis Bacon, "Of Usury," in *Francis Bacon's Essays* (London: Dent, 1906), 124.

Venice is a mercantile society and Antonio trades for profit. As W. H. Auden puts it, "he is a merchant and the Aristotelian argument that money is barren and cannot breed money, which he advances to Shylock, is invalid in his own case."[22] The case against Shylock is misrepresented if it is understood merely in the moral terms of an opposition of certain to uncertain returns on capital.

III

The resonances of the story of Jacob and Laban that Shylock tells to make sense of his practice of usury run deeper than their immediate context. Shylock swears "by Jacob's staff" (2.5.35), and his wife's name is that of Jacob's first wife, Leah. The blind Old Gobbo's mistaking the back of his son Lancelet's head for a beard parodies the deception of the blind Isaac by Jacob, who clothes his arms in kid's skin in order to steal the blessing intended for his hairy brother Esau. Furthermore, the elopement of Jessica, stealing her father's jewels, parallels that of Rachel fleeing with Jacob from Laban and stealing "her father's idols."[23] Thus Shylock "becomes Laban, his daughter and idols stolen, or Esau, bereft of blessing and compelled to witness a younger people thrive, rather than the Jacob he had been."[24] All of this situates Shylock as a character from the Old Testament, the world of law that is opposed to the world of grace represented by the New Testament. The connection between the two worlds is made explicit in Shylock's denunciation of the Christian Lorenzo with whom his daughter has eloped:

> I have a daughter:
> Would any of the stock of Barabbas
> Had been her husband rather than a Christian.
>
> (4.1.291–93)

---

22. W. H. Auden, "Brothers and Others," in *Selected Essays* (London: Faber, 1964), 79.

23. Gen. 31:19 (GNV). (All Biblical citations in this chapter henceforth refer to the Geneva version.)

24. Engle, "'Thrift is Blessing,'" 32.

Barabbas, the thief pardoned in place of Christ, here represents Jewish culpability for Christ's death; and that sacrificial death is thematized in the play's recurrent metaphors of flesh and blood.

Invoking the harmony of the spheres in act 5, Lorenzo adjures Jessica to "Look how the floor of heaven / Is thick inlaid with patens of bright gold" (5.1.58–59). Patens are the plates on which the Eucharist is laid: the body of Christ, his flesh and blood consumed in the sacrament. If, in the play's imaginary, Shylock is the one who bears responsibility for the crucifixion of Christ, the sacrificial victim is Antonio. "I am a tainted wether of the flock, / Meetest for death" (4.1.113–14), Antonio says to Bassanio when his death at Shylock's hands seems certain: he is a diseased and castrated ram, a sacrificial scapegoat, at once Christ as the lamb of God and Abraham's ram, sacrificed in the place of Isaac. Shylock, conversely, is a "wolf," a "bloody creditor" (4.1.72, 3.3.34); his desires are "wolvish, bloody, starved and ravenous" (4.1.137), and he greets Antonio by exclaiming, "Your worship was the last man in our mouths" (1.3.56). When Bassanio describes the paper on which Antonio's letter is written as "the body of my friend, / And every word in it a gaping wound / Issuing life-blood" (3.2.263–65), it is, Tennenhouse writes, "as if Shylock has already begun to feed on Antonio."[25]

Bodies are a unity of flesh and blood, but Portia's strictly literal construal of Shylock's bond threatens to separate them: Shylock may have the flesh, but not the blood. Indeed, Shylock prepares the way for this interpretation when he reads the contract as saying nothing about stanching the bleeding when the flesh is cut ("I cannot find it; 'tis not in the bond" [4.1.258]). But flesh and blood may be separated in other ways: Jessica says she is "a daughter to Shylock's blood" but "not to his manners" (2.3.18–19); and Salanio makes the distinction more literal: "There is more difference between thy flesh and hers than between jet and ivory, more between your bloods than there is between red wine and Rhenish" (3.1.34–36). Yet for Shylock, Jessica is "My own

---

25. Tennenhouse, "The Counterfeit Order of *The Merchant of Venice*," 60.

flesh and blood" (3.1.31). When Salanio mockingly takes this to refer to Shylock's penis ("My own flesh and blood to rebel"), Shylock corrects him: "I say my daughter is my flesh and blood" (3.1.33). Above all, Shylock understands himself as tortured flesh: "If you prick us do we not bleed? . . . If you poison us do we not die?" (3.1.58–60). The balance of sacrifice falls each way.

IV

In addition to its Christian and sacrificial senses, the metaphor of blood carries its humoral sense of youthful passion and its genetic sense of aristocratic lineage. Blood is "warm" (1.1.83); it is equivalent to "a hot temper" (1.2.18); the "redness" of the Prince of Morocco's blood proves his courage (2.1.7); and wild colts are characterized by "the hot condition of their blood" (5.1.74). The two senses are fused in Bassanio's response to Portia after his successful choice of the casket:

> Madam, you have bereft me of all words.
> Only my blood speaks to you in my veins.

$$(3.2.175–76)$$

Here, blood is the speech of the body itself; Bassanio's blood "speaks" to Portia not only sexually but in the sense that they have made a match of their respective social standings—a shared gentility that brings with it a complex of aristocratic values.

Stephen Greenblatt reads *The Merchant of Venice* as being constructed around a series of tensions between the old and the new Law, justice and mercy, revenge and love, calculation and recklessness, thrift and prodigality, and more generally between "Jewish fiscalism and Gentile mercantilism."[26] But it also re-volves around a conflict between the regimes of value associated respectively with Shylock and Portia: whereas he possesses liquid rather than landed capital, and his relation to his environment is

---

26. Stephen Greenblatt, "Marlowe, Marx, and Anti-Semitism," in *Learning to Curse: Essays in Early Modern Culture* (New York: Routledge, 1990), 42.

calculative and instrumental, the "special values" associated with Portia have to do with the *non*instrumental relation to her environment that Belmont represents. "Her world is not a field in which she operates for profit, but a living web of noble values and moral orderliness."[27]

The world of Belmont is that of a gift economy, and the play is suffused with the ethos of the gift. Portia as Balthazar is named for one of the three magi, a bearer of gifts to the Christ child. She brings a gift of freedom to Antonio and is effectively the restorer of his lost fortune; and she is herself a gift to Bassanio:

> Myself, and what is mine, to you and yours
> Is now converted. But now, I was the lord
> Of this fair mansion, master of my servants,
> Queen o'er myself; and even now, but now,
> This house, these servants, and this same myself,
> Are yours, my lord's. I give them with this ring. . . .
>
> (3.2.166–71)

Bassanio in turn has pursued his wooing of Portia with "gifts of rich value" (2.9.90). The Duke makes Shylock the gift of his life and then requires him to draw up a "deed of gift" bequeathing his property to Lorenzo and Jessica (5.1.292). Bassanio asks Balthazar to "Take some remembrance of us as a tribute, / Not as fee" (4.1.418–19). When Balthazar then asks for Portia's ring, Bassanio demurs that "there's more depends on this than on the value" (4.1.430) and explains that the ring was given him by his wife; but Balthazar—enforcing the rules of free giving—sarcastically retorts, "That 'scuse serves many men to save their gifts!" (4.1.440). The gift that is then made of the ring is, in Jacques Derrida's sense, an *absolute* gift, since in giving it Bassanio risks losing his wife; on the other hand, however, "not to give the ring away would be tantamount . . . to converting a gift to capital, and it is clear that the security, material comfort, and suppression of

27. Greenblatt, "Marlowe, Marx, and Anti-Semitism," 43.

liveliness connected with capital are in *The Merchant of Venice* associated with Shylock and contrasted negatively to Antonio's and Portia's imaginative economy of gift."[28]

That economy is most fully realized in the inscription on the casket of lead: "Who chooseth me must give and hazard all he hath" (2.7.9). Shakespeare derived the story of the choice between three caskets from the *Gesta Romanorum*, a translation of which appeared in 1595; in that tale the three mottoes are "Who so chooseth me shall finde that he deserveth," "Who so chooseth mee shall find that his nature desireth," and "Who so chooseth mee shall find that God hath disposed for him."[29] The first of these corresponds completely to the inscription given in the play for the silver casket ("Who chooseth me shall get as much as he deserves") (2.7.7); the second, less closely, to that for the gold casket ("Who chooseth me shall gain what many men desire") (2.7.5); the third substitutes for God's disposition the admonition to "give and hazard all he hath"—not an acceptance of God's ways but an active and absolute embrace of risk and sacrifice. Giving and hazarding are the strict opposite of calculation and of the "certain gains" of usury. They inform the lottery by which the choice of Portia's partner is made—a lottery in which men come "to hazard for my worthless self" (2.9.17); they inform Antonio's practice as a merchant, venturing his capital against uncertain returns and allowing him to turn Bassanio's indebtedness into Antonio's gift; and they inform the ethos of mercy that "blesseth him that gives and him that takes" (4.1.183). "The quality of mercy is not strained" (4.1.180): it is not constrained by law, not a matter of instrumental calculation, but it can only be freely given; whereas Shylock's standing on justice will render him "merely justice and his bond" (4.1.335). As C. L. Barber puts it, "It has been in giving and taking, beyond the compulsion of accounts, that Portia, Bassanio, Antonio have enjoyed the something-for-

---

28. Sharp, "Gift Exchange and the Economies of Spirit," 257.
29. Cited in Danson, *The Harmonies of* The Merchant of Venice, 98.

nothing that Portia here summarizes in speaking of the gentle rain from heaven."[30]

V

Venice, we might say, is the city of contract, and Belmont the place of the gift. This is the gist of those readings of the play that take it as an allegory of Christian values. For Barbara Lewalski, the cues given by the play's biblical allusions allow her to read it through Dante's four levels of allegorical meaning as being "ultimately concerned with the nature of Christian life."[31] For Frank Kermode, "*The Merchant of Venice* is 'about' judgement, redemption and mercy; the supersession in human history of the grim four thousand years of unalleviated justice by the era of love and mercy. It begins with usury and corrupt love; it ends with harmony and perfect love."[32] Two forms of bond are contrasted: the contractual bond and the freely given "gentle bond" of love;[33] the old covenant of the Jews and the new covenant of the Christians.

Roberto Mangabeira Unger turns the opposition of these two forms of life into an illustration of the principles underlying Western contract law:

> The idea that there is a field of experience outside the serious world of work, in which communal relations flourish, can be made to justify the devolution of practical life to the harshest self-interest. The premises to this devolution recall the contrast between Venice and Belmont in *The Merchant of Venice*. In Venice people make contracts; in Belmont they exchange wedding rings. In Venice they are held together by combinations of interest, in Belmont by mutual affection. The wealth and power of Venice depend upon the willingness of its

30. Barber, *Shakespeare's Festive Comedy*, 186.

31. Barbara K. Lewalski, "Biblical Allusion and Allegory in *The Merchant of Venice*," in Marcus, *The Merchant of Venice*, 169–70.

32. Frank Kermode, *Shakespeare, Spenser, Donne: Renaissance Essays* (London: Routledge & Kegan Paul, 1971), 251.

33. Sigurd Burckhardt, "*The Merchant of Venice*: The Gentle Bond," in Wilders, *The Merchant of Venice: A Casebook*, 222.

courts to hold men to their contracts. The claim of Belmont is to provide its inhabitants with a community in which contracts remain for the most part superfluous. Venice is tolerable because its citizens can flee occasionally to Belmont and appeal from Venetian justice to Belmontine mercy. But the very existence of Belmont presupposes the prosperity of Venice, from which the denizens of Belmont gain their livelihood. This is the form of life classical contract theory aims to describe and seeks to define—an existence separated into a sphere of trade supervised by the state and an area of private family and friendship largely though not wholly beyond the reach of contract. Each half of this life both denies the other and depends upon it. Each is at once the other's partner and its enemy.[34]

The fantasy of a "living web of noble values and moral orderliness" that is Belmont is predicated on a strictness of adherence to contract that far outdoes Shylock the Jew's insistence on his bond. This is one of the play's central paradoxes (or perhaps its central joke): that the generous and noble Portia is more legalistic, more cunning, more ruthless than her opponent.

Let me now turn to that paradox in order to map one route out from my reading of the play. What I have been doing to this point is, roughly, a summary of what Ross Chambers calls "commentary," by which he means the ways in which a text implicitly or explicitly makes sense of itself. These include its unspoken assumptions, but also the various forms of *allegoresis* (allegory, metaphor, mythology), the embedding of narrative or descriptive segments which mirror the textual whole, the use of paratextual materials to signal the text's genre, and explicit commentary such as the "moral" of a fable.[35] What Chambers calls "interpretation" may be a redundant repetition of this intratextual commentary, or it may recontextualize it, and this is what I seek to do now by moving out to a broader interpretive context: in the first place, that of the law.

34. Roberto Mangabeira Unger, *The Critical Legal Studies Movement* (Cambridge, MA: Harvard University Press, 1986), 63–64.

35. Ross Chambers, *Meaning and Meaningfulness: Studies in the Analysis and Interpretation of Texts* (Lexington, KY: French Forum, 1979), 142–43.

The Merchant of Venice is coeval with a major transformation of the English common law of contract, and much of the legally oriented commentary on the play reads it as an allegory of the struggle between the common-law courts, with their literalist interpretation of bonds, and the equitable forms of interpretation that characterize the Court of Chancery.[36] Danson, for example, reads the jurisdictional disputes between common lawyers and the chancellor as "a local, secular stage of the endless debate between Mercy and Justice."[37] This account, which "finds Shylock gravitating toward common-law literalism and Portia toward equitable conscience," fits neatly with a dominant literary view of Shylock as the puritanical, humorless, calculating, and literal-minded pursuer of vengeance and "the harshest self-interest," and of Portia and the Venetians as the representatives of "a festive, graceful, generous, loving, interpretive vitality."[38] Molly Mahood agrees with E. P. J. Tucker, however, in rejecting "the equation of common law with strict legalism and Chancery with mercy" as "an oversimplification of Elizabethan legal thinking."[39] Charles Spinosa, whose analysis I follow closely in this section, similarly refuses it, both because it anticipates the outcome of a struggle between the common-law courts and Chancery that broke out only in 1613—namely, "that equity and the equitable right of redemption would take precedence over the narrow common law and its strict reading of bonds and contracts"[40]—and because it

36. Cf. Thomas C. Bilello, "Accomplished with What She Lacks: Law, Equity, and Portia's Con," in *The Law in Shakespeare*, ed. Constance Jordan and Karen Cunningham (Basingstoke, UK: Palgrave Macmillan, 2007), 109–10; Peter G. Platt, *Shakespeare and the Culture of Paradox* (Farnham, UK: Ashgate, 2009), 112–15.

37. Danson, *The Harmonies of* The Merchant of Venice, 84.

38. Charles Spinosa, "The Transformation of Intentionality: Debt and Contract in *The Merchant of Venice*," *English Literary Renaissance* 24, no. 2 (1994), 371.

39. M. M. Mahood, "Introduction," in *The Merchant of Venice*, ed. M. M. Mahood (Cambridge: Cambridge University Press, 2003), 17; cf. E. P. J. Tucker, "The Letter of the Law in 'The Merchant of Venice,'" *Shakespeare Survey* 29 (1976), 93–101. Tucker demonstrates that "while there was indeed a dispute between the common law courts and Chancery, it was purely a jurisdictional conflict and never based upon a clash of fundamental principles" (94).

40. Spinosa, "The Transformation of Intentionality," 370; hereafter cited in the text.

misses that central paradox about the interpretive positions taken by Shylock and Portia.

The core of Spinosa's argument is that the evolution of contract doctrine in late-Elizabethan England corresponds to and in part drives a shift in everyday practice from the tacit frameworks of a customary social order to the explicit forms of obligation that underpin a society of contract. The legal case that crystallizes this shift is *Slade's Case* (1597–1602), which definitively recognized a form of implicit obligation, the *assumpsit*, as a component of a customary bargain and sale: that is, it recognized that when I undertake to pay you at some future date for a good or service that you provide me, whether or not we commit this deal to a formal document, I also thereby make a binding *promise* to do so. The effect of the triumph of *assumpsit* is to read implicit contractual promises into a range of customary practices and then to make those implied promises legally enforceable.

The action of *assumpsit* is an alternative to a traditional action of debt, which it had gradually been displacing, although not without resistance from the Exchequer Chamber, which repeatedly overruled the King's Bench, insisting that the proper cause of action for breaches of contract was that of debt (enforceable by wager of law: the swearing of an oath, supported by eleven oath helpers, who could be hired for the occasion) and that overlapping remedies should not be allowed.[41] The medieval and early-modern law of debt is concerned with things, not with the intentions of the parties; as Luke Wilson puts it, in traditional conceptions of debt, "contract is conceived as a relation between things and where they are located relative to where they ought to be located":[42] what counts is the restitution of the object, regardless of whether the delay in returning it causes a financial loss (because the price of grain has risen, for example, or an opportunity has been lost). It is in that sense that the traditional law

41. A. W. B. Simpson, *A History of the Common Law of Contract: The Rise of the Action of Assumpsit* (Oxford: Clarendon Press, 1975), 293–95.

42. Luke Wilson, "Ben Jonson and the Law of Contract," *Cardozo Studies in Law and Literature* 5, no. 2 (1993), 291.

of debt is precapitalist, taking no account of the temporality of capital. Instead of thinking of debt as something brought about by the parties to the contract and with a delay between a promise and its execution,

> contract is conceived in atemporal terms. Rather than an interval between promise and performance there is only a condition which signifies by its structure that money or goods bargained for are not in the possession of the person who has a right to them. Everything happens at the moment of the bargain: a failure of the items to pass from one person to the other must be corrected by the law because it is, in some sense, *unreal.* Circumstances must be brought into line with the relations that obtain legally: the plaintiff *really* has the thing sued for, therefore he *should* have it.[43]

In the transition from relatively informal bargains and sales to the entrenching of contractual expectations in everyday life, Spinosa argues, we can see a shift "from a culture whose institutions treated everyday transactions in terms of skills and competence to one whose institutions treated everyday transactions as replete with explicit intentions and knowledge" (380). Traditional societies are built around inexplicit expectations of others: if I do you a favor, you will return it at some point, but I have no right to insist on your doing so, or to take you to court if you don't. In the same way, in a face-to-face community, disputes over debts will be resolved in the first instance through informal negotiations among your fellows, and then in a local court where you are personally known; this is why asking oath helpers to support your case (that is, to testify to your honesty) is a workable procedure, although in more formal and less personal settings it will become more open to abuse.

As the doctrine of *assumpsit* takes hold, however, intentional conceptions of transactions come to be rooted in the law and in daily life. At the heart of this process is the doctrine of consideration, which decides whether an informal promise is actionable

---

43. Wilson, "Ben Jonson and the Law of Contract," 291.

or not "by reference to the circumstances in which the promise in question is made,"[44] that is, by reference to the motives or intentions that cause me to make it. The law is suspicious of any "naked" act of will—any purely arbitrary decision to do something; it takes seriously those motives which can be grounded in a specific interest or obligation. Thus "a promise to do something which one is already under an obligation to do, the promise being made in consideration of the circumstance giving rise to the obligation, is the paradigm or central case of a binding promise" (322). I owe you a debt, and *in consideration of* this debt I agree to repay it. What is curious about the common law, writes A. W. B. Simpson, is not that it enforces business agreements or binding promises but "that the actionability of informal promises is made to turn upon an analysis of the motivating reasons which induced the promisor to make the promise" (326). *Slade's Case* is the moment when the logic of intentionality comes to assume "a new degree of importance in conceptualizations of person and action in the theater and in the shapes of popular consciousness generally."[45]

Part of what is involved in this shift is that people become intensely aware of their own motives: "They focus on those aspects of life which may be easily accounted for with clear, determinate intentions, and they learn how to represent these intentions."[46] They may also become rather sophisticated at misrepresenting intentions, or at playing a multiplicity of roles. The theater translates that ethos of intention into cultural models, and it is doubly a pedagogic institution: it teaches us to analyze the way other people (other characters) represent themselves, and how to be actors ourselves.

On Spinosa's reading, *The Merchant of Venice* gives a sympathetic view of the contractual mode of life where intentions are fully on display. The characters who are at home in this world

44. Simpson, *A History of the Common Law of Contract*, 317; hereafter cited in the text.
45. Wilson, "Ben Jonson and the Law of Contract," 291.
46. Spinosa, "The Transformation of Intentionality," 377; hereafter cited in the text.

are the non-Jewish Venetians, who tend to dramatize their own intentions and assumptions. In making his choice of casket, for example, Bassanio examines the possible motives that might be brought to bear in making the choice, seeing himself as though he were another: he "looks at himself as a typical agent and examines how that agent is solicited to act. Consequently, he becomes able to isolate his intention and compare it with other possible intentions in the situation. He then chooses on the basis of a roughly figured but abstract, computational probability" (388). The loquacious and self-reflexive Venetians are "the exemplary citizens in the world organized by the ethos of the assumpsit" (391), and their key representative is Portia, who is able to reveal an intention to take Antonio's life in Shylock's claiming of his bond: an interpreter such as her "could always import unusual intentions into any of competence's acts and show that they had been there all along even if nothing like such intentions had ever been dreamt of" (404).

The alien Shylock, by contrast, inhabits an earlier, customary world where everyday transactions are treated in terms of skills and competence rather than being "replete with explicit intentions and knowledge" (380); he is, as Walter Cohen puts it, "a figure from the past: marginal, diabolical, irrational, archaic, medieval."[47] He may seem to be calculating, listing all the reasons why he shouldn't rely on Antonio's credit (Antonio's overweighting of "the high-risk portion of his portfolio" and its inadequate diversification);[48] yet he then proceeds to accept the bond, sensing that it is a way "to explore and deepen his bitter relations with Antonio" (393). So little is he a calculating usurer that he sets no interest on the loan, and when offered repayment, even of twice the amount, he refuses it, insisting on the forfeit. Pressed for his reasons, he offers only that "it is my humour," just as

47. Walter Cohen, "*The Merchant of Venice* and the Possibilities of Historical Criticism," *ELH* 49, no. 4 (1982), 771.

48. Spinosa, "The Transformation of Intentionality," 392; hereafter cited in the text.

Some men there are love not a gaping pig!
Some that are mad if they behold a cat!
And others, when the bagpipe sings i'th' nose,
Cannot contain their urine . . . .

(4.1.42, 46–49)

My reasons are unreasonable, nonsensical, known only to myself, he says. Having little reflective distance from his own motives, and so unable to see his activities "as directed by clear determinate intentions that play a part in a network of others' clear determinate intentions" (394), Shylock reads the story of Jacob and Laban as an account of skillful cunning rather than conscious deceit: men flourish by using their native abilities, without thinking too hard about the moral implications of their acts. That he is a figure of customary life comes out most clearly in his forensic arguments, where

> he does not simply say that Antonio owes him the flesh or even that the pound of flesh is already his and that Antonio merely detains it. Rather, true to the notions behind the bond, Shylock speaks as though flesh embodies for him what is most his own and as though controlling what is his own is the basis of human relations. Shylock exemplifies these claims by identifying himself with his own flesh, which itself cries out for the pound of Antonio's flesh. Shylock does not speak with any independence from his body. (397)

"I am a Jew," he cries out:

> Hath not a Jew eyes? Hath not a Jew hands, organs, dimensions, senses, affections, passions? Fed with the same food, hurt with the same weapons, subject to the same diseases, healed by the same means, warmed and cooled by the same winter and summer as a Christian is? If you prick us do we not bleed? If you tickle us do we not laugh? If you poison us do we not die? And if you wrong us shall we not revenge? (3.1.53–60)

Revenge, the *lex talionis* that requires an eye for an eye, is a precontractual law of custom, and here it is immediately tied to bodily being. Shylock "understands his actions as unmediated fleshy responses to solicitations of the environment" (398). His feeling of unmediated hurt is of course a rationalization, and we should read it with the appropriate dramatic irony; but in the most general sense Shylock's habits of thinking and acting belong to the moral economy that governs the gift rather than to the market that governs the exchange of commodities; to the world of tacit obligation rather than the world of contract.[49] In *Time and Commodity Culture* I wrote of these two forms of life that

> the one supposes and enacts a continuity between persons and things and thus the formation of chains of reciprocal obligation by means of the transfer of objects; the other supposes and enacts a discontinuity between persons and things and thus a reciprocal independence in relatively more abstract processes of transfer.

And I then added that "in no real society . . . are these contexts entirely distinct; and each is present in all real societies."[50] The world of Belmont, with its "imaginative economy of gift"[51] and its "living web of noble values and moral orderliness,"[52] is a world entirely formed by and dependent upon its contractual (and patriarchal) conditions of existence. Conversely, the usury that Shylock practices, for all its apparent ruthlessness, is a part of what Marcel Mauss calls an "antiquated and dangerous gift economy, encumbered by personal considerations" and by a close and deeply ambivalent relationship between lender and debtor.[53]

VI

This reading of the play attempts to make sense of a particular historical context, that of a major cultural shift which ex-

---

49. Cf. Michael Polanyi, *The Tacit Dimension* (Chicago: University of Chicago Press, 1966).

50. John Frow, *Time and Commodity Culture* (Oxford: Clarendon Press, 1997), 131.

51. Sharp, "Gift Exchange and the Economies of Spirit," 257.

52. Greenblatt, "Marlowe, Marx, and Anti-Semitism," 43.

53. Marcel Mauss, *The Gift: Forms and Functions of Exchange in Archaic Societies*, trans. Ian Cunnison (New York: Norton, 1967), 52.

tends across the whole of early modernity but which we can, in its legal crystallization, localize to the late sixteenth century and the moment of the play's first production. Yet the historicity of the play reaches well beyond that context, both forward and backward.

Walter Cohen's seminal essay "*The Merchant of Venice* and the Possibilities of Historical Criticism" cites a passage from Fredric Jameson's *The Political Unconscious* in which Jameson notes that the operation of thinking historically must choose between

> study of the nature of the "objective" structures of a given cultural text (the historicity of its forms and of its content, the historical moment of emergence of its linguistic possibilities, the situation-specific function of its aesthetic) and something rather different which would instead foreground the interpretive categories or codes through which we read and receive the text in question.[54]

Jameson goes on to opt, "for better or for worse," for the second of these alternatives: for understanding that texts always come mediated "through sedimented layers of previous interpretations, or—if the text is brand-new—through the sedimented reading habits and categories developed by those inherited interpretive traditions."[55] Cohen's argument, in brief, is to hope that it is possible to have it both ways. *The Merchant of Venice* has been subject to a plethora of interpretations, being read

> as the unambiguous triumph of good Christians over a bad Jew; as the deliberately ambiguous triumph of the Christians; as the unintentionally ambiguous, and hence artistically flawed, triumph of the Christians; as the tragedy of Shylock, the bourgeois hero; and as a sweeping attack on Christians and Jews alike.[56]

What is needed, then, is "not so much to interpret as to discover the sources of our difficulty in interpreting, to view the play as a symptom of a problem in the life of late sixteenth-century

---

54. Fredric Jameson, *The Political Unconscious: Narrative as a Socially Symbolic Act* (London: Methuen, 1981), 9.

55. Jameson, *The Political Unconscious*, 9.

56. Cohen, "*The Merchant of Venice* and the Possibilities of Historical Criticism," 767.

England."[57] But there are two difficulties with this argument. The first, as Laurence Lerner puts it, is that the appeal to a past "system of thought" can inform our judgment "only if some kind of direct access to the past is possible; if it produces the same kind of arguments as already rage about the plays, we may find ourselves reasoning in a circle."[58] The second is that this strategy undoes the force of Jameson's insight into the *multiple* historicities of a text: reducing *The Merchant of Venice* to its late sixteenth-century context does away with precisely those "interpretive categories or codes through which we read and receive the text in question." And it thereby does away with the "peculiar contingency of the work of art, whose meaning is dependent upon its context but never definitively determined by any one context—least of all its original context."[59] In Georges Didi-Huberman's words, "everything past is definitively *anachronistic*: it exists or subsists only through the figures that we make of it; so it exists only in the operations of a 'reminiscing present', a present endowed with the admirable or dangerous power, precisely, of *presenting* it, and, in the wake of this presentation, of elaborating and representing it." At the same time, however,

> the past, too, functions as a constraint. First as a *Zwang* [constraint, compulsion] in Freud's sense, for the past offers itself to the historian as a sovereign obsession, a structural obsession. Second, because it sometimes imposes itself as an alienating element of the historical interpretation itself—a vexing paradox. What would be gained, in fact, by fully realizing the program of interpreting the realities of the past using only the categories of the past, supposing that this has any concrete meaning? We would perhaps gain an interpretation of the Inquisition armed solely with the arguments . . . of the inquisitor. Even if it were also armed with the arguments (the defenses and

57. Cohen, "*The Merchant of Venice* and the Possibilities of Historical Criticism," 767.

58. Laurence Lerner, "Wilhelm S and Shylock," in Marcus, *The Merchant of Venice*, 212.

59. Amy Knight Powell, *Depositions: Scenes from the Late Medieval Church and the Modern Museum* (New York: Zone Books, 2012), 14.

screams) of the tortured, this interpretation would nonetheless become a vicious circle.[60]

My second route out from a reading of the play to a broader interpretive context (that of the conditions of possibility of any particular interpretation) tries to take seriously the question of how we should construct the changing categories through which the text becomes intelligible to subsequent generations. At its heart is the question of how we are to deal, and how the institution of the theater has historically dealt, with the apparently anti-Semitic force of the figure of Shylock. Since 1945, writes Dennis Kennedy—that is, since our full awareness of the attempt by German fascism to exterminate European Jewry in its entirety—"we have been in possession of a new text of the play, one which bears relationships to the earlier text but is also significantly different from it."[61] Shylock embodies a fantasy about Jewishness that has been central to English self-understanding from the early medieval period onwards and which is closely cognate with the cultural fantasies informing that genocidal rage in Nazi Germany.

Here is a slightly earlier embodiment of that fantasy, Christopher Marlowe's Jew of Malta, Barabas, boasting to the slave Ithamore about his exploits:

> I walk abroad a nights
> And kill sicke people groaning under walls:
> Sometimes I goe about and poyson wells;
> And now and then, to cherish Christian theeves,
> I am content to lose some of my Crownes;
> That I may, walking in my Gallery,
> See 'em goe pinion'd along by my doore.

60. Georges Didi-Huberman, *Confronting Images: Questioning the Ends of a Certain History of Art*, trans. John Goodman (University Park: Pennsylvania State University Press, 2005), 38–39.

61. Dennis Kennedy, *Looking at Shakespeare* (Cambridge: Cambridge University Press, 1993), 200; cited in Drakakis, "Introduction," 129.

Being young I studied Physicke, and began
To practise first upon the Italian;
There I enrich'd the Priests with burials,
And alwayes kept the Sexton's armes in ure
With digging graves and ringing dead men's knels:
And after that I was an Engineere,
And in the warres 'twixt *France* and *Germanie*,
Under pretence of helping *Charles* the fifth,
Slew friend and enemy with my strategems.
Then after that was I an Usurer,
And with extorting, cozening, forfeiting,
And tricks belonging unto Brokery,
I fill'd the Jailes with Bankrouts in a yeare,
And with young Orphans planted Hospitals,
And every Moone made some or other mad,
And now and then one hang himselfe for griefe,
Pinning upon his breast a long great Scrowle
How I with interest tormented him.[62]

Marlowe's Barabas is, as one editor notes, "an increasingly hysterical caricature—a zany, wickedly funny, homicidal (in truth, genocidal), immensely intelligent and realistically implausible creation who runs through in five acts practically all the choices actors have made over the centuries for Shylock: comic monster, buffoon, tragic victim, flawed and overwronged ordinary human, sadistic genius."[63]

If we understand the theater as an evolving interpretive institution, the history of performances of *The Merchant of Venice* (which in practice largely means the history of the ways in which Shylock is played) is a document of those often contradictory interpretive choices. We can understand these choices as inherent in the character itself, as Molly Mahood does:

62. Christopher Marlowe, *The Rich Jew of Malta*, in *The Complete Works of Christopher Marlowe*, vol. 1, ed. Fredson Bowers (Cambridge: Cambridge University Press, 1973), 174–98.

63. A. R. Braunmuller, "Introduction," in *The Merchant of Venice*, ed. A. R. Braunmuller (New York: Penguin, 1970), xxxv.

[Shylock] meets several different expectations. At one moment he is the ogre of medieval romance, at another the devil of the morality play, at another the usurer of citizen comedy; from time to time also the proud, even awesome, remnant of the House of Jacob from the Book of Genesis. He may even appear to us fleetingly as the Pantaloon of the *commedia dell'arte*, who was an avaricious Venetian householder with a large knife at his side, plagued by a greedy servant and an errant daughter.[64]

Or we can understand them as a chronological series, unfolding unevenly and often recursively over more than four centuries. Crucially, however, we know almost nothing of the beginning of that series: *The Merchant of Venice* was recorded as being played twice before King James in February 1605; it then disappeared for a century, reappearing in 1701 in the form of George Granville's extensively and crudely rewritten adaptation *The Jew of Venice*, in which Shylock was played as a comic villain.

The assumption has long been prevalent that *The Merchant of Venice* was first played in an atmosphere of hostility toward Jews fostered by the trial of Elizabeth's physician Roderigo Lopez and by the revival of Marlowe's *Jew of Malta* in 1595; that Shylock was played as a stereotypical stage Jew; and that the Elizabethan audience would have felt that the conditions of Shylock's pardon—his forced conversion and forced renunciation of usury—"completed the Duke's god-like act of mercy because they made it possible that Shylock 'should see salvation.'"[65] John Gross, for example, writes that

> to an Elizabethan audience, the fiery red wig that he almost certainly wore spelled out his ancestry even more insistently than anything that was actually said. It was the same kind of wig that had been worn by Marlowe's Barabas and before that by both Judas and Satan in the old mystery plays.[66]

64. Mahood, "Introduction," 12.
65. Mahood, "Introduction," 18.
66. John Gross, *Shylock: A Legend and Its Legacy* (New York: Simon and Schuster, 1992), 27.

And William Poel's attempt to restore a historically authentic performance in 1898 had him playing Shylock as a low-comic role, in red wig and shabby clothes—"a grotesque and unsympathetic villain."[67] In fact, there is little evidence for the red wig, or even that Judas in the mystery plays had red hair; there is little evidence of an English theatrical tradition of anti-Semitic stereotyping; Lopez's Jewishness was never an issue at his trial or in public demonstrations, since he was identified at the time with a supposed Catholic plot; Shylock's forced conversion, rather than being seen as a path to salvation, might well have reminded an audience of the forced conversion of the Jews in Spain a century earlier; and, in short, there is little archival basis for the view that the Elizabethan Shylock was played as the type of the despised Jew.[68] Rather, as Emma Smith argues, this anti-Semitically conceived Shylock is a Victorian back-projection, constructed as a contrast to Henry Irving's long-running portrayal of "a tragic figure cruelly wronged in a world of racial intolerance," and "many of the connotations of Jewishness that criticism has wanted to locate in the early modern period turn out to be symptoms of Victorian racial 'science.'"[69]

The key eighteenth-century productions—Macklin's "sullen, malevolent, implacable Jew"[70] in a Drury Lane performance that ran for a half century starting in 1741, and John Philip Kemble's Shylock of 1789—played him as a serious villain and a figure alien to the sympathies of the audience. A major turn, to "the sympathetic Shylock, psychologically human and essentially a martyr to Christian intolerance,"[71] was effected (although there is some

67. Charles Edelman, *Shakespeare in Production: The Merchant of Venice* (Cambridge: Cambridge University Press, 2002), 36.

68. Cf. Edelman, *Shakespeare in Production*, 2ff; Charles Edelman, "Which Is the Jew That Shakespeare Knew? Shylock on the Elizabethan Stage," *Shakespeare Survey* 52 (1999), 99–106; Emma Smith, "Was Shylock Jewish?" *Shakespeare Quarterly* 64, no. 2 (2013), 188–219.

69. Smith, "Was Shylock Jewish?," 188–90.

70. Mahood, "Introduction," 43.

71. Stephen Orgel, *Imagining Shakespeare* (Basingstoke, UK: Palgrave Macmillan, 2003), 145.

argument about how radical the break was) by Edmund Kean, whose reading of the role in 1814 "took the Romantic preoccupation with individual passion and applied it to Shylock, allowing audiences to experience sympathy and pity for the antagonist."[72] Michael Ragussis notes that the period from the French Revolution to the publication of Scott's *Ivanhoe* in 1819 was one in which "'the Jewish question' emerged as a pressing European concern,"[73] and Kean's performance doubtless reflects this new awareness of the struggle for Jewish emancipation, as does Hazlitt's warm reception of it, which David Bromwich links to Hazlitt's 1831 essay "Emancipation of the Jews."[74]

But without doubt the crucial transformation in the character of Shylock was Henry Irving's complex, wounded, dignified Shylock; his production opened at the Lyceum in London in 1879, with Ellen Terry as Portia, and ran for over a thousand performances in England and the United States, finally closing in 1905; it continues to shape the theatrical understanding of Shylock as a tragic hero. Naturalizing "the emotionally volatile, theatrically vengeful Shylocks popularised by Macklin and Kean," Irving's Shylock "was very much the product of his age, a man marked by an intense pathos and a keen sense of injury that bespoke the refined sensibilities of his race, a businessman whose dignity and intelligence, to the outrage of some, rivalled those of a Rothschild."[75] Perhaps the most famous scene in Irving's production was an interpolated and pathos-laden episode at the end of act 2, scene 6, in which Shylock returns to his house. Irving's grandson describes it as follows:

72. Jonathan Bate, "*The Merchant of Venice* in Performance: The RSC and Beyond," in *The Merchant of Venice*, ed. Jonathan Bate and Eric Rasmussen (London: RSC/Macmillan, 2010), 117. For the contrary view, cf. Edelman, *Shakespeare in Production*, 13–14.

73. Michael Ragussis, "Writing Nationalist History: England, the Conversion of the Jews, and *Ivanhoe*," *ELH* 60, no. 1 (1993), 182.

74. David Bromwich, *Hazlitt: The Mind of a Critic* (New York: Oxford University Press, 1983), 406–7; cf. Jonathan Bate, *Shakespearean Constitutions: Politics, Theatre, Criticism 1730–1830* (Oxford: Clarendon Press, 1989), 180–81.

75. James Bulman, *Shakespeare in Performance: The Merchant of Venice* (Manchester, UK: Manchester University Press, 1991), 28, 33.

The last scene of this act was Shylock's house by the bridge. After the elopement of Jessica and Lorenzo, the curtain fell slowly as the maskers, sweeping across the stage, swallowed them up. After a second or two it rose again upon an empty stage. Shylock was seen returning over the bridge. He crossed to his house and, unsuspecting, knocked upon the door. A second and a third knock echoed through the empty house. The curtain fell again as, without word or outward sign, Irving conveyed to the audience Shylock's crushing realization of his daughter's perfidy.[76]

The extent to which the play became, in Irving's reading, a character study of Shylock is indicated by his dropping act 5 completely after 1880.

Irving's interpretation dominated the next half century of performances of *The Merchant of Venice*. Edelman notes its influence on Max Reinhardt's 1905 production at the Berlin Deutsches Schauspielhaus, with Rudolf Schildkraut playing Shylock:

A full-blooded actor and a conscious Jew, he entered into the feelings of a hunted, tormented and therefore unbalanced being, through whom generations of Jews voiced their shrill protest against their persecutors of all times. At the same time, Schildkraut imbued the character with an unspeakable melancholy, which was elemental compared with the ennui of Antonio. Injustice was round him like a shroud.[77]

Post-Holocaust productions worked even harder to redeem the play from the imputation of anti-Semitism: Erwin Piscator's 1963 version for the West Berlin Freie Volksbühne incorporated projected statistical information about the conditions in which the Jews of early-modern Venice lived. A 1966 production at the Berkshire Festival in Massachusetts by Georg Tabori, most of whose family had been murdered in Auschwitz, was called *The Merchant of Venice as Performed at Theresienstadt* and staged as

76. Laurence Irving, *Henry Irving: The Actor and His World* (London: Faber & Faber, 1951), 341; cited in Edelman, *Shakespeare in Production*, 154.

77. Edelman, *Shakespeare in Production*, 32, quoting the reminiscences of Hermann Sinsheimer.

a play performed by prisoners in the concentration camp, with Shylock at the end breaking out of his role to attack a guard and then kill himself.[78] And Charles Marowitz's 1977 rewriting of the play as *Variations on The Merchant of Venice* has the trial scene concluding with Shylock's Jewish supporters—Chus, Tubal, and others—suddenly revealing themselves as armed Zionist resistance fighters as a prelude to Shylock's "I am a Jew" speech.[79]

A number of commentators call attention to the disruptive force of Theodore Komisarjevsky's 1932 production for the Stratford Festival, which attacked "the moral sententiousness that had characterised *Merchants* for more than fifty years,"[80] playing it with a kind of carnivalesque abandon. Tyrone Guthrie's 1955 performance at the Stratford Festival of Canada initiated a tradition of emphasizing the homosexual dimension of the relation between Antonio and Bassanio and construed the Venetians as persecutors of the Jew. And Don Selwyn's 2002 film *The Māori Merchant of Venice* (*Te Tangata Whai Rawa o Weniti*) draws an explicit parallel between the persecution of Venetian Jews and the colonial subjugation of Māori. But two modern productions above all stand out for their challenge to Irving.

The first is Jonathan Miller's "great watershed production"[81] at the National Theatre in 1970, in which Laurence Olivier's Shylock is a Victorian financier—a well-dressed banker striving for assimilation, and the mirror image of Antonio ("Which is the merchant here, and which the Jew?"), apart from a small yarmulke that he wears beneath his top hat. Yet this Shylock is still an outcast: by undermining the romance of Belmont, Miller foregrounds the "explosion of frank, murdering, tribal hatred at the core of it";[82] and with the Victorian setting he contests those supposedly enlightened values that Irving implicitly opposed to a

---

78. Edelman, *Shakespeare in Production*, 62–64.

79. Charles Marowitz, *The Marowitz Shakespeare* (New York: Marion Boyars, 1990).

80. Bulman, *Shakespeare in Performance*, 54.

81. Orgel, *Imagining Shakespeare*, 146.

82. *The Observer*, April 3, 1970; cited in Bulman, *Shakespeare in Performance*, 99.

barbaric Elizabethan past. Olivier's offstage howl of despair after the trial scene and the singing of the Kaddish that closes the play sharpen the tension between the norms of romantic comedy and Shylock's tragic destiny within them.

Antony Sher's Shylock in Bill Alexander's 1987 production for the Royal Shakespeare Company, by contrast, is played as a grotesque stereotype, with Antonio and Bassanio cast as lovers. Deliberately provoking the audience's "discomfort with swarthy Semites and closet queens,"[83] Alexander closes off the possibility of identification with the wronged Jew. The production invites an anti-Semitic and homophobic response, and indeed, it received it: rather than reflecting on the systemic roots of bigotry, the audience cheered at the moment of Shylock's undoing. The theatrical emotions set in play by *The Merchant of Venice* channel larger structures of group identification that are not easily contained.

It is little surprise, then, that productions of *The Merchant of Venice* in Israel, the Occupied Territories, and the Arab world "do not universally evoke the discomforting ambivalence that Western audiences have come to expect, and instead are often marked by their thematic clarity," reflecting a political polarization in which both Israelis and Palestinians understand themselves as historical victims.[84] On one side, the stereotype of the bloodthirsty Jew informs both Khalil Moutran's 1922 translation of the play into Arabic for a Cairo theater company, identifying Shylock not as a confessional but as a racial enemy, and Ali Ahmed Bakathir's anti-Zionist rewriting of the play in 1945 as *The New Shylock*; on the other, numerous Israeli productions portray Shylock as a heroic victim of the Gentiles, a remnant of an older order who can now be defended only by a strong and intransigent Jewish state. The Habima National Theater's 2012 staging of the play in Hebrew at the London Globe opens with a mime scene in which joyous Venetians in white robes surround

83. Bulman, *Shakespeare in Performance*, 142.

84. Mark Bayer, "*The Merchant of Venice*, the Arab-Israeli Conflict, and the Perils of Shakespearean Appropriation," *Comparative Drama* 41, no. 4 (Winter 2007–2008), 466.

Shylock, snatch away his skullcap and phylactery bag, tie him with its leather straps, and kick him savagely; one of the assailants then removes his mask to reveal himself as Antonio, still overcome with laughter, who speaks the play's opening lines: "In sooth, I know not why I am so sad."[85] Shylock as victim or Shylock as malevolent Jew: the criteria used to validate each interpretation "can only be generated from inside particular—and antithetical—interpretive communities. . . . The authority presumably conferred by *The Merchant of Venice* is, in a sense, illusory and severely limited by its ubiquity and by its simultaneous employment for contradictory agendas."[86] Regimes of interpretation, I have said, are not necessarily reducible to the interests of particular social groups; in the case of the stark polarities brought about by the Israeli occupation of Palestine, such a reduction is inevitably difficult to avoid.

VII

Shylock is not Marlowe's Barabas, but *The Merchant of Venice* mobilizes many of the same stereotypes that inform Marlowe's play, most centrally that of the "Jewish crime" of ritual murder as it heightens the representation of usury. In James Shapiro's reconstruction, a central component of the myth of ritual murder is the circumcision of the victim before his death; Shylock's desire to cut a pound of Antonio's flesh is an occluded threat of circumcision, since "flesh" works here as a euphemism (as it does in the Geneva Bible and in *Romeo and Juliet*) for the penis;[87] and

85. Michael Handelzalts, "Shylock in the Shadow of the Shoah," *Haaretz*, May 15, 2012, https://www.haaretz.com/israel-news/culture/shylock-in-the-shadow-of-the-shoah-1.5155859; John Nathan, "Review: Habima's Bravura *Merchant of Venice*," *The Jewish Chronicle*, May 31, 2012, https://www.thejc.com/culture/theatre/review-habima-s-bravura-merchant-of-venice-1.33673.

86. Bayer, "*The Merchant of Venice*, the Arab-Israeli Conflict, and the Perils of Shakespearean Appropriation," 469.

87. James Shapiro, *Shakespeare and the Jews* (New York: Columbia University Press, 1996), 122; hereafter cited in the text.

circumcision in turn has immediate connotations of castration (hence, perhaps, Antonio's description of himself as a "tainted wether"). One of the play's precursor texts, Silvayn's *The Orator*, makes the equation explicit. Insisting to the judge that the pound of flesh should be handed over to him, the Jew says: "What a matter were it then if I should cut of his privy members, supposing that the same would altogether weigh a just pound" (126). But the displacement of the flesh from the genitals to the part of the body "nearest the merchant's heart" (4.1.229) is in fact, as Shapiro demonstrates, a double displacement, invoking as it does the Pauline metaphor of the "circumcision of the heart," the spiritual rather than merely fleshly circumcision that marks the difference of the Christian from the Orthodox Jew; "viewed in light of this familiar exegetical tradition, Shylock's decision to exact his pound of flesh from near Antonio's heart can be seen as the height of the literalism that informs all of his actions in the play" (127).

The Merchant of Venice, Shapiro writes, "is . . . not 'about' ritual murder or a veiled circumcising threat any more than it is about usury, or marriage, or homosocial bonding, or mercy, or Venetian trade, or cross-dressing, or the many other social currents that run through this and every other one of Shakespeare's plays" (121). Plays are not sermons. But this one does thematize some of the darkest currents of English national life, from the blood libel of Hugh of Lincoln onward, and it has in turn been mobilized time and again to racist ends, providing "confirmation of the insidious threat Jews posed to the economic, sexual, and religious life of the nation" (200). If it speaks to us about contract and the increase on capital, it does so by representing the Jew, the representative of a customary world of direct transaction, as the villain of an emergent capitalist order whose true, intentionally reflexive representatives are passed off as embodiments of the economy of the gift. Alternatively, however, as Derrida argues, the play sets up an entire history of relations between the Christian and the Jew in such a way that Shylock comes to figure as the one who is to be mercifully forgiven, and so to understand "that he is in the process of being had . . . in the name of the sublime transcendence of grace"; the accusation of anti-Semitism does not apply to a work "that stages with an unequalled power all the great motives of Christian anti-Judaism."[88]

These are the "sedimented layers of previous interpretations" through which the text reaches us; the Shoah adds a devastating layer to the text's semantic history, opening an interpretive abyss between past and present audiences; and the Israeli occupation of Palestine adds one more.

There are many uses to which we can put this play; each of them depends upon the interests we bring to it—"interests" in the broad sense of what we have a stake in: what is of personal or political or economic concern to us—and on the sedimented interests the text bears with it. The questions we may ask of it are not dictated by the text, nor by the chain of previous interpretations, but by the interplay between past and present interests as they are mediated by that chain. Those interests are governed by a particular history, but the quantum of possible conjunctions of past and present histories cannot be limited by normative criteria of appropriateness. They might, in this case, have to do with everything that is at stake in thinking about Jewishness and the cultural fantasies associated with it; or about usury and the grounds of economic value and debt; or about the overdetermined relations between sexual, social, and economic fantasies; or about the organization of everyday life by relations of custom and contract; or about societies of the gift and societies of the commodity. Usury and Jewishness have been and remain condensed moments of social tension, concentrating larger historical structures of interest, and *The Merchant of Venice*, in its very unreadability, helps us read those structures. At the same time, however, it is crucial to ask the question of how to *avoid* simply reading back from our own historically structured concerns: how to imagine a world in which contempt for usurious Jews makes

88. Jacques Derrida, "What Is a 'Relevant' Translation?" trans. Lawrence Venuti, *Critical Inquiry* 27 (2001), 188, 191.

good sense and in which the concept of anti-Semitism does not exist. This is the world of a late-medieval Christian order in which the Jew has no good place, and it is also a world in which Shakespeare, a dramatist working collaboratively in a popular and nonprestigious poetic form, is not yet the cultural fetish that he will subsequently become. We cannot ignore the intervening history in which that becoming—of "Shakespeare," and of our contemporary apprehension of anti-Semitism—takes place and which sets the parameters of our reading; nor can we privilege the particular interests of our historical moment over all of those which preceded it.

3

Icon, Iconoclasm, Presence

A special artist is needed to paint the eyes on a holy figure. It is always the last
thing done. It is what gives the image life. . . . The artificer puts the brush over
his shoulder and paints in the eyes without looking directly at the face. He uses
just the reflection to guide him—so only the mirror receives the direct image
of the glance being created. No human eye can meet the Buddha's during the
process of creation.

«MICHAEL ONDAATJE, *Anil's Ghost*[1]»

In pictures of the human or divine face it is above all through the
eyes that the soul seems most clearly to shine forth. Iconoclastic
attacks on images or sculptures frequently seek to erase the eyes,
and W. J. T. Mitchell tells of a colleague who persuades his dis-
believing students of the magical relation between an image and
what it represents by asking them to take a photograph of their
mother and cut the eyes out.[2] The notion of a "magical relation"
here designates not a conventionally constructed likeness but an
identity or fusion between an image and what it designates: the
picture is in some sense infused with the being of the god or the
saint or the person it pictures. Indeed, the very vehemence of

1. Michael Ondaatje, *Anil's Ghost* (London: Picador, 2000), 97, 99.
2. W. J. T. Mitchell, *What Do Pictures Want? The Lives and Loves of Images* (Chicago:
University of Chicago Press, 2005), 9.

iconoclastic attacks suggests a kind of perverse belief in the force of the image, its occupation by a demonic presence which has usurped that of the god or the saint or the person. The icon is really an idol; the images attacked by iconoclasts "are dead matter, but they do, unsettlingly, act as if they were alive."[3] Indeed, how dead is the stone or the wood of which a statue is made if the saint's effigy is, as sometimes happened during the Reformation, decapitated by the town executioner?[4] Hatred of the image is the obverse of the faithful's belief in its inhabitation by the god, or of our deep reluctance to deface an image of our mother.

When our heart rate, our respiration, and our skin conductivity increase during moments of suspense in a movie, or when we are aroused by an erotic image, we are responding to the image as though it had this kind of magical force; belief that an image is in some sense animate is not restricted to children or the pious illiterate but permeates every aspect of our interaction with pictures. What we respond to is typically (but not exclusively) a figural representation, a likeness of the human person, no matter how roughly or schematically executed, that seems to possess a person's animation. David Freedberg suggests that there is

> a cognitive relation between looking and enlivening; and between looking hard, not turning away, concentrating, and enjoying on the one hand, and possession and arousal on the other. The argument from convention then becomes irrelevant in that it is insufficient, although it is evidently not wrong.[5]

The power and efficacy of the image derive from that cognitive sleight by which we conflate the likeness with the prototype it represents: the god, the dead ancestor, the loved one. Death masks and funerary portraits evoke one kind of response to the

---

3. James Simpson, *Under the Hammer: Iconoclasm in the Anglo-American Tradition* (New York: Oxford University Press, 2010), 60.

4. Joseph Leo Koerner, *The Reformation of the Image* (Chicago: University of Chicago Press, 2004), 109.

5. David Freedberg, *The Power of Images: Studies in the History and Theory of Response* (Chicago: University of Chicago Press, 1989), 325.

lifelike, a fear that the person survives their death in the image. Statues of the god or the saint evoke another, a sense of awe or dread that "its divine powers belie its human appearance, and its animate quality denies its inanimate materiality."[6]

The affective force of the image, then, is not a matter of symbolization. It is a matter of the ontological ambivalence of likenesses, to which we respond somewhere along a continuum between treating them as conventional constructions and treating them as direct manifestations or emanations of the human or divine person they represent. Hans-Georg Gadamer thus argues that in a real sense "a picture is not a copy of a copied being, but is in ontological communion with what is copied";[7] what he calls "picture magic" "depends on the identity and non-differentiation of picture and what is pictured" (139). Although Gadamer associates this "picture magic" with the "prehistory" of the picture, he nevertheless posits that the picture, or at least the figural picture, can never entirely escape that magical fusion of image with prototype: "Non-differentiation remains essential to all experience of pictures. The irreplaceability of the picture, its fragility, its 'sacredness' are all explained in the ontology of the picture here presented. Even the sacralization of 'art' in the nineteenth century . . . rests on this basis" (139).

I ask two questions in this chapter: Is it possible to take seriously the existence of effects of presence in the work of art? And how do the different regimes of religious and museum-based art (each of which is interpretive in the fundamental sense that it decides what rightfully belongs in the category and what doesn't) deal with the charged and disruptive force of these effects of presence? I explore these questions through dual but interconnected accounts of the struggles in the Byzantine and Reformation eras between iconoclasts and iconophiles, and of the desacralization

6. Freedberg, *The Power of Images*, 74.

7. Hans-Georg Gadamer, *Truth and Method*, 2nd ed., trans. Joel Weinsheimer and Donald G. Marshall (New York: Continuum, 1998 [1960]), 143; hereafter cited in the text.

of the image in the passage from the church to the art museum, from cult practice to exhibition. I conclude with a discussion of the art produced, with modern materials and in direct relation to the contemporary institutions of art, by Australian Indigenous painters for whom traditional sacred knowledges are a living reality.

I

The modern, Western category of art emerges from, *and continues to be implicated in*, the crisis of the image[8] that we call iconoclasm. That crisis is driven by doctrinal disputes, but it also involves what James Simpson calls "the image's passage from church to museum as part of the larger, violent drama of Protestant modernity and abstraction, a drama of which doctrinal positions are symptoms as much as motors of change."[9] More precisely, perhaps, this drama is that of a progressive secularization, always incomplete, of the function of the image, its detachment from the service of the cult and its transfer to private or public exhibition. In this sense, the struggles of the Reformation over the place and value of the image are preceded by the shift in the Renaissance from the church to private patronage and the emergence of the genres of the personal portrait and the plastic representation of figures from classical mythology; and they are succeeded both by the language of Enlightenment taste and the "system of the fine arts,"[10] as well as the birth of the art museum, which we may for convenience date from the establishment of the Louvre in August 1793.

To speak more precisely, the museum is itself an Enlighten-

8. I use the term "image" in this chapter as a shorthand for both two- and three-dimensional visual representations.

9. Simpson, *Under the Hammer*, 5.

10. The classic essay is Paul Oskar Kristeller, "The Modern System of the Arts: A Study in the History of Aesthetics, Part I," *Journal of the History of Ideas* 12, no. 4 (1951), 496–527, and "Part II," *Journal of the History of Ideas* 13, no. 1 (1952), 17–46. Cf. also Larry Shiner, *The Invention of Art: A Cultural History* (Chicago: University of Chicago Press, 2001).

ment institution. Its modern history begins "with the opening of existing princely and papal collections and the simultaneous ordering of such collections in a novel, historical, intellectual way,"[11] together with the creation of new kinds of social space (zoos, libraries, parks, concert halls) which helped bring the modern category of "the public" into being. The Vatican's art collections opened in 1723, 1749, and 1772; the Sloane Collection, which formed the basis of the British Museum, opened in 1759; all Viennese court-owned pictures were displayed to the public three days a week in 1781; and the Louvre opened, as the Muséum Français, on August 10, 1793, exactly a year after the imprisonment of Louis XVI.

The Louvre, built around the royal collection and confiscated church property, and supplemented after Napoleon's campaigns by the plunder of foreign (especially Italian) wars, was envisaged at once as an instrument of moral regeneration of and by the people and as a democratic replacement for the Royal Academy of Painting and Sculpture. Its central roles are thus pedagogic rather than, in any simple way, aesthetic, and Jacques-Louis David defines them through his successive confrontations with the Academy and the Museum Commission that replaces it. Attacking the organization of the museum as a spectacle of amassed treasures rather than as a properly educational institution arranged chronologically and by artistic schools, he brings to the fore a clash between two alternative modes of display: one built on the principles of a timeless aesthetic, the other historical and grounded in a scientific taxonomy. "The former," writes Andrew McClellan, "aimed to concentrate the beholder's attention first and foremost on pictorial qualities within the frame, whereas the latter encouraged appreciation of a given painting in terms of its place in a diachronic, national sequence."[12] The new

11. Philip Fisher, *Making and Effacing Art: Modern American Art in a Culture of Museums* (Cambridge, MA: Harvard University Press, 1991), 6.

12. Andrew McClellan, *Inventing the Louvre: Art, Politics, and the Origins of the Modern Museum in Eighteenth-Century Paris* (Cambridge: Cambridge University Press, 1994), 103.

museum displays relations between objects rather than objects in themselves, and its dominant mode is the tour, the walk-through past successive works of art, rather than meditation on an isolated work. When pictures are lined on walls, the room is flattened and the museum "becomes a perfect image of history, or rather of the single, linear motion of history preferred since Winckelmann"; its culmination, Philip Fisher suggests, is the downward-spiraling walkway of the New York Guggenheim, a "pure path, without rooms."[13]

The regime of vision at work in the Louvre is thus continuous with the statist principles of its former organization as the public display rooms of the sovereign, and yet it initiates a semiotic recoding that is interwoven with the new configurations that develop throughout the nineteenth century to "allow new concepts and realities to be figured forth into the sphere of visibility."[14] Those new configurations have to do with that double process of estrangement of works from their original functions and their resituation in a quite different form of historical time filled with the presence of "rival or even hostile works" that Malraux describes in *The Voices of Silence.*[15]

The attempt to use the Louvre as an instrument not only for celebrating the Republic and the glory of France but also for the formation of a new mode of "civic seeing"[16] throws up almost immediate contradictions. The political purification of the museum in 1794 seeks to purge works closely associated with the Old Regime (like Rubens's Medici cycle, which was seen to be ideologically incompatible with Revolutionary ideals), or religious art, or Flemish genre scenes, "deemed inconsistent with the didactic, moralizing aims of the museum during the Terror," because "in

13. Fisher, *Making and Effacing Art*, 9.

14. Tony Bennett, *The Birth of The Museum: History, Theory, Politics* (London: Routledge, 1995), 38.

15. André Malraux, *The Voices of Silence*, trans. Stuart Gilbert (1954; repr., St Albans: Paladin, 1974), 14.

16. Cf. Tony Bennett, "Civic Seeing: Museums and the Organisation of Vision," in *Companion to Museum Studies*, ed. S. MacDonald (Oxford: Blackwell, 2006), 263–81.

strict Republican eyes the activities of farmyard and tavern would not mold and inspire the young artist or citizen along desired lines."[17] In practice, however,

> a solution to the apparent contradiction between Revolutionary ideology and the purpose of much past art lay in the secularizing power of the museum and the reidentification of iconic paintings as art objects occupying a place in the history of art. A transformation from *imago agens* to work of art, a shift in emphasis from function to form, from signified to signifier, would, it was suggested, result from displacement to a museum and an arrangement of the collection by school and chronology. This was implicit in the October 1793 law outlawing vandalism of significant art objects bearing feudal signs: the alternative to destruction was removal to the "nearest museum." The power of the museum to elide original meanings and to substitute for them new aesthetic and art historical significances is well understood today, but it is an attribute of museums first recognized and exploited during the Revolution.[18]

We could describe this process as one of resocialization, as the religious icon or the painting that celebrates an aristocratic lineage is inserted into a new and different community of objects, an array of access and uses and contexts that makes of it a new and different kind of cultural or technical or stylistic example and inserts it into a new historical sequencing. Fisher speaks of three stages in the silencing of earlier functional characteristics. The first is the deconsecration of the image. In the second, "the European museums began to include and exhibit objects converted into art by their presence in a museum, objects from alien societal, religious, and artistic communities."[19] This is not an assimilation but a preservation of difference, not a forgetting but an ignorance of the object's original context. The third stage, the last in a sequence of the silencing of images from our own and then from other cultures, is the genesis of those modern abstract objects

---

17. McClellan, *Inventing the Louvre*, 111.
18. McClellan, *Inventing the Louvre*, 112–13.
19. Fisher, *Making and Effacing Art*, 20.

that have as their single, overt design, the desire to join history. Once the past has been organized as a past, a new type of cunning object began to appear, one that was no longer naively historical. . . . These sentimental objects, as Schiller would have called them, have as their intention to come to rest in history, to become at some future point the past, to become not things but art.[20]

The process that culminates in the birth of the art museum is thus the evolution of a new way at once of looking at and, in that gaze, of constituting the work of art. We could think of it as a way of breaking the force of the sacred image—the exemplary type, at the moment of the birth of the museum, of the functional image—by replacing it with the absolute human figure, or the word (rather than the image) of God, or a self-sufficient and disinterested aesthetic form. Each of these substitutes for the sacred image carries the memory of what it has displaced. The whitewashed, unadorned walls of the Protestant church or chapel evoke the images that once hung there and that will hang again on the plain white walls of the art gallery; the flat picture plane of abstract art, "a sign of non-mediation with the absolute," mimics those violently cleansed walls of the Reformation church.[21] The language of Enlightenment taste, "at every point inflected by recurrent fear of idolatry," adapts, and adapts to, iconoclasm by "a massive work of image neutralization" (120). New genres of disenchanted art—still lifes, landscapes, or, in eighteenth-century England, "portraits of self, family, or horses" (14)—drain the image of its dangerous energy. And a critique of the museum that is nearly contemporaneous with its birth accuses it of tearing art out of the "network of ideas and relations that made the works alive with interest":[22]

Loss of context, loss of cultural meaning, destruction of a direct connection with life, promotion of an esthetically alienated mode of

20. Fisher, *Making and Effacing Art*, 6.
21. Simpson, *Under the Hammer*, 32–33; hereafter cited in the text.
22. Antoine-Chrysostome Quatremère de Quincy, *Considérations morales sur la destination des ouvrages de l'art* (1815); cited in Didier Maleuvre, *Museum Memories: History, Technology, Art* (Stanford: Stanford University Press, 1999), 15.

observation, instigation of a passive attitude toward the past and of a debilitating mood of nostalgia—the museum seemed to embody all these ills of the modern age, an age that by its own account had forsaken the immanent ties with tradition that had blessed every previous era.[23]

Yet the secularization and aestheticization of the image is not a simple linear process, a "church-to-gallery drama" in which modern easel painting became detached from "a stable prevenient condition of integrated art."[24] Walter Benjamin analyzes the transition by way of the concept of aura and the dialectic of the categories of cult value and exhibition value. The "highly sensitive core" of the work of art is its authenticity, "the quintessence of all that is transmissible in it from its origin on, ranging from its physical duration to the historical testimony relating to it"; and that core is threatened by technological reproducibility, which "detaches the reproduced object from the sphere of tradition," substituting "a mass existence for a unique existence."[25] The aura that is destroyed by a reproducibility that "extracts sameness even from what is unique" (256) is equivalent at once to that uniqueness and to the historicity that marks the self-identity of the work through time.

The artwork is unique and authentic by virtue of "its embeddedness in the context of tradition" (256), although that context changes as the work passes through historical time: a Greek cult statue may become a sinister idol when it is re-embedded in the medieval period. What persists through historical recontextualization is the ritual underpinning of the artwork:

> Originally, the embeddedness of an artwork in the context of tradition found expression in a cult. As we know, the earliest artworks originated in the service of rituals—first magical, then religious.

23. Maleuvre, *Museum Memories*, 101–2.

24. Alexander Nagel, *Medieval Modern: Art Out of Time* (London: Thames and Hudson, 2012), 51.

25. Walter Benjamin, "The Work of Art in the Age of Its Technological Reproducibility," Third Version, in *Selected Writings Vol. 4: 1938–1940*, ed. Howard Eiland and Michael W. Jennings (Cambridge, MA: Harvard University Press, 2003), 254; hereafter cited in the text.

And it is highly significant that the artwork's auratic mode of existence is never entirely severed from its ritual function. In other words: *the unique value of the "authentic" work of art has its basis in ritual, the source of its original use value.* This ritualistic basis, however mediated it may be, is still recognizable as secularized ritual in even the most profane forms of the cult of beauty. (256)

This is to say, just as Gadamer argues about the nineteenth-century sacralization of the artwork, that there is a continuity rather than a simple dichotomy between the cult value of the work and its aesthetic value.[26] Artistic production has its origins in worship, when it is more important for the image to be present than to be seen. Cult objects tend to be physically grounded in a holy site, whereas the emancipation of artistic practices from the service of ritual allows for a greater mobility and for more extended opportunities for display. That mobilization of the artwork is extended and transformed into something quite different when the exhibition value of art modulates into the technological reproducibility of, for example, the photograph. This is the further dialectical reversal that carries through the shift from the regime of cult value to that of exhibition value: "Insofar as the age of technological reproducibility separated art from its basis in cult, all semblance of art's autonomy disappeared forever" (258).

Technological reproducibility, with everything that it entails—the substitution of sameness for uniqueness, the destruction of the quasi-religious aura of the artwork—is thus for Benjamin an entirely positive value (although we might note the undertones of melancholy with which he speaks of the loss of aura). Yet the desacralization of art that it promises is, with the hindsight afforded by our image-saturated society of the spectacle, not so

---

26. Alexander Nagel thus argues that the conception of the work of art as authentic and unique must be understood in paradoxical relation to the modality of the medieval *relic*, an absolute singularity that cannot be replicated and the authenticity of which derives from its direct association with the sacred—the body of the saint, the true cross. Nagel, *Medieval Modern*, 235.

easily accomplished as he believed: we now know with absolute clarity that the industrialized production of images can achieve the most powerfully auratic effects, and even in the Middle Ages there was a widespread belief that replicas of icons, manufactured on an almost industrial scale, carried with them the magic powers of the original.[27] "Reproduction both enables and facilitates repetition; and repetition, sheer repetition . . . engenders a new and compelling aura of its own."[28] Belief in the power of technological reproducibility to effect a passage from ritual to exhibition and thereby to strip the artwork of its aura repeats the failure of every previous iconoclasm.

II

The Western world has known two major (and many more minor) outbreaks of destructive anger against the image: the successive Byzantine attacks on religious images in the eighth and again in the ninth centuries, and those that accompanied the Reformation in Northern Europe in the sixteenth and seventeenth centuries. These were theological struggles about the "ontological communion" of the picture with the thing copied; but although the doctrinal debates were abstruse, they were also, in each case, the essential form taken by much broader socioeconomic and institutional struggles, and, in the case of the Christian states of the eighth century, by "the crevasse that had opened between their rich Late Antique past and an anxious present overshadowed by the armies of Islam."[29] Theologically, the Byzantine and Reformation debates were very different, but there are clear lines of continuity between their respective questioning of the weight to be given to the inherence of the godhead in the "natural" image,

27. Hans Belting, *Likeness and Presence: A History of the Image Before the Era of Art*, trans. Edmund Jephcott (Chicago: University of Chicago Press, 1994), 6.

28. Freedberg, *The Power of Images*, 126.

29. Peter Brown, "A Dark-Age Crisis: Aspects of the Iconoclastic Controversy," *The English Historical Review* 88, no. 386 (1973), 4–5.

in the doctrine of the incarnation and the ritual of the Eucharist, and in the artificial image: the icon or the devotional picture.

Christian art in the first few centuries of the common era was restricted to a few sacred symbols—the fish, the lamb, the vine scroll, the cross—and only gradually, between the fourth and sixth centuries, did it develop a richer iconographic tradition of images of Christ, of the Madonna and child, and of the saints. The portrait icon plays a crucial role in mediating the human and divine, since, unlike Islam, which refuses intercession, the Byzantine Church's "belief in intercession, and the consequent psychological need to focus one's attention and hopes on the face of the intercessor, was the lever that shifted the religious art of the early Byzantine world. The earliest icons are those that make plain the mechanism of intercession,"[30] that is, the hierarchy of saints, angels, and the Virgin, who can relay messages and prayers to the highest power.

This emerging iconographic tradition drew heavily on (and eventually competed with) the imperial iconography of the post-Constantine era: the scene of the offering of gifts to the emperor was transformed into that of the visitation of the Magi; the apotheosis of the emperor became the Resurrection; the image of the emperor and empress on the throne surrounded by their entourage became the image of Christ and the Virgin among the saints.[31] Imperial image theory fuses the emperor with his portrait, which represents him and is identified with him in his absence. Honors paid to the image are transferred to the emperor himself, since, in the words of Athanasius of Alexandria,

> in the image [of the emperor] there is the idea (*eidos*) and form (*morphē*) of the emperor. . . . The emperor's likeness is unchanged in the image, so that who sees the image sees the emperor in it, and again who sees the image, recognizes him to be the one in the image. . . . The image might well say: "I and the emperor are one." "I am

30. Brown, "A Dark-Age Crisis," 14.

31. Alain Besançon, *The Forbidden Image: An Intellectual History of Iconoclasm*, trans. Jane Marie Todd (Chicago: University of Chicago Press, 2000 [1994]), 110.

in him and he is in me." Who therefore adores the image adores in it also the emperor. For the image is the form of the latter and his idea.[32]

This fusion of image and person is transferred directly to the christological context, where it generates a tension between understanding the cult image as a *secondary representation* of the primary identity of Christ with God and understanding it as a *direct manifestation* of the presence of Christ (or the Virgin, or a saint) in the image, just as the portrait of the emperor embodies his real presence. This dichotomy corresponds to a tension between regarding respect for the icon as a form of veneration (*proskynesis*) or as a form of adoration or worship (*latreia*), which should be reserved only for God;[33] the iconoclastic struggles emerge in the space opened by these tensions.

The history is contested but clear in its general outlines. In the traditional version, a policy of iconoclasm[34] was implemented in 726 by the emperor Leo III when he removed the image of Christ from the Chalke Gate of the imperial palace and replaced it with a cross and an inscription denouncing the worship of dead and inanimate matter; in 730, he issued an edict ordering the destruction of all cult images (although not of images of the emperor).[35]

---

32. Athanasius of Alexandria, *Oratio III contra Arianos* 5, cited in Freedberg, *The Power of Images*, 392.

33. Ernst Kitzinger, "The Cult of Images in the Age before Constantine," *Dumbarton Oaks Papers* 8 (1954), 91.

34. The word itself was only coined much later, in 1571, and was first applied to the Byzantine struggles over the image only in the 1950s. Leslie Brubaker, *Inventing Byzantine Iconoclasm* (London: Bristol Classical, 2012), 120.

35. Cf., for example, George Ostrogorsky, *History of the Byzantine State*, trans. Joan Hussey (New Brunswick: Rutgers University Press, 1969), 162–63; and Stephen Gero, *Byzantine Iconoclasm During the Reign of Leo III: With Particular Attention to the Oriental Sources* (Louvain: Secrétariat du Corpus Scriptorum Christianorum Orientalium, 1973), 94; both Ostrogorsky and Gero rely primarily on what the latter calls Theophanes' iconophile but "quite sober and factual" account in the *Chronographia*. Cf. also Marie-France Auzépy, "State of Emergency (700–850)," in *The Cambridge History of the Byzantine Empire c. 500–1492*, ed. Jonathan Shepherd, Cambridge Histories Online, http://universitypublishingonline.org/cambridge/histories/ (2009), 281. For a sharp critique of the traditional version, cf. Leslie Brubaker and John Haldon, *Byzantium in the Iconoclast Era c. 680–850: A History* (Cambridge: Cambridge University Press, 2011), 79–155.

Alternatively, while the struggle over images had begun in the 720s, it was only during the 750s, in the reign of Constantine V (741–75), that an imperial initiative to ban the production of religious portraits was introduced; this policy of iconoclasm was endorsed, reversed, and reinstated over the reign of several rulers until the synod of 843 restored the veneration of icons.[36]

What is at stake in that veneration—and the sources we have for the doctrinal struggles are almost entirely the writings of the iconophile polemicists—is the possibility of representing a God who is by definition and by Mosaic law unrepresentable. If "the divine, being unmaterial and uncircumscribable, cannot be represented in material and circumscribable form,"[37] then all images of a divine object are necessarily idolatrous. This is the "apophatic" conviction, in most iconoclastic thought, of the absolute transcendence and thus invisibility of God and of the priority of the spirit and the word over matter and the image. Indeed, the conviction is shared by many iconophiles, who think, however, in terms of a series of graded mediations between the poles of matter and spirit. The iconophile John of Damascus defines God by a series of "alpha-negations": God is without being, uncreated, immortal, unassailable, eternal, everlasting, bodiless, incomprehensible, invisible, uncircumscribed, formless. . . .[38] Understanding God in this way lends force to the rejection of visual form, unless matter and the visual can be rescued by way of the doctrine of the incarnation and of the providential economy that underpins it. John of Damascus again:

> Of old God the incorporeal and uncircumscribed was not depicted at all. But now that God has appeared in the flesh and lived among men, I make an image of the God who can be seen. I do not worship matter but the creator of matter, who for my sake became material

36. Brubaker, *Inventing Byzantine Iconoclasm*, 4–5, 27–28.

37. Freedberg, *The Power of Images*, 62.

38. Kenneth Parry, *Depicting the Word: Byzantine Iconophile Thought of the Eighth and Ninth Centuries* (Leiden: E. J. Brill, 1996), 115.

and deigned to dwell in matter, who through matter achieved my salvation.[39]

For the iconoclasts, conversely, the icon is at once dead and yet threatening matter, infused with the dangerous presence of the idol. The compound word *eidōlon latreia*, the worship of an idol, is found only in the New Testament; *eidōlon* in the Septuagint translates some thirty Hebrew words—"statue," "cast metal," "abomination," and so on—but comes to acquire the sense of "the image, statue, or symbol of a false god."[40] What makes the image of a god "false," however, is the fact that idols are the abode of demons who are mistaken for true gods, along with the pagan belief that the idol and the god are of the same essence: that is, it is the overinvestment in the truth of the image that produces error, "a deadly adoration of nothing."[41] Hence the iconophiles' objection to the iconoclastic theory that "the image must be consubstantial with its prototype to be a true image":[42] the pagan idol has no prototype, whereas the Christian image does but is not consubstantial with it (it has a formal but not an essential resemblance to the godhead; image and prototype are distinct). The iconophiles thus devalue the image, emptying it of the immanence of the sacred, in order to save it, and they do so by constructing a hierarchy between the "natural" image and the artificial image or icon.

The natural image, unlike the icon, involves a double relation of consubstantiality, or *homoousia*; it is to be found in the similitude of Father and Son and in the Eucharist, where the bread and the wine are indeed the real body of Christ but there is no icon as such. Christ is himself twice an image, first of the Father

39. John of Damascus, *Oratio de imaginibus* 1, cited in Freedberg, *The Power of Images*, 403.

40. Besançon, *The Forbidden Image*, 65.

41. Marie-José Mondzain, *Image, Icon, Economy: The Byzantine Origins of the Contemporary Imaginary*, trans. Rico Franses (Stanford: Stanford University Press, 2005 [1996]), 70.

42. Parry, *Depicting the Word*, 44.

and then, in his fleshly incarnation, of humankind: "Philip saith unto him, Lord, shew us the Father, and it sufficeth us. Jesus saith unto him . . . he that hath seen me hath seen the Father. . . . Believe me that I *am* in the Father, and the Father in me."[43] And Paul writes that Christ is "in the form of" (*morphē*) God, but "made himself of no reputation, and took upon him the form of a servant, and was made in the likeness of men";[44] he is "the image of the invisible God"[45] but also a man who dies. This double resemblance corresponds to that initial act of resemblance in which "God said, Let us make man in our image, after our likeness,"[46] a likeness that is redeemed by Christ's incarnation and that makes visual representation possible (but that also ties picturing inexorably to dying).[47]

What characterizes the Christian icon is not the immanence of the god in the image but its authenticity, meaning its spiritual fidelity to its prototype, the figure it represents. It has nothing to do with imagination or aesthetic form or "the servitude of reproduction and representation":[48] it is not a copying but a conformity to the prototype, a secondary representation of the natural image. The icon's spiritual fidelity is acquired in one of two ways. On the one hand, there is the authenticity of acheiropoietic images, those not "made by human hands" but rather "connected to their referents through processes of quasi-mechanical replication,"[49] either directly impressed from the face of Christ onto a cloth or rendered in the images of the Virgin made in her presence by St Luke and then faithfully reproduced by others.[50] On the other hand, fidelity can be doctrinal, a matter of the unchanging

43. John 14:8–11.
44. Phil. 2:6–7.
45. Col. 1:15.
46. Gen. 1:26.
47. Amy Knight Powell, *Depositions: Scenes from the Late Medieval Church and the Modern Museum* (New York: Zone Books, 2012), 105.
48. Mondzain, *Image, Icon, Economy*, 70.
49. Nagel, *Medieval Modern*, 228.
50. Belting, *Likeness and Presence*, 47–49.

and "'abstract' relation that characterizes the formal, deliberate resemblance of the icon to its model."[51] Formal resemblance is *homoiôsis*, and according to Nikephoros the icon has stamped on it "the whole of the visible form of what it is a likeness of," but it is different in substance from that being that it resembles.[52]

It is Christ's assumption of human form that institutes the possibility of a meaningful order of visuality. Christ in the flesh is the god made mortal and visible, a human shape[53] that symbolizes and yet is radically heterogeneous to the transcendental substance of the godhead. The abject and dying god is paradoxically remote from the divine and yet is what makes it possible to apprehend it. It is his incarnation that justifies the icon. This justification is made explicit in the 82nd Canon passed by the Quinisext Council at Constantinople in 692, which prescribed that Christ should be represented not by a lamb but in human form, "so that we may perceive through it the depth of the humiliation of God the Word and be led to the remembrance of His life in the flesh. . . ."[54] The canon is thus designed, as Ernst Kitzinger puts it,

> to place the connection between Christ and His image on a transcendental level. The image had begun to be thought of not simply as a reminder of the Incarnation, but as an organic part, an extension, or even a re-enactment thereof. Slowly concepts had begun to evolve whereby the Byzantine religious image was to become a means of demonstrating the Incarnation not merely as a past history but as a living and perpetual presence. The role of the image ceased to be purely didactic and was in the process of becoming sacramental like the Sacrifice of the Mass.[55]

---

51. Mondzain, *Image, Icon, Economy*, 85.

52. Mondzain, *Image, Icon, Economy*, 86.

53. "When Christ is referred to in his carnal economy, he appears as *eidos*, that is, a visible form, *morphē*, a perceptible form, *skhēma*, a figure, *charactèr*, a line of the face or the silhouette, *tupos*, an image as a sign or imprint, and therefore less strictly iconic than a symbol." Mondzain, *Image, Icon, Economy*, 86.

54. Cited in Kitzinger, "The Cult of Images," 121.

55. Kitzinger, "The Cult of Images," 142–43.

The incarnational justification of the icon is linked to a further distinction, between the orders of theology (the immanent and eternal being of God) and providential economy. Economy (*oikonomia*) covers such concepts as incarnation, design, administration, providence, responsibility, duty, history, and a number of others;[56] it is translated into Latin as *dispensatio* or *dispositio*, terms that illustrate its "distributive, organic, and functional sense,"[57] and it thus comprises those doctrines that deal with "the dispensation of God in history in relation to all of creation."[58] Paul uses the concept of economy to talk about "the plan of the incarnation,"[59] and it refers to "the entirety of the incarnational plan and to divine providence."[60] The icon is subsumed within the doctrine of incarnation, and the church fathers repeatedly state that "*whoever rejects the icon rejects the economy*, that is, Christ himself and the totality of the incarnational plan in history,"[61] since "for iconophiles, the more spiritually minded position of the iconoclasts results in the devaluation of the material world and hence the devaluation of the incarnation."[62] The concept of economy thus designates that level of being at which the divine is made sensibly intelligible and takes on its historical and worldly form. Governing the divine order that underlies the natural, fallen world, it concerns "an organism or an internal arrangement whose visibility becomes accessible to us."[63]

Nothing in this implies an evacuation of the sacred from the image; there is no passage of the Byzantine image from cult value to exhibition value, no birth of an autonomous aesthetic realm.

56. Giorgio Agamben traces the semantic evolution of the concept in *The Kingdom and the Glory: For a Theological Genealogy of Economy and Government*, trans. Lorenzo Chiesa (Stanford: Stanford University Press, 2011), 17–52.

57. Mondzain, *Image, Icon, Economy*, 13–14.

58. Jaroslav Pelikan, *Imago Dei: The Byzantine Apologia for Icons* (Princeton: Princeton University Press, 1990), 98.

59. 1 Cor. 11:7; 2 Cor. 4:4; Col. 1:15.

60. Mondzain, *Image, Icon, Economy*, 14.

61. Mondzain, *Image, Icon, Economy*, 14–15.

62. Parry, *Depicting the Word*, 71.

63. Mondzain, *Image, Icon, Economy*, 21.

At the heart of the icon is the double mystery of the becoming-flesh of Christ and its converse, the transformation in the Eucharist of the host and the wine into the body and blood of Christ as they are incorporated into the body of the communicant. Yet the hierarchical subordination of economy to theology, and correspondingly of the icon to the natural image, does stage a *partial* desacralization of the icon: neither empty matter nor idolatrous fullness, the picture represents a sacred mystery that lies beyond it and which it reads through the duality of Christ, whose hypostatic union with the godhead leaves intact his carnal and historical being.

III

Like the Byzantine iconoclasms, those of the Northern European Reformation at once condemn and overvalue the image. Here again we can distinguish two major outbreaks, from the first iconoclastic riots in Wittenberg in 1522 and Zurich in 1523 to the episode of widespread image destruction (the *beeldenstorm*) in the northern Netherlands in 1566. Iconoclasm is central to the politics of the Reformation and its relation to the state: Luther reaches an early accommodation with both the image and the princely state, struggling to contain the image-breaking zeal of Karlstadt, Zwingli, Müntzer, and (to a lesser extent) Calvin. In England and Scotland, injunctions against the idolatrous image are enunciated as official state policy in bills and proclamations of 1538, 1547, 1550, and 1559, and a further wave of iconoclasm is unleashed a century later during the English Civil War. As in Byzantium, the theological content of the struggle over images centers on the relation of spirit to matter, the word to the image, but that content is fully overdetermined by the broader political and institutional struggles of the sixteenth century.

At the heart of Luther's rebellion against the Catholic Church is the question of mediation. Rather than being the representative of Christ on earth, interceding between the planes of the earthly and the divine, the Reformation church is the invisible and placeless site of a direct, personal, and private spiritual encounter between a believing individual and their God. If "no one can die for another," then faith and salvation are matters for me alone, and it is my faith alone, not the work of intercession (the invocation of the help of a saint or the Virgin, or the buying of pardons and indulgences, for example) that can reconcile me with the divine. To believe is to form my own interpretation of and my own intimacy with the Word that is God, the word that interprets itself because of its "miraculous power to effect the understanding by which alone we are saved."[64]

That refusal of mediations extends to the image. For the Protestant theologians,

> the eye no longer discovers evidence for the presence of God in images or in the physical world; God reveals himself only through his word. The word as bearer of the spirit is just as abstract as is the new concept of God; religion has become an ethical code of living. The word does not depict or show anything but is a sign of the covenant. God's distance prohibits his presence in a painted representation, sensually comprehended. The modern subject, estranged from the world, sees the world as severed into the purely factual and the hidden signification of metaphor. But the old image rejected reduction into metaphor; rather, it laid claim to being immediate evidence of God's presence revealed to the eyes and senses.[65]

For radicals like Thomas Müntzer, even Scripture itself is a form of mediation, and it could only be validated by direct experience of "God's inner voice in us."[66] For more mainstream be-

---

64. Koerner, *The Reformation of the Image*, 201. James Simpson, however, makes clear the deep distrust of "private interpretation" on the part of Luther and Tyndale; the truth of Scripture is grounded in an appeal to the authority not of the established church but of the invisible and self-selecting True Church of the elect. James Simpson, *Burning to Read: English Fundamentalism and Its Reformation Opponents* (Cambridge, MA: Harvard University Press, 2007), 139.

65. Belting, *Likeness and Presence*, 15.

66. Koerner, *The Reformation of the Image*, 164; hereafter cited in the text. Bruno Latour defines "the conviction that mediations may be bypassed" as the core of any fundamentalism. *Iconoclash: Beyond the Image Wars in Art and Science*, ed. Bruno Latour and Peter Weibel (Karlsruhe and Cambridge, MA: ZKM and MIT Press, 2002), 41.

lievers, the word of God physically replaces visual representations on the walls and windows of the church; images are overwritten with texts, but, in a striking paradox that helps to redeem the image, the written texts in turn are seen to point beyond themselves to the scenes and persons they signify. Thus, as Luther writes in his anti-iconoclastic treatise *Against the Heavenly Prophets*, the image of Christ arises spontaneously in my heart when I hear the words of Scripture: this is "the picture that is the word's meaning"; the picture "*entwirft sich*," "'projects itself' in the head in the way an object casts a shadow" (160–61) or generates a reflection in a mirror. Iconoclasm is therefore based on a false semiology, since this "inner" image arises directly from words; and, just as, in Byzantine theology, the "artificial" icon is a secondary representation of the "natural" image, so for Luther the pictorial or sculptural representation follows naturally from the psychological representation I make of the scenes and persons I imagine as I read the text of Scripture.

To say that words depend upon a deeper layer of images and imaging is to say that the meanings of texts are a matter not just of spiritual significance but of the embodied forms through which that significance is made manifest. The incarnate and fallen nature of Christ is essential to the way in which the revelation of his divinity is made humanly and historically visible: he is the abject god who dies on a cross and who returns from the dead not as spirit but as a mortal and fleshly human being. Incarnation underpins the image, which enables the immediacy of identification with the suffering god. This, at least, is the line that Luther seeks to maintain between, on the one hand, the Catholic veneration of the image and the holy relic, and on the other, the more radical forms of Protestant hostility which reject the finite and the visual in favor of the pure spirituality of the word.

These are questions about the form of presence of the god in the image (either the real presence that, in Protestant eyes, amounts to idolatry, or a mediated and figurative presence, or indeed a complete absence of the godhead from material representations); and these questions are in turn bound up with that of one of the central mysteries of the Christian faith: the form of presence of the god in the Eucharist. The Protestant refusal of mediation entails a refusal of the Catholic liturgy in which the priest is "deemed continually to repair a broken covenant with God by offering Christ's sacrifice on man's behalf" (328): a spectacle of the ritual eating of the god that repeats both the sacrificial killing and the gift that it embodies. That spectacle is valid regardless of whether it is understood, regardless of the belief of the priest or the observer; whereas for Luther what matters, and what effects the transformation of the host and the wine into the real presence of Christ, is the faith of the communicant, their belief in the reality conveyed by the ritual. Luther continues to insist that the sacrament of the Eucharist is not merely a symbol: the words "This is my body" are to be read literally; the body of Christ is present "substantially and essentially" in the host as it is received in faith in the sacramental union. In this Luther remains close to the Catholic doctrine of the real presence of Christ in the elements of the Eucharist. For the more radical reformers and iconoclasts the presence of Christ is to be understood in a more figurative sense, as a metonymy, an "exalted mnemonic device,"[67] detached from the literal, material reality of the bread and wine. As the goal of communication replaces the performative function of language ("This is my body"), the link between the Last Supper and the Eucharist is broken: "Signs became distinct from the entities to which they refer" and "the bread and wine thus pointed to, without mingling with, Christ's body; Communion happened elsewhere, a union occurring in the spirit. Sacrament merely symbolized this union."[68] To a greater or lesser degree, the Reformation contributes to a disenchantment of the cult in the withdrawal of the sign from its ontological fusion with its object. And that ethos of disenchantment extends to

67. Catherine Gallagher and Stephen Greenblatt, *Practicing New Historicism* (Chicago: University of Chicago Press, 2000), 146.

68. Koerner, *The Reformation of the Image*, 311.

the cult image, which is feared for its animation, invested with a kind of personhood, and violently stripped of its dangerous force.

IV

One way of stripping the image of its danger is to place it in a private collection or, later, in an art museum, where it becomes an object of the aesthetic gaze (and thus of a wholly different modality of interpretation). This is indeed what saved many church pictures from iconoclastic destruction in the course of the Reformation. In the passage from the church to the museum their function is redescribed: what matters now is their formal beauty and the skill of their execution. This is a familiar account: a model of the disenchantment, neutralization, and secularization of the image, and then of its resacralization, as the aesthetic image itself acquires a cult value rooted in its authenticity and uniqueness, akin to that of the relic. The dialectic of enchantment and disenchantment comes in turn to be closely intertwined with the play between the market value of the sacralized work of art and the successive waves of iconoclastic reaction against its commodified form.[69] (In other cultures, of course, the line between the aesthetic, the commercial, and the sacred is drawn very differently: I am thinking here, for example, of the work of Kajri Jain and Christopher Pinney, each of whom demonstrates the role of mass-produced popular visual culture in articulating a messianic or "sacred" order of temporality at the heart of the commercial life of the bazaar and Hindu nationalist politics.[70])

At once a defensive response to early-modern iconoclasm,

69. These waves of reaction give rise to that "death of painting" that "has been infamously protracted, in part, because successive waves of abstract art have courted that death while . . . holding it at bay as a still impossible dream for the future." Powell, *Depositions*, 113.

70. Kajri Jain, *Gods in the Bazaar: The Economies of Indian Calendar Art* (Durham, NC: Duke University Press, 2007); Christopher Pinney, *Photos of the Gods: The Printed Image and Political Struggle in India* (London: Reaktion Books, 2004).

then, and its continuation, the Western art museum is the institutional ground of this transformation of the artwork. It is "the fundamental social space towards which art in the modern period orients itself, from which it draws its monetary and cultural value, and in which it intends ultimately to come to rest."[71] Demarcating aesthetic from both sacred and worldly space, it constructs a site for the staging of aesthetic value and of interpretive conflict. It creates a normative way of looking at the artwork: silent, reverent, disinterested, appreciative. It selects the normative objects of this gaze and, thus, the criteria of value and discrimination inherent in that selection. It juxtaposes framed objects, separated from each other and from the world, according to an order which may or may not be made explicit. It sets up a continuous dialectic between valued objects and their historical predecessors and successors, but it does so within a regular, homogeneous, and timeless space. It thus creates a time outside of time, in which the work of art is separated from its context of origin but at the same time alienated from the present by the museum's monumentalizing strategies. The ordering principle of the display may be historical, but that order is nevertheless ahistorical in raising the artwork above historical becoming and fixing it in an aesthetic eternity.

Yet, as Didier Maleuvre argues, the decontextualization operated by the museum is precisely what allows the distance and difference of the past to become available to us, and it allows what he calls the "strong historical inauguralness" of the artwork to have effect both in and against the time of the museum.[72] The work of art is irreducible to its historical time because, creating and becoming its own rule of making and thus falling outside the horizon of the already known, it actively shapes historical time: in it, "history stops looking like itself," and it "encapsulates the ahistorical way in which history takes place" (66). One metaphor that Maleuvre develops for this ahistoricity of the historical is

71. Fisher, *Making and Effacing Art*, 92.
72. Maleuvre, *Museum Memories*, 74; hereafter cited in the text.

Panini's 1740 painting *Alexander the Great before Achilles' Tomb*, in which Alexander walks in a landscape of ruins, as though the past of antiquity were already to be seen only as a past, staged "as it would become in the retrospective glance of modern times. . . . The past, as a product of the present, is always a ruin because it always appears *anachronistically* in the present" (61). Paradoxical or even absurd as that staging of the past as always-already a ruin may seem, the truth it reveals is that "the historical past does not precede its transplantation in the present: history is precisely the recognition that the past does not exist outside the reminiscing present. . . . The past belongs to the present" (271). Indeed, what took place in the past was not the past: it was the then-present, which means that "to treat the past as past is a perversion of the fact [that] the past once took place as a present. . . . The past event is always recollected, not as it happened, but as it is seen happening from the alienated standpoint of the present" (272). The museum is at once the expression of and a technology for the production of a sense of the past as the flash of remembrance in which the historical being of the work of art becomes possible: a historical being that is of the order neither of the past from which it has been separated nor of the present in which it resists assimilation.

Within an aesthetic regime, that flash of remembrance—the rescue of a fragment of the past in what Benjamin calls a messianic *Jetztzeit*—is one of the forms that the manifestation of presence in the artwork may take.[73] The attitude of aesthetic disinterest which the art museum has worked (along with other institutions) to form as a general cultural disposition and which informs its exhibitionary ethos has, however, largely displaced the presence of the sacred except in the attenuated form of the sacralization of the aesthetic itself. The aesthetic regime is an order of applied irony. Of course, there has been a continuous production of religious art within or athwart the Western "aesthetic"

73. Walter Benjamin, "On the Concept of History," in Eiland and Jennings, *Selected Writings Volume 4*, 391, 395.

tradition: the Baroque art of the Counter-Reformation; Blake; Stanley Spencer. . . . But the art museum initiates an economy in which the aesthetic is sharply distinguished both from the sacred and from the commercial. Sacred images may be displayed in the art museum, but they are stripped of their cult value;[74] works of art have a market value,[75] and art museums buy them in the marketplace and are a crucial part of their value chain,[76] but the art museum (unlike the commercial art gallery) is not a place where images are traded.

Yet the magical force of the image survives the irony of the aesthetic. It survives in every representation of the human body, because we have never lost our sense that the human image is an incarnation: millennia of religious training have instilled in our irreligious culture (and in my own secular and irreligious ethos) a continuing apprehension of what the Byzantine theologians called economy, that level of being at which the divine is made sensibly intelligible and takes on its historical and worldly form. It survives in nonfigurative art in the form of the iconoclastic refusal of presence. And it survives most powerfully in myriad

74. Gadamer argues that "an ancient image of the gods that was not displayed in a temple as a work of art in order to give aesthetic, reflective pleasure, and is now on show in a museum, retains, even as it stands before us today, the world of religious experience from which it came," and thus that "its world still belongs to ours." But the fact is that it belongs only in a secondary degree: we do not worship it in the museum. Gadamer, *Truth and Method*, xxxi. In Hegel's words: "No matter how excellent we find the statues of the Greek gods . . . we bow the knee no longer." G. W. F. Hegel, *Aesthetics: Lectures on Fine Art*, vol. 1, trans. T. M. Knox (Oxford: Clarendon Press, 1975), 103.

75. Which is formed through the convertibility of singular and incommensurable artifacts into commensurable values by means of "multiple and debatable" sources of interpretive knowledge and judgment grounded in a range of evaluative "judgment devices" acting as forms of distributed authority and trust. Lucien Karpik, *Valuing the Unique: The Economics of Singularities*, trans. Nora Scott (Princeton: Princeton University Press, 2010), 37, 44.

76. On the tax and asset-enhancement advantages of allowing privately owned artworks to reside on temporary loan in museums, cf. Georgina Adam, *Dark Side of the Boom: The Excesses of the Art Market in the Twenty-First Century* (London: Lund Humphries, 2017), 184–86.

other modes of engagement with the image, above all in the public sphere of photographs, movies, television, kitsch religious images, and social media. As formal portraiture has become a more or less academic subgenre of painting, the radiance of the face has migrated to the nonaesthetic arts: above all, to the semidivine face of the star and celebrity systems, which in turn govern and are increasingly being displaced by the publicly private facial image—the mass-produced self-portrait, a "hybrid phenomenon of vernacular photography and social media,"[77] the transiently enchanted selfie.

V

A number of influential theorists have tried over the last few decades to take seriously the magical force of the image by opposing affective intensity or the unrepresentable sublime to the detached aesthetic gaze. At the more nuanced end of the spectrum David Freedberg calls attention to "the investiture of visual imagery with a power and efficacy that transcends its status as mere representation,"[78] or Georges Didi-Huberman mounts a critique of Panofsky's rationalist iconology, which, presupposing "the mimetic transparency of the iconic sign,"[79] delivers images "to the tyranny of the concept, of definition, and, ultimately, of the nameable and the *legible*."[80] In somewhat less nuanced terms, Keith Moxey speaks of a "*pictorial* and *iconic turn*" in studies of visual culture which attends "to that which cannot be read, to that which exceeds the possibilities of a semiotic interpretation, to that which defies understanding on the basis of convention,

77. Alise Tifentale and Lev Manovich, "*Selfiecity*: Exploring Photography and Self-Fashioning in Social Media," http://selfiecity.net/.

78. Freedberg, *The Power of Images*, 134.

79. Georges Didi-Huberman, *Confronting Images: Questioning the Ends of a Certain History of Art*, trans. John Goodman (University Park: Pennsylvania State University Press, 2005), 240, emphasis removed.

80. Didi-Huberman, *Confronting Images*, 122.

and to that which we can never define."[81] And in Hans Ulrich Gumbrecht's recent writings, the work of art is said to generate both "meaning-effects" and "presence-effects," but interpretation as the identification or attribution of meaning-effects and as an endless loop of self-reflexivity has become the "exclusive core practice" of the humanities.[82] The effect of this predominance of interpretation has been a "loss of world," a feeling "that we are no longer in touch with the things of the world" (40); and the remedy is a kind of passive openness—the term Gumbrecht uses is the Heideggerian *Gelassenheit*—to the immediacy of presence in the work. "Presence" is an aspect of the materiality of the work, but it has a necessarily theological force: in George Steiner's terms, the work of art "quicken[s] into presence the continuum between temporality and eternity, between matter and spirit, between man and 'the other.'"[83] Gumbrecht's major examples of "presence cultures" are thus religious: on the one hand contemporary Afro-Brazilian cults, with their ecstatic inscription of bodies into the rhythms of the cosmos,[84] and on the other the sacramental culture of the pre-Reformation Catholic Church, for which the Eucharist is "a ritual of magic because it makes God's body physically present as the central part of a past situation" and thus intensifies "the already existing real presence of God" (85). It is from such cultures that we can learn new ways of grasping phenomena of presence in the work of art, new ways of grasping Being "outside the networks of semantics and other cultural distinctions," Being in its "unconcealment . . . in the happening of truth" (70).

The last stage of my inquiry in this chapter asks whether we

81. Keith Moxey, *Visual Time: The Image and History* (Durham, NC: Duke University Press, 2013), 54.

82. Hans Ulrich Gumbrecht, *Production of Presence: What Meaning Cannot Convey* (Stanford: Stanford University Press, 2004), 1–2, 92; hereafter cited in the text.

83. George Steiner, *Real Presences* (Chicago: University of Chicago Press, 1991), cited in Gumbrecht, *Production of Presence*, 59. For a critique, cf. Georges Didi-Huberman, *Ce que nous voyons, ce qui nous regarde* (Paris: Les Editions de Minuit, 1992), 153.

84. Gumbrecht, *Production of Presence*, 79–80; hereafter cited in the text.

can understand the conditions of possibility of the "ontological communion" between the image and what it represents without relying on a quasi-theological regime of reading. I turn here to a domain of art that is intricately bound up with the apprehension of the sacred and of ancestral presence and yet fully integrated into the commercial art market on a global scale. I investigate how the lines between the aesthetic, the commercial, and the sacred are drawn within the symbolic economy that orders contemporary Australian Indigenous art, using as my focus the work of a single artist, to try to complicate the question of ontological communion in two ways. First, this artist does not work with the figure of the human or divine body, and yet her work is clearly bound up with the representation of a sacred cosmos; second, the complexity of the regimes that order this domain of aesthetic production seems to me to preclude any simple invocation of effects of presence or of the sacred to explain it. In particular, the relation of this body of work to the art museum and to Western traditions of abstract art, to which it bears a close and perhaps misleading resemblance, makes it difficult to understand in isolation from the market-based aesthetic regime that allocates a place and a value to all contemporary art.

Dorothy Napangardi (also known as Dorothy Napangardi Robinson) was a Warlpiri artist born in the early 1950s in an area known as Mina Mina, which includes a part of the vast Lake Mackay (Ngayurru), a salt-encrusted claypan with two huge soakages, that stands at the intersection of the Great Sandy Desert, the Gibson Desert, and the Tanami Desert in the arid heart of Australia. Napangardi had no contact with white people until she was seven or eight, when her family was forcibly resettled in the township of Yuendumu; they subsequently escaped the settlement and returned to Mina Mina. Christine Nicholls attributes Napangardi's "extraordinary spatial abilities," which enable her to organize complex patterns of ordered variations and discontinuities across very large canvases, to her having grown up in a world with virtually no natural features and without built structures other than "bough shelters and makeshift dwellings that enabled [her and her family] to see the full 360 degrees, as an uninterrupted vista, virtually all the time."[85] Napangardi began painting in Alice Springs in 1987, and her early work represented vividly colored and elaborately symmetrical designs of bush plums and bush bananas; a major stylistic break in 1997 led to a late style characterized by a radically restricted palette (often just black and white) and abstract, repetitive patterns often based on the flow and intersection of straight or curving dotted lines across a grid. Napangardi died in a car accident in Alice Springs in 2013.

As a member of the Napangardi skin group Dorothy was a custodian of the Mina Mina women's Dreaming site. The Jukurrpa, or "Dreaming," that she was authorized to reproduce is the Kana-Kurlangu Jukurrpa, which in Warlpiri literally means "digging-stick-possessing Dreaming" and is also sometimes called Karnta-Kurlangu Jukurrpa, or "women-belonging Dreaming."[86] The Jukurrpa is a complex of story, ritual, dance, body decoration, and song, and a temporal structure that is at once ancestral and present, transcendental and yet immanent in daily life; it maps out a relation to country for which "the sacred" would be one (inadequate) term and "law" another. The story that underlies Napangardi's painting is that of a group of ancestral women who dance their way across country (to Australian Aboriginal people, "country" without an article refers to their ancestral lands; the usage has been adopted by non-Aboriginal Australians), sometimes entering the ground, sometimes encountering other Dreamings and other ancestral beings, and using their digging sticks to incise distinctive features into the landscape. The most salient of these features for Napangardi's work are the markings on the

85. Christine Nicholls, "Thinking Big: Spatial Conception in the Art of Dorothy Napangardi," *Artlink* 23, no. 3 (2003), 44–50; excerpted in *How Aborigines Invented the Idea of Contemporary Art: Writings on Aboriginal Contemporary Art*, ed. Ian McLean (Sydney: Institute of Modern Art/Power Publications, 2011), 253.

86. Punayi (Jeannie) Herbert Nungarrayi, in conversation with Christine Nicholls, "Introduction," in *Dancing Up Country: The Art of Dorothy Napangardi* (Sydney: Museum of Contemporary Art, 2003), 6.

dried-up salt lake—what Jeannie Nungarrayi describes as "a series of criss-crosses, lots of criss-crosses—like grid patterns and
all that. Or even sort of like an intricate pattern of interwoven
string"[87]—and the patterns made by the surrounding sandhills.
One way of reading her paintings, then, is as a representation
of the "intricately interwoven Dreaming networks" along which
the ancestral women danced, and which form the "elaborate grid
pattern, animated, alive, breathing" of Mina Mina.[88] In Napangardi's later paintings,

> the optical effects of distortion, of tension, compression, flow, re-
> lease and movement created across the two-dimensional surface
> mirror the transformation of place by the Ancestor Women, creat-
> ing the country, changing the shape and form of it and of them-
> selves. The optical effects are not incidental but linked conceptually
> to the Dreaming and its relation to place. The re-creation across a
> painted surface evokes place in an almost cartographic sense as the
> lines operate like compass points or directional markers, both spatial
> and moral.[89]

A variation on this cartographic account would see the paintings as "a mapping not of a territory but its passages, the traces
it leaves in the landscapes it uncovers."[90] But both versions are
certain that a landscape is there: many of the paintings' titles say
so, and most of them make reference to the immanence of the
Dreaming in country, to a depth of meaning and belonging that
inform the landscape that lies beneath the paint.

Yet that certainty acts as an interpretive supplement that, in
reducing the paintings to an iconographic premise, constitutes
them as the illustration of a narrative. Barbara Bolt cites Benjamin Genocchio's reading of Napangardi's paintings as "symbolic
maps as well as ciphers for the Jukurrpa. . . . The long flowing

87. Nungarrayi, "Introduction," 8.

88. Christine Nicholls, "Grounded Abstraction: The Work of Dorothy Napangardi,"
in *Dancing Up Country*, 62.

89. Vivienne Webb, "Form and Content," in *Dancing Up Country*, 74.

90. Erin Manning, "Relationscapes: How Contemporary Aboriginal Art Moves
Beyond the Map," *Cultural Studies Review* 13, no. 2 (2007), 135.

lines in Napangardi's paintings represent the movement of the female figures as they dance their way across the country, while the small white dots reflect the indentations made in the desert sands by their feet over the sandy ground."[91] This is the kind of reading that Eric Michaels denounces as the construction of a "readable" gloss by the abstraction of certain figurative meanings from their ceremonial and social settings. It is not that "design elements of variously readable iconicity"[92] are absent from the paintings he is discussing but that they are not readable by an outside observer:

> I do not "understand" these paintings, not in terms of the meanings the painters put there. . . . These meanings are complex, implicit, even restricted. To understand them, one would need to be a full member of a particular Warlpiri kin group, initiated and competent in the stories and ceremonies and landscapes that are intimately associated with the sources of these paintings. Even then, some meanings would remain inaccessible until the painter, reciprocating some ancient or contemporary obligation, passed on the design to another. The ability to interpret these paintings is inseparable from the right or the obligation to paint them.[93]

To be outside the culture, to have no access to its secret and sacred materials, or even to be a member of the culture but not to be initiated into particular Dreamings, the rights to which are distributed by gender, by skin name, by filial descent, and by seniority, and which are vulnerable to the cultural loss that afflicts all Australian tribal communities, is to lack the interpretive tools to read the iconography—to lack them *entirely*, such

91. Benjamin Genocchio, "Traditional Abstracts," *The Weekend Australian Review*, January 25–26, 2003, 13; quoted in Barbara Bolt, "Rhythm and the Performative Power of the Index: Lessons from Kathleen Petyarre's Painting," *Cultural Studies Review* 12, no. 1 (2006), 58.

92. Eric Michaels, "Western Desert Sandpainting and Postmodernism," in *Bad Aboriginal Art: Tradition, Media, and Technological Horizons* (Minneapolis: University of Minnesota Press, 1994), 57.

93. Michaels, "Western Desert Sandpainting and Postmodernism," 55.

that no amount of ethnographic information can compensate for our exclusion. The digests of mythical narratives that commonly accompany the paintings produced by members of traditional Aboriginal communities tell us something, but they have little or nothing to do with either the paintings' "custodial and commemorative intent"[94] or the work that they do *as paintings.*

And indeed, in one strong sense these paintings are not "sacred" at all but are rather commercial and secular artifacts; or, more precisely, they exist within an economy that orders relations between the sacred, the commercial, and the aesthetic in a way that renders them at once fully at home within the institutions of Western art—the gallery, the museum, the auction house, the catalogue, the discourses of art appreciation and art history—and yet in some sense outside or in excess of them. There is a history here: modern Indigenous acrylic paintings have often drawn on the designs, and on techniques such as cross-hatching and dotting, that characterize traditional ceremonial ground painting and body painting; yet the acrylics made the passage from the category of the ethnographic to that of fine art relatively quickly. But the link between secret and sacred designs and the artwork produced for commercial sale is a complex one: sometimes (in the case of many urban Aboriginal artists, for example) it is absent, or present only as a felt loss; at other times the connection is so intimate that offense may be taken at the revelation of knowledge that should not have been made public.[95] Painting differs from ritual decoration for a ceremony, but "both the design forms and the dots in acrylics are understood as being equivalent to simi-

94. Rex Butler, "The Impossible Painter," *Australian Art Collector* 2 (1998), 42–45; excerpted in McLean, *How Aborigines Invented the Idea of Contemporary Art*, 228.

95. "When a group of paintings was exhibited at a Perth museum in 1975, visiting Pitjantjatjarra men requested that 44 of the 46 paintings be turned toward the wall as inappropriate for exposure. Subsequently, they demanded and received compensation from the Papunya Pintupi painters because the acrylic designs were images that belonged to them jointly." Fred R. Myers, *Painting Culture: The Making of an Aboriginal High Art* (Durham, NC: Duke University Press, 2002), 65.

lar usages in ritual,"[96] and both have a numinous force. Indeed, it may be that the characteristically abstract design elements of Indigenous art conceal and displace an underlying figural representation. Whereas early Papunya artists, for example, worked with the representation of "Ancestor Figures, often fully dressed for ceremony, painted up and bearing sacred implements, set out on bare ground and arranged symmetrically for maximum legibility," under pressure over the use of recognizably sacred stories they began to remove such narrative detail from their paintings, replacing it with "elements of background, in-fill, and incident."[97] Abstraction may conceal from outsiders an embodied sacred presence.

Fred Myers casts this tension between the two worlds in which the paintings circulate as an articulation of regimes of value that are not fully compatible or commensurate: first, a regime that he calls "revelatory"; second, the "regimes of value organized around the concepts of art and commodity, on the one hand, and identity and the politics of indigeneity, on the other."[98] If there is tension, however, there is also a symbiosis between that revelatory regime and the art market, which authenticates contemporary Indigenous paintings as an integral part of the world of fine art precisely by affirming their indigeneity. This mode of authentication is not exactly a primitivism, but it does involve an othering of this art—this sophisticated and commercially driven art—as a condition of its recognition: traditional Indigenous paintings may be "fine" rather than "ethnographic" art, but they are displayed in the art museum as Indigenous art, not as Australian art or as modern or modernist art. And their authentication by the art institution thus renders the very great diversity of Indig-

---

96. Myers, *Painting Culture*, 58.

97. Terry Smith, "Creating Value between Cultures: Contemporary Australian Aboriginal Art," in *Beyond Price: Value in Culture, Economics and the Arts*, ed. Michael Hutter and David Throsby (Cambridge: Cambridge University Press, 2008), 28.

98. Myers, *Painting Culture*, 6.

enous cultures and of individual relations to them, always caught between an endangered tradition and a destructive modernity, impossibly homogeneous.

Dorothy Napangardi's paintings, like those of Rover Thomas or Emily Kngwarreye, make little or no use of traditional ceremonial designs, and none of the technique of cross-hatching. The art of her later period is severely abstract, built out of intersecting straight or curved dotted lines; out of the play between empty and more or less densely filled space, between larger and smaller points of dotted intensity, and between black and white or subdued and tonally related colors; and out of the play of vectors across a grid. What is most striking, perhaps, about paintings like the series entitled Salt on Mina Mina is the spaces of blackness, like tears in fabric, left by the incomplete gridding effected by the white lines, but also the almost starlike intensity of the white dots of uneven sizes that form them. The lines themselves waver between the promise and the refusal of a regular grid, above all because of the irregularity of the parallels and the slightly curving lines that cut across them. These are often huge canvases, and it is difficult to describe the intensity they convey when you're standing in front of one of them, overwhelmed by its sheer scale and the astonishing formal complexity of its organization of space.

Writing of Napangardi's use of the grid as a structural device in her late work, Vivienne Webb notes that her "distorted grid structure" and serial repetition of modules closely, but misleadingly, resemble the classic modernist grid which, in Rosalind Krauss's formulation, announces "modern art's will to silence, its hostility to literature, to narrative, to discourse. . . . The grid states the autonomy of the work of art. Flattened, geometricized, ordered, it is antinatural, antimimetic, antireal."[99] But the apparent affinity between the "abstract" art of Napangardi or Kngwarreye and modernist abstraction rests on what Roger Benjamin calls the

99. Rosalind Krauss, *The Originality of the Avant Garde and Other Modernist Myths* (Cambridge, MA: MIT Press, 1985), 9.

"fallacy of isomorphism: that similar meanings can be ascribed to images that happen to have similar visual configurations."[100] To the contrary, Webb argues: Napangardi's paintings,

> although superficially similar, directly contradict and subvert the modernist implication of the grid, and in so doing confront the viewer with cultural difference. Her works are narrative-based, mimetically tracing the movements and activities of the Women Ancestors as they dance their way through spinifex and over sandhills. They also repeat nature and the natural formations of the environment and as such deal very much with the "real" as opposed to the "abstract." Whilst contemporary they nevertheless draw upon age-old tradition and cultural knowledge as well as a complex and articulated religion.[101]

There is little doubt that these paintings, and the acrylic paintings of tribal Indigenous Australians more generally, are grounded in a set of traditional knowledges and practices that we might call "religious," or that what the painters themselves value is as much the Dreaming that the paintings represent as the formal surface of the works. For the Pintupi painters with whom Fred Myers worked, "the bigger or more important the story—the greater the value attached to the designs in traditional context—the more valuable the painting should be monetarily,"[102] and "the painters expected that buyers would recognize that payment was for the revelation of Dreamings and not for the mere execution of the painting."[103] What we read as formal features—cross-hatching and dotting, for example—are used to express the presence of ancestral power. Writing about the Yolngu art of northwestern

100. Roger Benjamin, "A New Modernist Hero," in *Emily Kame Kngwarreye: Ahalkere: Paintings from Utopia*, ed. Margo Neale (Brisbane and Melbourne: Queensland Art Gallery and Macmillan, 1998), 47–54; extracted in McLean, *How Aborigines Invented the Idea of Contemporary Art*, 227.

101. Webb, "Form and Content," in *Dancing Up Country*, 73.

102. Myers, *Painting Culture*, 72.

103. Fred Myers, "Some Properties of Art and Culture: Ontologies of the Image and Economies of Exchange," in *Materiality*, ed. Daniel Miller (Durham, NC: Duke University Press, 2005), 99.

Arnhem Land, Howard Morphy describes a quality of brilliance that is called *bir'yun*, "the shimmering effect of finely cross-hatched paintings which project a brightness that is seen as emanating from the *wangarr* [ancestral] beings themselves."[104] The quality of *bir'yun* produces an optical effect "in which the surface shines. . . . The underlying pattern is clearly defined yet the surface of the painting appears to move; it is difficult to fix the eye on a single segment without interference from others—indeed, in some paintings the image seems unstable, almost threatening to leave the surface of the painting."[105]

Although Morphy's analysis refers only to Yolngu art, the widespread use both of the techniques of cross-hatching and dotting and of the kinds of shimmering optical effect that make many Australian Indigenous paintings formally resemble the Op-Art canvases of Bridget Riley suggests that we can generalize from his analysis to a more widespread sense of ancestral presence in Aboriginal acrylics. That sense of presence indicates a relation between painting and Dreaming that is ontological, not representational. However inaccessible that ontological relation might be to the viewer from outside the culture, it is a crucial dimension of the act of painting; and its point of access is not the sacred face, not the eyes initiating a "magical relation" between the image and what it figures, not the mediating presence of a god or a saint or an ancestral being in human form, but something less personal that inheres in the formal techniques of representation themselves.

Yet the relationship of these paintings to the institutions of contemporary art seems to me at the same time to be more complex, more ambiguous than this statement would suggest. The ambiguity is brought out in two directly contradictory state-

---

104. Howard Morphy, "From Dull to Brilliant: The Aesthetics of Spiritual Power Among the Yolngu," in *Anthropology, Art and Aesthetics*, ed. Jeremy Coote and Anthony Shelton (Oxford: Clarendon, 1992), 209–44; extracted in McLean, *How Aborigines Invented the Idea of Contemporary Art*, 238.

105. Howard Morphy, *Becoming Art: Exploring Cross-Cultural Categories* (Sydney: UNSW Press, 2008), 92.

ments that Eric Michaels makes in two different essays. In the first, writing about classical Western art's former claim to "some privileged universality, some capacity for a communication less mediated than the linguistic," he rejects as untenable the idea that phenomena can "communicate directly, unmediated, their history and meaning"; and yet, he continues, this is precisely the claim made by these paintings from the Western Desert, "that the landscape does speak, and that it speaks directly to the initiated, and explains not only its own occurrence, but the order of the world."[106] It is a claim that, given his involvement with Warlpiri painters, he finds no basis to refuse. Yet in a subsequent essay he writes:

> Because these [Warlpiri] designs claim sources in a religious iconography, a "cult ritual" (satisfying Benjamin's definition of "aura"), it may somehow be imagined that they carry intact from the primitive (Dreamtime) some exemption from the modern/postmodern condition and its unbearable (if oblique) view of chaos. But such claims require also an exemption from recognizing the relations and conditions of their production, and their own historical (not prehistorical) construction. But this asserts that dangerous fantasy of authenticity that all our other critical terms resist. I have argued the opposite: that these works are to be judged first and foremost in terms of the social practices that produce and circulate them—practices that promote issues of authority, not authenticity.[107]

Both of Michaels's positions—a humility before the claim to the ontological truth of Indigenous acrylics, and a deep suspicion of the "dangerous fantasy of authenticity"—seem to me valid and compelling. They are equally valid because they stem from distinct regimes of value: a "sacred" or "revelatory" regime that informs the relation of the painters to their work and generates diverse effects of presence for different actors, and a critical regime that informs the stance of Western intellectuals. To these we could add the kind of aesthetic stance that flows from the commodity-driven regime of the institution of art, and a formal-

---

106. Michaels, "Western Desert Sandpainting and Postmodernism," 59–60.
107. Michaels, "Bad Aboriginal Art," in Michaels, *Bad Aboriginal Art*, 162.

ist mode of reading that contextualizes these works in relation to the field of Western art as a whole. These distinct regimes—and the overlaps and intersections between them—are a product of the distinctive and historically particular economy that distributes relations between the sacred, the commercial, and the aesthetic in our world, together with their disparate and incommensurable temporalities.

VI

Dorothy Napangardi worked closely with and under the sponsorship of the Gallery Gondwana in Alice Springs, run by her friend and business collaborator Roslyn Premont. Her career was shaped by this protective commercial relationship and by a series of major exhibitions: her first major solo exhibition, *Dancing Up Country: The Art of Dorothy Napangardi*, was held at the Museum of Contemporary Art in Sydney and later toured in Asia; another was held at the Hosfelt Gallery in San Francisco in 2005; and she participated in group shows in Vienna and Köln and at the Seattle Art Museum and the 2012 Sydney Biennale. In many ways her career conforms to the classic modernist format of a strategic relation to the market in which the artist differentiates herself as a brand in order to further her candidacy for the art museum—and indeed, Napangardi's work is widely held in major collections throughout the world. If it is the case that the art museum governs the fundamental values, both aesthetic and monetary, of the contemporary art world, it is nevertheless also the case that for many Indigenous artists from remote communities there is either a lack of interest in or a refusal of "those forms of artistic creativity required for the competitive struggle for field-specific forms of capital," and thus that "the temporal dynamics of the Australian art field cannot be reduced to a singular accumulating time of modernity."[108] The art museum, the

108. Tony Bennett, "Adjusting Field Theory: The Dynamics of Settler-Colonial Art Fields," in *Routledge International Handbook of the Sociology of Art and Culture*, ed. M. Savage and L. Haniquet (London: Routledge, 2015), 257–58.

institutional order of art, is the condition of possibility for the display of ancestral presence, but it is precisely its display that, in a kind of reverse iconoclasm, makes that presence inaccessible to outsiders, both Indigenous and non-Indigenous. It exists, it can be glimpsed, only as a trace within historical time, and as the performance of an entirely aesthetic effect.

4

Construing Climate Change

Ice storm rolls from Texas to Tennessee—I'm in Los Angeles and it's freezing.
Global warming is a total, and very expensive, hoax!
«DONALD J. TRUMP»

The mean annual concentration of carbon dioxide in the atmosphere has now passed 400 parts per million. For the foreseeable future that figure is irreversible: the best we can hope is that human activity will not exacerbate it. We know with great clarity what the effects of that concentration of greenhouse gases will be. The world will experience greater extremes of temperature in the context of an overall warming of the climate. There will be a greater frequency and intensity of extreme weather events: drought, floods, tornadoes; cyclones may be less frequent but will be more intense; monsoons will become less frequent and more unpredictable. As the oceans become warmer and more acidic, they will lose their capacity to absorb heat from the atmosphere, and their oxygen levels will be depleted; sea levels will rise as glaciers and ice sheets melt and as the ocean waters expand with warming. Coral reefs will bleach and die; marine life will migrate and die. The eventual disappearance of the Himalayan and Tibetan glaciers will dry up the great river systems that irrigate the South Asian subcontinent. Low-lying islands will disappear, and rising sea levels will make the Asian mega deltas uninhabitable. The loss of forest cover will create new deserts and diminish the capacity of the earth to breathe. The thawing of the Siberian and northern Canadian permafrost will release vast quantities of methane, which will induce positive feedback in the climate system. Groundwater will become saltier, topsoils will erode, pests will infest crops, and harvests will fail. Land species will migrate and many will become extinct. Humankind will suffer an increase in disease and mortality; there will be mass migration within and across national borders, wars for the control of more fertile land, and an increased incidence of terrorism and civil disorder. Policing will become more militarized. The rich will barricade themselves in gated communities; the wretched of the earth will carry the burden of suffering.

I

The science that predicts these effects is, in its broad outlines, unambiguous. There is no reasonable doubt that human pollution of the atmosphere with greenhouse gases will warm the planet and make it less hospitable to the flourishing of life. Nor is there any doubt that, given the long residence time of carbon dioxide in the atmosphere, it is now too late to prevent these consequences. The problem has been too hard, the interests at play too deeply entrenched. As the editors of an influential handbook put it:

> The stakes are massive, the risks and uncertainties severe, the economics controversial, the science besieged, the politics bitter and complicated, the psychology puzzling, the impacts devastating, the interactions with other environmental and non-environmental issues running in many directions. The social problem-solving mechanisms we currently possess are not designed, and have not evolved, to cope with anything like an interlinked set of problems of this severity, scale, and complexity.[1]

1. John S. Dryzek, Richard B. Norgaard, and David Schlosberg, "Introduction," in *The Oxford Handbook of Climate Change and Society*, ed. John S. Dryzek, Richard B. Norgaard, and David Schlosberg (Oxford: Oxford University Press, 2011), 3.

One of the more bewildering aspects of the public discussion of climate change has been the sharp disjunction between the strong consensus among climate scientists that anthropogenic climate change is a real and imminent danger[2] and the ambivalence or even indifference of the lay population, most strongly expressed in the most heavily polluting countries.[3] This looks like a question about knowledge—about who knows what and who knows best—just as the political resistance to meaningful action to address greenhouse-gas emissions looks like a failure of understanding and of will. Certainly one part of this complex of problems has to do with the concerted undermining of the science. The larger issue, though, has to do with the material interests at stake in the transition from an economy and its enabling web of social relations which is based on the burning of fossil fuels (what Andreas Malm calls "fossil capital")[4] and which is steadily destroying its very conditions of existence, to an economy and an emergent set of social relations based on alternative sources of energy.

Questions of knowledge and judgment are folded into the slow and painful process of that transition, and the organization of and contest over those questions are the focus of this chapter. After discussing the denialist counterinstitutions of knowledge

2. Naomi Oreskes found no disagreement whatsoever among climate scientists with the conclusion that there is compelling evidence for human modification of the climate (Naomi Oreskes, "Beyond the Ivory Tower: The Scientific Consensus on Climate Change," *Science* 306, no. 5702 [2004], 1686); Doran and Zimmerman and Cook et al. found a robust consensus with a range of 90% to 100%, depending on the question asked and the sampling methodology used (Peter T. Doran and Maggie Kendall Zimmerman, "Examining the Scientific Consensus on Climate Change," *EOS* 90, no. 3 [2009], 22–23; John Cook et al., "Consensus on Consensus: A Synthesis of Consensus Estimates on Human-Caused Global Warming," *Environmental Research Letters* 11 [2016], 1–7).

3. Pew Research found in 2016 that fewer than 50% of Americans attributed global climate change to human activity, and only 27% acknowledged that "almost all" climate scientists agree on this. Cary Funk and Brian Kennedy, *Public Views on Climate Change and Climate Science*, report, October 4, 2016, http://www.pewinternet.org/2016/10/04/public-views-on-climate-change-and-climate-scientists/.

4. Andreas Malm, *Fossil Capital: The Rise of Steam Power and the Roots of Global Warming* (London: Verso, 2016).

about climate change in the following section, I move to consider how knowledge about something as complex and unstable as a "climate" is enabled, constructed, and authorized by the "official" institutions of science. I conclude by exploring how that knowledge then becomes available for a multiplicity of uses in the public realm.

II

The story of how individuals and institutions were funded by fossil-fuel corporations, in the United States and globally, to propagate uncertainty about the science of climate change is now well known. The strategy has been a simple one: sow doubt about the validity of the research; downplay the seriousness of the problem or its priority as a policy issue; argue against the need for regulation and corporate liability; find that applying the precautionary principle would be economically damaging; target politicians who think otherwise.[5] Each of these principles was pioneered by the tobacco industry in order to undermine research on the carcinogenic effects of tobacco smoke. A clear line of continuity runs from the notorious 1969 Brown and Williamson memo noting that "doubt is our product since it is the best means of competing with the 'body of fact' that exists in the mind of the general public"[6] to a less succinct but equally cynical statement posted on the ExxonMobil website in 2006:

> While assessments such as those of the IPCC have expressed growing confidence that recent warming can be attributed to increases in greenhouse gases, these conclusions rely on expert judgment rather than objective, reproducible statistical methods. Taken together, gaps in the scientific basis for theoretical climate models and the interplay of significant natural variability make it very difficult to determine

5. Coral Davenport and Eric Lipton, "How G.O.P. Leaders Came to View Climate Change as Fake Science," *New York Times,* June 3, 2017.

6. *Smoking and Health Proposal,* 1969, BN: 680561778, Legacy Tobacco Documents Library; cited in Naomi Oreskes and Erik M. Conway, *Merchants of Doubt: How a Handful of Scientists Obscured the Truth on Issues from Tobacco Smoke to Global Warming* (New York: Bloomsbury, 2010), 34.

objectively the extent to which recent climate changes might be the result of human actions.[7]

There is also a clear continuity of personnel: a core group of scientists like Frederick Seitz and Fred S. Singer, many of them clustered in the George C. Marshall Institute, moved smoothly from providing comfort to Big Tobacco to providing comfort to fossil-fuel interests by challenging the peer-reviewed scientific literature.

As with tobacco, the work of climate-change denial has been carried out by an extensive network of conservative advocacy groups and think tanks which acted to generate and to amplify the views of a small group of dissident scientists. The strategy of "astroturfing," initially developed by a PR company working for Philip Morris, involved setting up a large number of apparently independent front organizations in order to give the impression of a grassroots movement opposed to environmental regulation.[8] These organizations included the Global Climate Science Team, the Advancement of Sound Science Coalition, the National Center for Public Policy Research, the Competitive Enterprise Institute, the Cato Institute, the American Enterprise Institute, and the Heritage Foundation. They were, and in many cases continue to be, funded either directly, by ExxonMobil, Koch Industries, the Scaife family, and other corporate donors, or, more recently, by Donors Trust/Capital Funding, which acts to anonymize donations.[9] (ExxonMobil is one of the world's largest

---

7. ExxonMobil, "Corporate Citizenship Report," 2005 http://www.exxonmobil.com/corporate/citizenship/ccr5/climate_science.asp; cited in Union of Concerned Scientists, "Smoke, Mirrors & Hot Air: How ExxonMobil Uses Big Tobacco's Tactics to Manufacture Uncertainty on Climate Science," January 2007, 17, https://www.ucsusa.org/sites/default/files/legacy/assets/documents/global_warming/exxon_report.pdf. On the discrepancy between Exxon's internal scientific reports and its publicly funded advertorials, cf. Geoffrey Supran and Naomi Oreskes, "Assessing ExxonMobil's Climate Change Communications (1977–2014)," *Environmental Research Letters* 12 (2017).

8. Clive Hamilton, *Scorcher: The Dirty Politics of Climate Change* (Melbourne: Black Inc. Agenda, 2007), 128.

9. Robert J. Brulle, "Institutionalizing Delay: Foundation Funding and the Creation of U.S. Climate Change Counter-Movement Organizations," *Climatic Change* 122 (2014), 690.

publicly traded corporations, with 2016 revenues of $216 billion, down from a 2011 peak of $467 billion but still exceeding the gross domestic products of most nations.[10] It is also one of the world's largest producers of carbon pollution, with emissions in 2015 of 122 million CO_2-equivalent metric tons.[11] Its internal research has been clear about the reality of anthropogenic climate warming since as early as 1977,[12] and it has acted to preserve key investments against the effects of climate change.[13] Koch Industries is a conglomerate of more than twenty companies involved in petroleum refining, fuel pipelines, coal supply and trading, oil and gas exploration, chemicals and polymers, fertilizer production, and agribusiness, with revenues in 2016 of around $100 billion.)[14]

The proliferation of institutions (there are well over one hundred conservative "climate change counter-movement"[15] organi-

10. ExxonMobil, "ExxonMobil's revenue from 2001 to 2017 (in million U.S. dollars)," https://www.statista.com/statistics/264119/revenue-of-exxon-mobil-since-2002/.

11. ExxonMobil, "Mitigating Emissions in Our Operations," Sustainability Report, http://corporate.exxonmobil.com/en/community/corporate-citizenship-report/charts/greenhouse-gas-emissions-net-chart.

12. Neela Bannerjee, Lisa Song, and David Hasemeyer, "Exxon's Own Research Confirmed Fossil Fuel's Role in Global Warming Decades Ago," *Inside Climate News*, September 16, 2015, https://insideclimatenews.org/news/15092015/Exxons-own-research-confirmed-fossil-fuels-role-in-global-warming; Katie Jennings, Dino Grandoni, and Suzanne Rust, "How Exxon Went from Leader to Skeptic on Climate Change Research," *Los Angeles Times*, October 23, 2015, http://graphics.latimes.com/exxon-research/; Lisa Song, Neela Bannerjee, and David Hasemeyer, "Exxon Confirmed Global Warming Consensus in 1982 with In-House Climate Models," *Inside Climate News*, September 22, 2015, https://insideclimatenews.org/news/18092015/exxon-confirmed-global-warming-consensus-in-1982-with-in-house-climate-models.

13. Amy Liebermann and Suzanne Rust, "Big Oil Braced for Global Warming While It Fought Regulations," *Los Angeles Times*, December 31, 2015, http://graphics.latimes.com/oil-operations/; Neela Bannerjee and Lisa Song, "Exxon's Business Ambition Collided with Climate Change Under a Distant Sea," *Inside Climate News*, October 8, 2015, https://insideclimatenews.org/news/08102015/Exxons-Business-Ambition-Collided-with-Climate-Change-Under-a-Distant-Sea.

14. *Fortune*, "Koch Industries," in *25 Most Important Private Companies*, http://fortune.com/most-important-private-companies/koch-industries-4/. Cf. also Greenpeace, "Koch Industries: Secretly Funding the Climate Denial Machine," https://www.greenpeace.org/usa/global-warming/climate-deniers/koch-industries/.

15. Brulle, "Institutionalizing Delay," 684.

zations in the United States, and they have extensive influence in other parts of the world) helps create the impression that there is widespread doubt about climate change and widespread disagreement among the scientists who study it. The quasi-scientific names of some of the think tanks similarly "help to suggest that serious researchers are challenging the consensus."[16] Most importantly, perhaps, conservative think tanks have been able to establish themselves as "a true 'counter-intelligentsia' that has achieved equal legitimacy with mainstream science and academia";[17] they are often preferred over academics by the media as a source of expert opinion, even though they are more like advocacy groups than scientific institutions and even though they tend (with the exception of the Marshall Institute) to be "populated primarily by economists, policy analysts and legal scholars rather than natural scientists."[18] They do not publish peer-reviewed papers; their job is to undermine the validity of the established science and to "stoke the ongoing fires of talk radio, cable news, the blogosphere and the like, all of which feed off contrarian story lines and seldom make the time to assess facts and weigh evidence";[19] indeed, a key tactic of this interpretive counterinstitution is to keep repeating "alternative facts" long after they have been discredited.[20] Singer and Seitz, together with the Exxon-funded Global Climate Coalition, led a vicious attack in 1996 (in the *Wall Street Journal* and elsewhere) on Benjamin Santer, the lead author of Chapter 8 of the IPCC's Second Assessment Report—a report that concluded, with careful qualifications, that "the balance of

16. George Monbiot, *Heat: How to Stop the Planet Burning* (2006; repr., London: Penguin, 2007), 28.

17. Peter J. Jacques, Riley E. Dunlap, and Mark Freeman, "The Organisation of Denial: Conservative Think Tanks and Environmental Scepticism," *Environmental Politics* 17, no. 3 (2008), 356.

18. Jacques, Dunlap, and Freeman, "The Organisation of Denial," 356.

19. Editorial, "Climate of Fear," *Nature* 464, no. 7286 (March 11, 2010), 141.

20. See, for example, Monbiot, *Heat*, 25–26, and Shaun W. Elsasser and Riley W. Dunlap, "Leading Voices in the Denier Choir: Conservative Columnists' Dismissal of Global Warming and Denigration of Climate Science," *American Behavioral Scientist* 57, no. 6 (2013), 767.

evidence suggests that there is a discernible human influence on global climate"—falsely accusing him of having corrupted the IPCC's peer-review process.[21] Many of the same organizations helped create the "Climategate" scandal, alleging that hacked emails from a server at the Climate Research Unit at the University of East Anglia proved that climate change was a hoax.[22] Although after numerous reviews the scientists involved have been exonerated of all charges against them, these emails were still being cited in late 2016 by President-elect Trump as proof of manipulation of climate data; and the outbreak of the scandal coincided with "a significant decline in the American public's beliefs that climate change is happening, human-caused, and a serious threat, along with declines in public trust in climate science and scientists."[23]

In all of this, the denialist counterinstitutions are of course closely supported by the conservative television and print media, in particular the Murdoch press. But this is not just a matter of political affiliation. The entirety of the US "prestige" press (*New York Times, Washington Post, Los Angeles Times, Wall Street Journal*) has failed to report climate change in a way that reflects the state of the science. While, for example, the 2009 Conference of Parties meeting in Copenhagen was widely reported in Europe for its message that worst-case scenarios were becoming a reality, in the United States there was virtually no coverage, and the *New York Times*'s environmental correspondent attended a quite different meeting organized by the Heartland Institute, closely connected to the Koch brothers and their network of right-wing

21. Paul N. Edwards and Stephen H. Schneider, "Self-Governance and Peer Review in Science-for-Policy: The Case of the IPCC Second Assessment Report," in *Changing the Atmosphere: Expert Knowledge and Environmental Governance*, ed. Clark A. Miller and Paul N. Edwards (Cambridge, MA: MIT Press, 2001), 219.

22. Cf. Lee Fang, "A Case of Classic SwiftBoating: How the Right-Wing Noise Machine Manufactured 'Climategate,'" ThinkProgress, December 9, 2009, https://thinkprogress.org/a-case-of-classic-swiftboating-how-the-right-wing-noise-machine-manufactured-climategate-bd7ab3b04988/.

23. Anthony A. Leiserowitz, Edward W. Maibach, Connie Roser-Renouf, Nicholas Smith, and Erica Dawson, "Climategate, Public Opinion, and the Loss of Trust," *American Behavioral Scientist* 57, no. 6 (2012), 821.

donors.[24] In the period from the mid-'90s to the present, over half of the climate-change stories in those newspapers of record represented the science as being "in dispute." In network television, "the contrast was even more extreme: 70% of the media reports portrayed climate scientists as being in strong disagreement on the topic."[25] Much of this failure can be explained by the journalistic norm of balanced reporting, which assumes an equivalence between peer-reviewed science and denialist discourse. In one influential analysis, more than half of a large sample of stories were found to give "'roughly equal attention' to the view that humans were contributing to global warming, and the other view that exclusively natural fluctuations could explain the earth's temperature increase."[26]

But the journalistic norm of balance is only part of the story. More importantly, the counterinstitution of climate denial has managed to acquire a legitimacy in the public sphere that is grounded in the politicization of science itself, that is, in a shift from rejection or distortion of particular scientific findings to a rejection of climate science as an institution. The validity of scientific knowledge has become an issue in the American culture wars that stand as a proxy for economic and political struggles. A 2010 editorial in *Nature* put it like this:

Denialism over global warming has become a scientific cause célèbre within the [Tea Party] movement. [Rush] Limbaugh, for instance, who has told his listeners that "science has become a home for displaced socialists and communists," has called climate-change science "the biggest scam in the history of the world." The Tea Party's leanings encompass religious opposition to Darwinian evolution and to stem-cell and embryo research—which [Glenn] Beck has equated with eugenics. The movement is also averse to science-based regula-

24. William R. Freudenburg and Violetta Muselli, "Reexamining Climate Change Debates: Scientific Disagreement or Scientific Certainty Argumentation Methods (SCAMs)?" *American Behavioral Scientist* 57, no. 6 (2013), 778; cf. Sourcewatch, "Heartland Institute," http://www.sourcewatch.org/index.php/Heartland_Institute.

25. Freudenburg and Muselli, "Reexamining Climate Change Debates," 779–80.

26. Maxwell T. Boykoff and Jules M. Boykoff, "Balance as Bias: Global Warming and the US Prestige Press," *Global Environmental Change* 14 (2004), 129.

tion, which it sees as an excuse for intrusive government. Under the administration of George W. Bush, science in policy had already taken knocks from both neglect and ideology. Yet President Barack Obama's promise to "restore science to its rightful place" seems to have linked science to liberal politics, making it even more of a target of the right.[27]

At least in the area of climate policy, that Tea Party world view has reached its apotheosis in the Trump regime. (President Trump's proposed budget for 2018[28] incorporates massive cuts to the National Science Foundation; the National Oceanographic and Atmospheric Administration, which records, analyzes, and curates much of the world's climate-science data; and the Environmental Protection Agency.)

One way of thinking about the politicization of science might be in terms of a more deeply rooted "civic epistemology" that informs the decision-making culture of the United States and that differs in significant respects from other decision-making cultures.[29] Founded in the common law's adversarial procedures, the US policy-making process brings together the procedural openness of legislative activity with the procedural openness of science—its constant reexamination of fundamental axioms and findings to assess them for error. Thus, for science-based policies, "two systems specifically designed to promote challenge-response-revision cycles multiply each other's effects"; the working assumption is that, while science itself is to be (at least in principle) accepted as "universal and impartial," the scientists who practice it are to be "treated as proxies for interest groups."[30]

27. Editorial, "Science Scorned," *Nature* 467, no. 7312 (September 9, 2010), 133.

28. David Malakoff, "Trump's 2018 Budget Will Squeeze Civilian Science Agencies," *Science* online, February 27, 2017, http://www.sciencemag.org/news/2017/02/trump-s-2018-budget-will-squeeze-civilian-science-agencies.

29. Sheila Jasanoff, "Cosmopolitan Knowledge: Climate Science and Global Civic Epistemology," in Dryzek, Norgaard, and Schlosberg, *The Oxford Handbook of Climate Change and Society*, 134–35.

30. Paul N. Edwards, *A Vast Machine: Computer Models, Climate Data, and the Politics of Global Warming* (Cambridge, MA: MIT Press, 2010), 405–7, emphases removed.

The intensity of the animus directed against climate scientists, as well as the intensity of public indifference towards their conclusions, attests something more profound than a dispute over knowledge: a deep-seated *ressentiment* directed against the "elite" knowledge class and everything it stands for in the fantasmatic imaginary of the American (and global) public sphere. That imaginary structures the reception of knowledge, and

> no form of knowledge establishes its truth simply by being stated. For classes and cultures, knowledge of the external world is a form of social organisation before it is a reality-testing or action-steering device; science, in our era, is both. It allows us to command nature, and it allows a class to exercise power.[31]

In the struggles over the science of climate change, complex socioeconomic conflicts are thus translated into the language of epistemological concern.

Denialists challenge climate models in two ways: "first, by exploiting uncertainties associated with modeling and, second, by denying that models are capable of yielding objective knowledge. Their enterprise is to stigmatize modeling as inferior science on philosophical grounds."[32] At its crudest, this means opposing the merely "theoretical" force of simulation modeling (based on "expert judgment") to empirical observation of the data—as though "the data" existed independently of the models that give them an interpretable form.[33] I discuss the complexities of climate modeling more fully in subsequent sections of this chapter, but let me note for now the difficulty of simply asserting that climate mod-

31. Guy Rundle, "Why Climate Change Activism Has Failed and How It Can Be Saved," *Crikey*, February 9, 2017, https://www.crikey.com.au/2017/02/09/rundle-why-climate-change-activism-has-failed/.

32. Stephen D. Norton and Frederick Suppe, "Why Atmospheric Modeling Is Good Science," in Miller and Edwards, *Changing the Atmosphere*, 67.

33. In the 1995 House hearings, for example, scientists like Patrick Michaels, Fred Singer, and Sallie Baliunas claimed that climate models were not borne out by empirical observation, that their own alternative models had been ignored by the scientific establishment, and that mainstream climate scientists had a vested interest in maintaining government funding. Cf. Edwards, *A Vast Machine*, 411–12, 418.

eling is of the same order as direct observation, that it is objective and value neutral. Such an assertion goes hand in hand with a conception of climate science as a willfully distorted truth. Thus the Union of Concerned Scientists writes that

> ExxonMobil's cynical strategy is built around the notion that public opinion can be easily manipulated because climate science is complex, because people tend not to notice where the information comes from, and because the effects of global warming are just beginning to become visible. But ExxonMobil may well have underestimated the public. The company's strategy quickly unravels when people understand it for what it is: an active campaign of disinformation.[34]

Alas, the strategy will not so quickly unravel when that mythical moment of understanding arrives. This Enlightenment image of science betrayed—a "public deficit model in which public indifference is interpreted as a direct consequence of dis- or misinformation"[35]—sets up a specular relationship between defenders of the science and denialists: either the science faithfully and objectively mirrors reality and is therefore true, or it is artificially constructed and is therefore value laden and false. Each side of that equation is wrongly formulated. The reality of climate change is not "a nature always already there" but "an assemblage to be slowly composed" within an institutional and social framework.[36] I now turn to explore, in some technical detail, the specific analytic procedures that compose that plausible and powerful regime of interpretation.

III

Climate modeling is a form of mathematical simulation of a reality that is treated in the manner of an experiment. It differs from many kinds of laboratory experiment in that the outcomes of its

---

34. Union of Concerned Scientists, "Smoke, Mirrors & Hot Air," 3.

35. Gert Goeminne, "Does the Climate Need Consensus? The Politics of Climate Change Revisited," *Symplokē* 21, no. 1–2 (2013), 159.

36. Leiserowitz et al., "Climategate, Public Opinion, and the Loss of Trust," 477.

manipulations cannot be compared with an unmodified control state; in a system as complex as the planetary climate there is no such control. Climate modeling constructs a range of counterfactuals in order to explore alternative states of the climate in a virtual environment; it is only through simulations that you can, in the words of Paul Edwards, "systematically and repeatedly test variations in the 'forcings' (the variables that control the climate system)," and only through modeling that you can "create a control—a simulated Earth with pre-industrial levels of greenhouse gases, or without the chlorofluorocarbons that erode the ozone layer, or without aerosols from fossil and agricultural waste combustion—against which to analyze what is happening on the real Earth."[37] Although it differs from traditional laboratory experiments, climate modeling "is like experimental work in that the behavior of the model or simulation is the subject of investigation. . . . Researchers make small changes—to parameters, initial conditions, the grain of calculation, etc.—and learn what results."[38]

Indeed, it might be argued that all scientific experiments are heavily dependent on virtual realities, in the sense that they work not upon an unmodified natural world but upon the "proximate systems" that they construct.[39] The objects on which experiments are performed rarely occur in their "natural" state: they are configured in a form that is amenable to analysis, and that form depends upon their malleability and the relations into which they can be induced to enter. What the scientist works with is "object images or with their visual, auditory, or electrical traces, and with their components, their extractions, and their 'purified' versions."[40] Astronomy, for example, constructs its object of

---

37. Edwards, *A Vast Machine*, 40.

38. Sergio Sismondo, "Models, Simulations, and Their Objects," *Science in Context* 12, no. 2 (1999), 255.

39. Roman Frigg and Julian Reiss, "The Philosophy of Simulation: Hot New Issues or Same Old Stew?" *Synthese* 169 (2009), 597.

40. Karin Knorr Cetina, *Epistemic Cultures: How the Sciences Make Knowledge* (Cambridge, MA: Harvard University Press, 1999), 27; hereafter cited in the text.

analysis by means of imaging technologies that yield digital renditions of traces of light from stellar bodies; the object is made manifest by human and technological agency and by the long history of the apparatus of experimental reason which renders it transparent. Similarly, laboratory-based sciences "subject natural conditions to a 'social overhaul' and derive epistemic effects from the new situation" (28).

Karin Knorr Cetina gives the extreme but informative example of experimental high-energy particle physics, for which the major laboratory is CERN's particle accelerator, the Large Hadron Collider. In this laboratory, where physicists working in very large teams are themselves configured and socialized in a particular way, as agents either of theory or of experimentation (16), the natural objects being investigated (subatomic cosmic particles and the scattered debris of particles smashed in collisions) are "unreal," "phantasmic": "they are too small ever to be seen except indirectly through detectors, too fast to be captured and contained in a laboratory space, and too dangerous as particle beams to be handled directly" (48). Most of them exist only for a billionth of a second, and their traces are problematized by the "noise" of vast numbers of false positives and random signals, the ghostly "fake tracks of particles misinterpreted as real tracks" (50–52), that mask the events of interest.

What the physicists who study these events scrutinize is thus the traces of the particles and debris registered in the detectors, traces which are then transmitted as signs to offline operations, where they are reconstructed into an interpretable shape from which physicists create variables that can be analyzed in terms of such templates as expected distributions. This is a world that is far removed from empirical observation: high-energy physics "moves in the shadowland of mechanically, electrically, and electronically produced negative images of the world—in a world of signs and often fictional reflections, of echoes, footprints, and the shimmering appearances of bygone events" (46). It derives its truth effects from operations that process the signatures of events, rather than the events themselves, which nowhere appear directly. Nor does it measure empirical events in the way most other fields of science do: few quantities can be measured directly, and measurements are always an effect of the particular detector; the data mean nothing in themselves but "are contingent upon the measurement apparatus, and are representations of this apparatus" (55). Crucially, then, experiential contact with the world of observable reality "appears to provide no more than an occasional touchstone that hurls the system back upon itself, and 'success' may well depend on how well—or how intricately—the system interacts with itself" (79). Thus, the epistemic practices of high-energy particle physics are focused on reflexive analysis of the system of representations that constitutes the experiment.

In this, these practices closely resemble the practices of simulation modeling. *Models* are "copies" that are "isomorphic to some aspect of a physical system";[41] they are analog and non-propositional; what they "copy" may be real or imaginary; and they "become epistemic instruments, and thus exemplary, if used or manipulated."[42] The concept of *simulation* refers to the construction of a model that involves "analytically intractable mathematics":[43] that is, it involves the "brute force solution"[44] of partial differential equations for which there is no analytic solution. Simulation modeling is characteristically applied to chaotic phenomena such as "a severe storm, a gas jet, or the turbulent flow of water" (257), where, although the underlying physical theories are well understood, the complexity of the interactions involved means the theories cannot be simply applied. The continuous differential equations that express the rates of change of such dynamic phenomena over infinitesimal intervals must be

---

41. Nancy J. Nersessian, "Model-Based Reasoning in Conceptual Change," in *Model-Based Reasoning in Scientific Discovery*, ed. Lorenzo Magnani, Nancy J. Nersessian, and Paul Thagard (New York: Kluwer Academic/Plenum, 1999), 15, 12.

42. Sismondo, "Models, Simulations, and Their Objects," 240.

43. Frigg and Reiss, "The Philosophy of Simulation," 596.

44. Eric Winsberg, "The Hierarchy of Models in Simulation," in Magnani, Nersessian and Thagard, *Model-Based Reasoning in Scientific Discovery*, 257; hereafter cited in the text.

converted into algebraic difference equations, which express rates of change in terms of discrete and discontinuous intervals and which can be computationally solved.

Such simulation involves the elaboration of a hierarchy of models, including a *mechanical* model that is "a bare bones characterization of a physical system that allows us to use the theoretical structure to assign a family of equations to the system"; a *dynamical* model that specifies "a class of parameters, boundary values, and initial conditions that restricts the theoretical model to a specific class of phenomena"; the conversion of that dynamical model into a *computational* model to overcome the problem of analytical intractability; and finally a "model of the *phenomena*" that assembles mathematical, visual, and textual information (258). Each of the steps represented by this hierarchy of models is an attempt "to infer, from existing theoretical knowledge, *new* knowledge about the system being simulated" (260). Simulation is often used for systems that are difficult to observe, and even if that is not the case, "often the simulation will bring a level of mathematical order where before there was only seemingly random detail" (262). It is often applied, too, to systems for which data are sparse, and this means that "comparison with real data can never be the autonomous criterion on which simulation results can be judged" (264), although they can be calibrated in other ways: by their reproduction of known analytical results, by comparison with the outputs of other simulations, and against experimental results.

Modeling is central not only to computational investigation but to all empirical science, since "neither raw data nor raw sensory experience carry their own interpretations. To be properly interpreted and deployed, data must be modeled."[45] By the same token, all experimental data must be reduced and simplified in order to be transformed into an interpretable order. Central to the workings of simulation modeling is the use of "ad hoc modeling assumptions to help make [the] computational models more

---

45. Norton and Suppe, "Why Atmospheric Modeling Is Good Science," 68.

tractable and manageable," including "such techniques as simpli-
fying assumptions, removal of degrees of freedom, and even substitution of simpler empirical relationships for more complex, but
also more theoretically founded laws,"[46] or eliminating certain
factors or influences because of the limitations of computational
power, and either ignoring them or finding ways to compensate
for their omission.

The assumptions brought to bear on the model "are added
to bring structural coherence to existing data, much as adding a
stain to a microscope slide brings into relief features otherwise
unseen,"[47] and they need not be true. Modelers routinely work
with idealized or even false assumptions, such as supposing that
the atmosphere is composed of discrete layers. Stephen Norton
and Frederick Suppe make a comparison with the artifacts introduced into maps of the earth by the projection of spherical data
onto flat surfaces; thus Mercator projections distort the polar
regions but produce maps which are suited to navigation. While
there is no "correct" way of projecting spherical data,

> objective knowledge can be retrieved from map models if claims
> are suitably adjusted to account for distorting effects. Similarly, the
> finite-layer assumption creates features not literally true. But, as with
> map models, if claims are selectively qualified to mask artifacts and
> reflect instrument resolution, modeled data reliably do support ob-
> jective knowledge claims. (84)

The counterview to that confidence about the possibility of
objective knowledge is the argument made by Naomi Oreskes
and her colleagues that "it is impossible to demonstrate the truth
of any proposition, except in a closed system,"[48] and that simulation models—which rely on incompletely known input param-

---

46. Winsberg, "The Hierarchy of Models in Simulation," 259.

47. Norton and Suppe, "Why Atmospheric Modeling Is Good Science," 100; hereafter cited in the text.

48. Naomi Oreskes, Kristin Shrader-Frechette, and Kenneth Belitz, "Verification,
Validation, and Confirmation of Numerical Models in the Earth Sciences," *Science*,
New Series, 263, no. 5147 (1994), 641.

eters, embedded assumptions, and data which are by definition "inference-laden signifiers of natural phenomena to which we have incomplete access"[49]—are never closed and are, therefore, at best heuristic representations. Even though we can talk about agreement of a model with observational data, there is always the possibility that more than one model will explain the available observations.

And indeed, it may be that the notion of agreement with the data is the wrong criterion to use, since there are no data independent of the models that shape them. This is the argument made by Ronald Giere (paraphrasing Patrick Suppes) that "higher level models are not compared directly with data, but with models of data which are lower down in a hierarchy of models."[50] In this view, then,

> when testing the fit of a model with the world, one does not compare that model with data but with *another model*, a model of the data. . . . It is this latter model, and not the data itself, that is used to judge the similarity between the higher-level model and the world. . . . It is models almost all the way down.[51]

IV

Climate modeling is a form of simulation modeling that grew out of a long history of analysis and forecasting of *weather*; in its earlier phases, climatology consisted primarily of local record-keeping and analysis of local trends.[52] The term "climate" is itself

49. Oreskes, Shrader-Frechette, and Belitz, "Verification, Validation, and Confirmation," 642.

50. Ronald N. Giere, "Using Models to Represent Reality," in Magnani, Nersessian and Thagard, *Model-Based Reasoning in Scientific Discovery*, 54, paraphrasing Patrick Suppes, "Models of Data," in *Logic, Methodology, and Philosophy of Science: Proceedings of the 1960 Conference*, ed. E. Nagel, P. Suppes, and A. Tarski (Stanford: Stanford University Press, 1962), 252–61.

51. Giere, "Using Models to Represent Reality," 55.

52. Paul N. Edwards, "Representing the Global Atmosphere: Computer Models, Data, and Knowledge about Climate Change," in Miller and Edwards, *Changing the Atmosphere*, 32.

a conceptual construct which evolved over time. In its most general sense it is an abstraction from our experience of the weather and from natural variation between years, seasons, and hours of the day. Its meaning shifted in the late 1970s, concurrently with the development of modeling techniques, from describing the average of the weather over a period of time to describing an integrated global system of great complexity:

> Governed by a combination of the laws of fluid dynamics, thermodynamics, radiative energy transfer and chemistry, the climate system is composed of the atmosphere, the oceans, ice sheets and land. Each of these four subsystems is coupled to each of the other three, through the exchange of immense quantities of energy, momentum and matter. Nonlinear interactions occur on a dizzying range of spatial and temporal scales, both within and between the subsystems, leading to an intricate and delicate network of feedback loops.[53]

The notion of climate *change* is an interpretive rubric applied against the background of great temporal and spatial variation.[54] While climate modeling takes account of natural variation, its urgency derives from the supposition that the climate system is being dramatically modified as a consequence of cumulative greenhouse-gas emissions. The theory of the greenhouse effect was first posited by Arrhenius in the nineteenth century and is now firmly established. Over long periods of time the global system maintains a global energy balance, and

> at equilibrium, the energy absorbed by the earth's surface from the sun would balance the energy radiated from the earth into space. However, the earth's surface radiates energy at longer wavelengths than it absorbs, which means that accumulations in the atmosphere of certain gases, like carbon dioxide and methane, will change the

53. Paul D. Williams, "Modeling Climate Change: The Role of Unresolved Processes," *Philosophical Transactions of the Royal Society: Mathematical, Physical and Engineering Sciences* 363, no. 1837 (December 2005), 2931.

54. Dale Jamieson, "The Nature of the Problem," in Dryzek, Norgaard, and Schlosberg, *The Oxford Handbook of Climate Change and Society*, 38.

equilibrium temperature by absorbing more energy at longer wavelengths than shorter ones.[55]

The system of variations on long-term equilibrium is studied by means of the construction of general circulation models (GCMs) which seek not just to predict future scenarios but to attribute the causes of variation. They do so by modeling the interaction between the major climate subsystems and extrapolating from trends, and by a counterfactual modeling of what the climate would have looked like without industrial greenhouse-gas concentrations.

In order to account for interactions and feedback loops within and between climate systems, GCMs must thus be "coupled," pulling together atmospheric, ocean, sea ice, and land surface models. The *atmosphere*, "a thin spherical shell of air that envelops the earth" which "is described by such variables as temperature, pressure, humidity, winds, and water and ice condensate in clouds,"[56] is analytically divided into a two-dimensional horizontal grid, typically of about 100 square kilometers, and discrete vertical layers of one or two kilometers in depth; the primitive equations describing this mesh of grid elements "are solved as a function of time on this mesh" (14). *Sea ice* models include the physics governing both the non-Newtonian flow of liquids and the transfer of heat and salt within ice, as well as models of the albedo (the reflection of incident sunlight) from snow and ice (21). Models of *oceanic circulation* "are coupled to the atmosphere and ice models through the exchange of heat, salinity, and momentum at the boundary among components" and are similarly divided into extensive horizontal grids and a smaller set of vertical layers (16). *Land surface* modeling represents fluxes in energy, precipitation, and drainage as well as exchanges of energy and

55. Sismondo, "Models, Simulations, and Their Objects," 251.

56. U.S. Climate Change Science Program and the Subcommittee on Global Change Research, *Climate Models: An Assessment of Strengths and Limitations*. U.S. Climate Change Science Program, Synthesis and Assessment Product 3.1, July 2008, 13; hereafter cited in the text.

moisture between the land surface, the vegetation canopy, and the atmosphere, as well as variability among soil types, the representation of snow, the different functions of snow in its interaction with soil, the representation of ice sheets and mountain glaciers, horizontal water flow through river routing, the freezing of soil, and the coupling of groundwater models into land models (18–20). In addition to modeling contemporary data, GCMs incorporate paleoclimatic data by "assembling, manipulating, and transforming various recalcitrant materials annually laid down in tree ring and ice cores, laminated lake and ocean sediments, and ocean corals,"[57] using them as a proxy for an otherwise unrecorded history.

Only the advent of digital computing has made it possible to deal with the massive size and complexity of the data sets required to calculate the interactions within and between these GCMs. The computing power needed is enormous: "GCMs recompute the state of the entire atmosphere every fifteen to thirty simulated minutes. . . . At each time step, hundreds to thousands of complex calculations must be performed on each of the tens of thousands of grid boxes. . . . A typical state-of-the-art GCM currently requires tens to hundreds of hours [of supercomputer time] for a full-length 'run' of twenty to a hundred simulated years."[58]

Before this stage is reached, however, the data sets must be constructed, and they must be interpolated into the grids in a way that makes them computable. Observations of temperature, precipitation, barometric pressure, and so on have been collected more or less systematically in certain parts of the world since the nineteenth century, using various systems of instrumentation and calibration. But practices of observation have varied from place to place; collection sites have moved, or their environment has been altered by urban encroachment; the formulae used to calculate means have changed; coding and transcription errors have crept

57. David Demeritt, "Science Studies, Climate Change and the Prospects for Constructivist Critique," *Economy and Society* 35, no. 3 (2006), 460.

58. Edwards, "Representing the Global Atmosphere," 55.

into data series; in short, measurements tend to be "asynchronous, inhomogeneous, incomplete, and of insufficient or excessive resolution."[59] A number of procedures have been deployed to generate clean and consistent data sets. The World Meteorological Organization was founded in 1950 to establish common formats and standards for weather data and to consolidate observing systems. Mathematical algorithms have been established to process historical records, and painstaking empirical adjustments have been made to them. Paradoxically, "the constant improvement of data analysis and assimilation techniques made it nearly impossible to use those techniques to study climatic change," since "frequent revisions of the models, made in the interest of improving their performance on forecasts, rendered any given set of data incommensurable with those generated earlier or later by a different analysis regime."[60] By the late 1980s, then, there was a move to use a single "frozen" system of reanalysis to reprocess sensor data over a long duration into a single consistent data set.

This refined model of the data corrects previous forecasts against current observations, checks the observations for errors and inconsistencies, and synthesizes the raw data. Because of the manner in which they were collected, observational data are sparse for many areas: the sea, because data are collected by ships and widely dispersed buoys; much of the underdeveloped world, where the observational infrastructure is limited; and the vertical dimension of the atmosphere, where observations are collected mainly from satellite imagery and from a small network of radiosondes transported by balloon. Grid-point values must be constructed for the areas for which observations are sparse by extrapolation from current observational data, which are weighted more heavily than the posited values, and these constructed values are then interpolated into the grid. The data images thus created may often be more accurate than the observations from which they were derived, and when systematic values are gener-

---

59. Norton and Suppe, "Why Atmospheric Modeling Is Good Science," 85.
60. Edwards, *A Vast Machine*, 253; hereafter cited in the text.

ated based not on the location of observation stations but on the abstract grid that covers the simulated planet, the majority of those values are taken from the analysis model rather than directly from observations (254). General circulation models "simulate their own climates" (337) and then compare these simulated climates with the outputs of other models; when data are sparse or unreliable, the reconstructed data images constitute an additional source of experimental data.[61]

In addition to the "smoothing" of gridded data by interpolation between data points and the "tuning" by which values are adjusted in order to produce an outcome that agrees more closely with observations or "more closely corresponds with the modeler's judgment about . . . the *physical plausibility* of the change,"[62] climate modeling relies on a number of work-arounds called *parameterizations*. In an ideal world, it should be possible to internally generate complex microphysical processes, such as those that make up clouds, on the basis of "endogenous mathematical representations of the first-order physical principles governing the interaction" of the components of a climate system.[63] In practice, however, a large number of basic atmospheric events cannot be directly simulated. Instead, the sub-grid-scale physics of such phenomena as ocean eddies (which transport heat, salt, and momentum over large distances and carry up to 99% of the ocean's kinetic energy); gravity waves in the atmosphere; land surface albedo (reflectance); or convection, convective clouds, and small-scale turbulence in the atmosphere's boundary layer are represented indirectly by means of parameterizations—"mathematical functions and constants that capture the large-scale effects of smaller-scale processes without modeling them directly."[64] Such unresolved chaotic processes are one of the main challenges for

61. Norton and Suppe, "Why Atmospheric Modeling Is Good Science," 99.

62. Edwards, "Representing the Global Atmosphere," 56.

63. David Demeritt, "The Construction of Global Warming and the Politics of Science," *Annals of the Association of American Geographers* 91, no. 2 (2001), 317.

64. Edwards, *A Vast Machine*, 146.

climate modeling, and, bizarre as this may sound, they may be most appropriately simulated by the addition of random noise to the model.[65] Different models will parameterize the same processes differently: it is here that judgment and interpretation most fully enter the construction of climate models.

Because of the complexity of parameterized processes, because the data against which models are verified are never fully independent of modeling assumptions, and because possible future political action on emissions cannot be known in advance, climate simulation modeling has an inevitable craft dimension. Most of its achievements result "from painstaking experimentation with the model, including iterative model- or data-adjustment and tweaking."[66] That iterative dimension is a strength: just as rolling a die seems "so strongly chaotic that we consider it random" but over a long sequence of throws we can nevertheless predict an average of 3.5 (with certainty increasing with the length of the series), so do numerical climate models make accurate climate predictions by "running the weather prediction model long enough or many times with different (randomly chosen) initial conditions."[67]

Iteration and multiplication are the two key resources of the craft, and perhaps of science more generally: "Proper scientific data interpretations never advance a single model of data, but rather claim that the true situation falls within some family of models indistinguishable from the offered model in relevant respects."[68] The IPCC thus relies on the intercomparison of GCMs in drawing its conclusions. The data images constructed

65. Williams, "Modeling Climate Change," 2933–34; T. N. Palmer, "Towards the Probabilistic Earth-System Simulator: A Vision for the Future of Climate and Weather Prediction," *Quarterly Journal of the Royal Meteorological Society* 138 (April 2012), 842.

66. Matthias Heymann, "Constructing Evidence and Trust: How Did Climate Scientists' Confidence in their Models and Simulations Emerge?" in *The Social Life of Climate Change Models: Anticipating Nature*, ed. Kirsten Hastrup and Martin Skrydstrup (London: Routledge, 2013), 218.

67. Peter D. Ditlevsen, "Predictability in Question: On Climate Modeling in Physics," in Hastrup and Skrydstrup, *The Social Life of Climate Change Models*, 187–88.

68. Norton and Suppe, "Why Atmospheric Modeling Is Good Science," 101.

by GCMs have proliferated as modeling techniques evolve and global data change; yet they have also converged on a clear trend that tells us with near certainty that the earth has warmed by about 0.85° in the period 1880–2012[69] and that the predicted pattern of rising temperature was a good match for the actual historical record—but "if and only if the rise of greenhouse gas levels was put into the models."[70] The science of anthropogenic climate warming is grounded in interpretation and what Pierre Bourdieu would call a "'feel' for the game,"[71] but the epistemic solidity of the craft of modeling is a function of the protocols and practices of knowledge formation that are rooted in the resources and constraints of the institution of science.

V

That institution can be thought of in terms of its normative cultural dimension, or as a particular kind of infrastructure. The locus classicus for thinking about science as a set of cultural imperatives is Robert Merton's 1942 paper "The Normative Structure of Science," which defines its ethos as

> that effectively toned complex of values and norms which is held to be binding on the man of science. The norms are expressed in the form of prescriptions, proscriptions, preferences, and permissions. They are legitimatized in terms of institutional values. These imperatives, transmitted by precept and example and reinforced by sanctions are in varying degrees internalized by the scientist.[72]

69. IPCC Fifth Assessment Report, *Climate Change 2014 Synthesis Report: Summary for Policymakers*, https://www.ipcc.ch/pdf/assessment-report/ar5/syr/AR5_SYR_FINAL_SPM.pdf, 2.

70. Spencer Weart, "The Development of the Concept of Dangerous Anthropogenic Climate Change," in Dryzek, Norgaard, and Schlosberg, *The Oxford Handbook of Climate Change and Society*, 73.

71. Pierre Bourdieu, *Practical Reason: On the Theory of Action*, trans. Randal Johnson et al. (Stanford: Stanford University Press, 1998), 25.

72. Robert K. Merton, "The Normative Structure of Science," in *The Sociology of Science: Theoretical and Empirical Investigations* (Chicago: University of Chicago Press, 1973), 268–69; hereafter cited in the text.

Four sets of institutional imperatives are held (along with technical norms of empirical evidence and logical consistency) to constitute the scientific ethos: those of universalism, communism,
disinterestedness, and organized skepticism.

Universalism is expressed in the prescription "that truth-claims,
whatever their source, are to be subjected to *preestablished impersonal criteria*: consonant with observation and with previously
confirmed knowledge" (270). The personal attributes of the scientist (for example, their race, gender, or political or religious
beliefs) are irrelevant to that prescription.

Communism, in the sense of the common ownership of goods,
or communalism, entails the priority of the scientific community
over the individual producer. The discovery of a law or theory
conveys no rights other than, perhaps, that of eponymy. Property rights are minimal, since scientists' claim to their intellectual "property" is "limited to that of recognition and esteem
which . . . is roughly commensurate with the significance of the
increments brought to the common fund of knowledge" (273).
Science is therefore incompatible with the patenting of knowledge, and the identification of scientific research with the public
domain entails an imperative for its full and open diffusion. "Se-
crecy is the antithesis of this norm; full and open communication
its enactment" (274).

The norm of *disinterestedness* is not to be explained in moral
or psychological terms (altruism or a passion for knowledge, for
example) but as an effect of the "rigorous policing" imposed by
the institution, which flows from the "public and testable character of science"; the translation of this norm into practice "is
effectively supported by the ultimate accountability of scientists
to their compeers. The dictates of socialized sentiment and of
expediency largely coincide, a situation conducive to institutional
stability" (276).

Finally, the norm of *skepticism*

> is both a methodological and an institutional mandate. The tempo-
> rary suspension of judgment and the detached scrutiny of beliefs in

terms of empirical and logical criteria have periodically involved science in conflict with other institutions. Science which asks questions of fact, including potentialities, concerning every aspect of nature and society may come into conflict with other attitudes toward these same data which have been crystallized and often ritualized by other institutions. The scientific investigator does not preserve the cleavage between the sacred and the profane, between that which requires uncritical respect and that which can be objectively analysed. (277–78)

Now, Merton's description looks in many respects very dated today. Its image of the (male) scientist as an enlightened hero fearlessly confronting superstition and particularism looks a little idealized at a time when so much scientific research is conducted under contract for corporations in the military-industrial or pharmaceutical or agribusiness domains; and the notion of an incompatibility between the public orientation of science and the holding of restrictive intellectual property rights seems quaint when so much scientific research is now directed precisely to the registration and exploitation of patents. Merton does, however, understand this complex of norms as a dimension of the *institutional* structure of science, and his insistence that they are not to be understood in psychological or moral terms opens a pathway into contemporary (let me say: post-Foucauldian) accounts of science as a complex of normative, practical, technological, and regulatory infrastructures: a machinery for the generation and certification of knowledge.

An institution is *an ordering of practice that has been made durable.* The natural sciences are the preeminent institution of knowledge in the modern world (which they have helped bring into being), but their authority and legitimacy are derived not from our admiration for their achievements *as knowledge* but from a long history of combining a heterogeneous group of components with a number of strategic sociotechnical alliances; that combination has been formed over and over in a struggle to give shape and stability to the institution and to fight off threats to its authority.

The key components that have gone into the making of the

natural sciences have been an *ontology* (the postulation of a division rather than an interplay between human activity and a stable and self-identical nature); a corresponding *methodology* (a process of gridding, marking, numbering, and disposing that brings phenomena into evidence; the performative construction of a world understood as external and prior to the observer, and the effacement of the observer before the object described; the experimental manipulation of the natural world; a temporality of knowledge which is cumulative and forgetful, unlike the interpretive regimes of the law or the theater or the museum, which operate in constant relation to past interpretive orders); a set of core *languages* (the methodical description of entities, processes, relations, and interactions, and the systematic inscription of those descriptions in verifiable form; the use of powerful mathematical languages to formalize and extrapolate from description to general principles; mathematical or textual axioms formulated as being applicable across a number of domains); a set of *technologies* and *techniques* (instruments and craft practices designed for the observation, recording, and experimental manipulation of natural objects); a set of restrictively constituted *agents* (accredited subjects of knowledge who act as components of the machinery of scientific method); *communities of knowledge* and *instruments of dissemination and authority* (academies, professional associations, journals, peer-review processes, citation indexes, career structures); *funding mechanisms* (publicly or privately funded institutes and laboratories, competitively awarded grants); and a *legal and regulatory infrastructure* (standards of measurement, ethical standards, intellectual property rights, sanctions against the falsification of data). The authority, credibility, and legitimacy of science come from the ongoing, continuously renegotiated entanglement of this infrastructure with capitalist relations of production. It is from the successful translation of knowledge either into the industrial instruments that, in transforming the time, space, and materiality of nature, directly generate profits for capital, or into the technologies of health and information that increase the productivity of workers—*not* as a set of knowledges abstracted from application—that the natural sciences have acquired their immense prestige. At the same time, however, it is precisely this success that has led to the fragmentation of "science" into a multiplicity of sciences, dividing and recombining as their working methods and their alliances change and develop.

The discipline of climatology was built on an entanglement of protocols of truth with the fossil economy and, more specifically, on the long, anonymous, and humble labor of millions of professional and amateur scientists taking daily observations of temperature, precipitation, and barometric pressure over nearly two centuries—a labor from which generations of data sets were then continuously constructed. As with so much scientific work, the discipline's key developments over this period pertained to its military and commercial applications, and much of the explosion of funding for the construction of computer-driven general circulation models came, paradoxically, from the insistence by the two Bush administrations on the need for greater certainty before taking, *and as a way of indefinitely deferring*, political action on climate change. But what is visible to us now is not that anonymous labor of construction of data, not the applications to warfare or agriculture or navigation or flight, not the politics of funding or the immensely sophisticated craft of modeling, but a knowledge whose credibility derives (like that of the Law) from the folding of its infrastructures into the black box of a closed and apparently timeless institution that generates an unending supply of controlled and applicable research.

The most salient contemporary form of the institution of climate-change science is the Intergovernmental Panel on Climate Change (IPCC). Established in 1988 under the auspices of the World Meteorological Organization and the United Nations Environment Programme, it was mandated by the United Nations General Assembly to assess knowledge about the impacts of and possible responses to human-induced climate change. The IPCC is governed by a panel made up of selected government representatives and supported by a trust fund that covers the costs of the secretariat. It conducts no original research but seeks to represent "the full range of credible scientific opinion," identifying a consensus view where possible but noting reasons for disagreement elsewhere.[73] Its work is governed by rules of procedure, which underwent substantial revisions in 1993 and 1999, the latter partly in response to controversies over Chapter 8 of Working Group 1 in the Second Assessment Report (the chapter that found a "discernible" human influence on climate change).[74]

Since 1990 the IPCC has issued five assessment reports (the sixth is due to be finalized in 2022), each containing three volumes, one written by each of its three working groups: climate science (WG1), impacts of climate change (WG2), and economic and social dimensions (WG3). All working groups are led by two co-chairs, one from the developed and one from the developing world, and the teams of authors are chosen from government nominations. Drafts of reports are published for open review, and each working-group report contains a "Summary for Policymakers," approved by the full working group, and an overall "Synthesis Report Summary for Policymakers," which is approved, word by word in a slow and often contentious review process, in a plenary session attended by national government representatives and a small number of the lead authors.

The IPCC is thus not a self-governing scientific body but a technical advisory body with strong political input.[75] The authoritative nature of its reports derives from the consensual nature of the research that it summarizes and from the deep-rooted institution of interpretation that underpins it, but its strength perhaps lies in the fact that it breaks down the division between a value-neutral discourse of science and a value-laden policy discourse, together with the linear sequence that supposedly leads from the one to the other. Its virtue has been its hybridity, on

73. Edwards and Schneider, "Self-Governance and Peer Review," in Miller and Edwards, *Changing the Atmosphere*, 220.

74. Mike Hulme and Martin Mahony, "Climate Change: What Do We Know about the IPCC?" *Progress in Physical Geography* 34, no. 5 (2010), 709.

75. Mike Hulme, *Why We Disagree about Climate Change: Understanding Controversy, Inaction and Opportunity* (Cambridge: Cambridge University Press, 2009), 95–96.

the one hand acting as an expert witness and allowing climate models "to inhabit public venues, displaying to all their epistemic claims of offering credible climate predictions, as well as a display of force (computational power, visualizations, endorsements by public figures . . .)";[76] on the other, however, forging a difficult epistemic community between scientists and governments, in "a co-production of scientific claims, political decisions and social order."[77]

IPCC reports must manage questions of the limits of knowledge with scrupulous care, particularly given the way denialists have exploited methodological caution as an admission of weakness in the science. Central to this management process is the calculation and representation of uncertainty. General circulation models are mathematically deterministic, meaning that "they calculate a unique solution for a given set of initial conditions," and the probability of a system state outcome therefore has to be estimated across a range of such calculations, each with slightly different variables.[78] Apart from the general issues of the chaotic nature of climate systems and the extent to which significant parameterized variables are "questionable, indeterminate, and untestable,"[79] there are different philosophical approaches to and means of calculating degrees of uncertainty.[80] IPCC reports are couched in the language of qualitative levels of confidence and probabilistic ranges of quantified likelihood, but Shackley and Wynne argue that there is a measure of strategic ambiguity

76. Mike Hulme, "How Climate Models Gain and Exercise Authority," in Hastrup and Skrydstrup, *The Social Life of Climate Change Models*, 33.

77. Reiner Grundmann, "Climate Change and Knowledge Politics," *Environmental Politics* 16, no. 3 (2007), 414.

78. David Demeritt, "The Construction of Global Warming and the Politics of Science," 318.

79. Simon Shackley and Brian Wynne, "Representing Uncertainty in Global Climate Change Science and Policy: Boundary-Ordering Devices and Authority," *Science, Technology, & Human Values* 21, no. 3 (1996), 283.

80. Cf. Rob Swart, Lenny Bernstein, Minh Ha-Duong, and Arthur Petersen, "Agreeing to Disagree: Uncertainty Management in Assessing Climate Change, Impacts and Responses by the IPCC," *Climatic Change* 92 (2009), 5.

or "condensation of uncertainty" in the language, acting as "a boundary-ordering device, allowing multiple interpretations by modelers and other scientists, policy analysts, and policymakers, while holding these different groups together under a semblance of mutual understanding and cooperation,"[81] and while still "ordering the relations between science and policy so as to sustain the special cultural authority of science."[82]

VI

That "special cultural authority" can no longer be taken for granted, however, in the area of policy discourse itself, particularly not when the countervailing regime of knowledge in this area is that of economics.

Economists understand the manner in which we deal with climate change as a collective action problem, meaning that it is assessed in terms of the self-interested action of individuals in managing the use of a finite resource (the environment). Unlike transactions occurring between individuals who are present to each other, dealing with climate change is a matter of an intergenerational transaction across multiple national territories between parties whose interests are in principle quite different, and "since every generation benefits from its own emissions but the costs are deferred to future generations, they have an incentive not to control their emissions."[83]

Whereas most climate scientists believe that the consequences of not taking immediate and substantial action to mitigate global warming will be immensely destructive, and therefore in a very real sense beyond price, most economists seek to put a price on the benefits and costs of present action and future consequences. They do so by calculating and thereby maximizing "the weighted

81. Shackley and Wynne, "Representing Uncertainty," 286.

82. Shackley and Wynne, "Representing Uncertainty," 280.

83. Dale Jamieson, "The Nature of the Problem," in Dryzek, Norgaard, and Schlosberg, *The Oxford Handbook of Climate Change and Society*, 47.

sum of the utilities of individuals over time, space, and in different states of nature (with associated probabilities)."[84] The mechanism for making this calculation is an assessment of how individuals would behave in a market that facilitates the transaction of their different interests (or "utilities") by applying a discount rate to present expenditure for long-term benefits. The discount rate is calculated by a combination of time preferences based on consumption (on the assumption that future generations will be wealthier than us and that the utility of each dollar spent now therefore declines with that increase in wealth) and on investment (on the assumption that building the real market return on capital into our calculation means the present value of a dollar invested will diminish with increasing returns); in a perfect market the two rates would coincide.[85] Thus, if I assume a discount rate of 3% and a $100 cost of damage to the climate a hundred years from now, then it would be worth it to me to pay $5.20 for the mitigation of that damage. Another way of putting this would be to say that investing in climate mitigation is a rational thing to do if and only if it offers a higher rate of return than prevailing interest rates. The influential economist William Nordhaus, whose modeling dominated this area over many years, advocates a high return on capital, on the order of 3%–5%, which tilts the balance between present costs and future benefits toward the future, whereas the Stern Review, which advocates more immediate and more urgent action in the present, sets a discount rate close to zero (while opting for 550 parts per million of CO_2e in the atmosphere as the lowest politically feasible target—one that yields a 30%–70% chance of temperature rises exceeding 3°C and a 24% chance of rises exceeding 4°C).[86]

84. Simon Dietz, "From Efficiency to Justice: Utility as the Informational Basis of Climate Strategies, and Some Alternatives," in Dryzek, Norgaard, and Schlosberg, *The Oxford Handbook of Climate Change and Society*, 296.

85. K. Arrow et al., "Determining Benefits and Costs for Future Generations," *Science* 341, no. 6144 (July 2013), 349.

86. Nicholas Stern, *The Economics of Climate Change: The Stern Review* (Cambridge: Cambridge University Press, 2007), 295; cf. William Nordhaus, "Critical Assumptions

Mainstream economic analysis has difficulty handling questions of value that cannot be monetized—which means not only that the fundamental question of the *ethical* obligations of one generation toward later generations falls outside its scope but that questions of the just distribution of costs and benefits are set aside as involving inappropriate judgments of relative value (even though "ignoring these issues meant that economic valuations and analyses tended to reproduce the status quo in the distribution of income, wealth, and power").[87] There are three distinct but related questions of social justice in play here: (1) a question of historical *responsibility* for climate change (given the long residence time of carbon dioxide in the atmosphere, some 75% of cumulative emissions have been generated by the OECD countries and the former Soviet Union, meaning that "in effect, the wealthy countries have largely consumed the capacity of the atmosphere to absorb the wastes of industrial metabolism");[88] (2) a question of the present *scale* of contribution to climate change (Should "luxury" emissions of greenhouse gases by the socially privileged be counted equally with "survival" emissions from agriculture in developing countries?[89] What consequences should follow from the estimate that the carbon legacy of every child born in the United States is 18,500 metric tons of CO_2, while that of a child born in Bangladesh is only 136 metric tons?);[90] and (3) a question of the unequal *impacts* of climate change ("The rich countries of

in the Stern Review on Climate Change," *Science* 317, no. 5835 (July 2007), 201–2, and W. D. Nordhaus and J. Boyer, *Warming the World: Economic Modeling of Global Warming* (Cambridge, MA: MIT Press, 2000). The term "CO_2e" indicates a measure of all greenhouse gases expressed as the equivalent quantity of carbon dioxide.

87. John S. Dryzek, Richard B. Norgaard, and David Schlosberg, *Climate-Challenged Society* (Oxford: Oxford University Press, 2013), 45.

88. Will Steffen, "A Truly Complex and Diabolical Policy Problem," in Dryzek, Norgaard, and Schlosberg, *The Oxford Handbook of Climate Change and Society*, 23–24.

89. David Demeritt, "The Construction of Global Warming and the Politics of Science," 313.

90. Paul A. Murtaugh and Michael G. Schlax, "Reproduction and the Carbon Legacies of Individuals," *Global Environmental Change* 19 (2009), cited in Clive Hamilton, *Requiem for a Species: Why We Resist the Truth about Climate Change* (Abingdon: Routledge, 2010), 43.

the North do most of the emitting, but the poor countries of the South do most of the dying").[91]

The application of discount rates in economic analysis also tends to presuppose that there is no cost to deferring action on mitigation, a presupposition that neglects "the longevity of atmospheric carbon dioxide perturbation and ocean warming" and the irreversibility of many of the changes to the climate that have already taken place.[92] And it neglects the fundamental precautionary principle that governs other areas of human life. This is particularly true in the case of the calculation of potentially catastrophic risk with a low or uncertain chance of occurrence: the Nordhaus style of analysis

> ignore[s] outcomes that are as likely as the floods for which dams have long been built by the public sector, far more likely than the rare but catastrophic fire against which homeowners regularly buy insurance, and many times more likely than the terrorist attacks against which some countries now protect themselves to the tune of billions or even trillions of dollars per year.[93]

How is it possible for these apparently marginal risks to be built into the forms of probability analysis that pose a problem both for the economic analysis of climate mitigation and for the science to which it responds?

VII

Climate simulation models "are mathematically structured so that processes are represented by continuous, smooth differences," with the effect that catastrophic events tend to be excluded from representation.[94] Richard Posner defines a catastrophe as "an event that is believed to have very low probability of material-

91. Dale Jamieson, "The Nature of the Problem," 44.

92. Susan Solomon, Gian-Kasper Plattner, Reto Knutti, and Pierre Friedlingstein, "Irreversible Climate Change Due to Carbon Dioxide Emissions," *Proceedings of the National Academy of Sciences of the United States of America* 106, no. 6 (2009), 1708.

93. Dryzek, Norgaard, and Schlosberg, *Climate-Challenged Society*, 54.

94. Brian Wynne, "Strange Weather Again: Climate Science as Political Art," *Theory, Culture and Society* 27, no. 2–3 (2010), 296.

izing but that if it does materialize will produce a harm so great and sudden as to seem discontinuous with the flow of events that preceded it."[95] A modus operandi based in compromise and in a cautious approach to risks which are severe but whose probability is difficult to calculate might well lead to the exclusion of such apparently outlying possibilities, and it may be that the IPCC's scientific consensus assessments, far from exaggerating the problem of climate change (as denialist critics charge), are not pessimistic enough.[96]

Sudden discontinuities are called tipping points, "abrupt moments of change" occurring in a nonlinear fashion when the climate system crosses a threshold, triggering "a transition to a new state at a rate determined by the climate system itself and faster than the cause";[97] such tipping points, occurring in many moments of planetary history, may or may not be caused by human activity and may be pushed by biogeophysical feedback mechanisms into "tipping cascades."[98] Recent research indicates that the risk of large-scale discontinuities becomes significant with a rise in global warming of around 1°C and starts to become severe at a rise of 2.5°C.[99] The latest IPCC Assessment Report addresses the issue, in its usual cautious way, as follows:

95. Richard A. Posner, *Catastrophe: Risk and Response* (New York: Oxford University Press, 2004); cited in Martin L. Weitzman, "On Modeling and Interpreting the Economics of Catastrophic Climate Change," *The Review of Economics and Statistics* 91, no. 1 (2009), 1.

96. Freudenburg and Muselli, "Reexamining Climate Change Debates," 790; cf. David Spratt and Ian Dunlop, *What Lies Beneath: The Scientific Understatement of Climate Risks* (Melbourne: Breakthrough, 2017).

97. National Research Council, *Abrupt Climate Change: Inevitable Surprises* (Washington: National Academy Press, 2002); cited in Timothy M. Lenton et al., "Tipping Elements in the Earth's Climate System," *Proceedings of the National Academy of Sciences of the United States of America* 105, no. 6 (2008), 1786.

98. Will Steffen et al., "Trajectories of the Earth System in the Anthropocene," *Proceedings of the National Academy of Sciences of the United States of America* 115, no. 33 (2018), 8255.

99. Joel B. Smith et al., "Assessing Dangerous Climate Change through an Update of the Intergovernmental Panel on Climate Change (IPCC) 'Reasons for Concern,'" *Proceedings of the National Academy of Sciences of the United States of America* 106, no. 11 (2009), 4133.

With increasing warming, some physical and ecological systems are at risk of abrupt and/or irreversible changes. . . . Risks associated with such tipping points are moderate between 0 and 1°C additional warming, since there are signs that both warm-water coral reefs and Arctic ecosystems are already experiencing irreversible regime shifts (*medium confidence*). Risks increase at a steepening rate under an additional warming of 1 to 2°C and become high above 3°C, due to the potential for large and irreversible sea level rise from ice sheet loss.[100]

Examples of subsystems of the earth system that may be switched into a qualitatively different state by small perturbations include Arctic sea ice, the Amazon rain forest, the Greenland ice sheet, the Indian summer monsoon, and the Atlantic thermohaline circulation that carries warm surface currents from equatorial waters to the North Atlantic. The synthesis of present knowledge carried out by Timothy Lenton and his colleagues concludes that "a variety of tipping elements could reach their critical point within this century under anthropogenic climate change. The greatest threats are tipping the Arctic sea-ice and the Greenland ice sheet, and at least five other elements could surprise us by exhibiting a nearby tipping point."[101] The crucial thing about this research is that "the portrayal of climate tipping points as 'high impact–low probability' events no longer seems justified if future global warming is >2°C and certainly not if warming exceeds 4°C. . . . If we look at 'business-as-usual' type emissions scenarios with a mid-range climate sensitivity they readily produce around 4°C warming at the end of this century, and staying under 2°C warming is looking less likely than exceeding it."[102]

So what are the best current predictions of the likely range of global warming—and how successful is mitigation likely to be? Again, we can only talk about probable ranges, since what is in

100. IPCC Fifth Assessment Report, Box 2.4, 72.
101. Lenton et al., "Tipping Elements in the Earth's Climate System," 1791.
102. Timothy M. Lenton and Juan-Carlos Ciscar, "Integrating Tipping Points into Climate Impact Assessments," *Climatic Change* 117 (2013), 588.

question here is chaotic systems and the uncertainty of political action. The IPCC's Fifth Assessment Report uses a set of Representative Concentration Pathways based on population size, economic activity, lifestyle, energy use, land use patterns, technology, and climate policy, to make projections of four different twenty-first-century pathways of greenhouse-gas emissions and atmospheric concentrations, air-pollutant emissions, and land use; they include a stringent mitigation scenario, two intermediate scenarios, and one scenario with continuing high levels of greenhouse-gas emissions.[103] The modeling of these scenarios finds that in the baseline scenarios (those without additional mitigation), global mean increases in temperature by the year 2100 range from 3.7°C to 4.8°C above the average temperature for the years 1850–1900; when climate uncertainty is included, they range from 2.5°C to 7.8°C. These projections are made with high confidence (20). In most of these scenarios, "warming is *more likely than not* to exceed 4°C above pre-industrial levels by 2100" (18–19). A later report, the US government's Fourth National Climate Assessment, issued in November 2018, makes a similar warning that "without significant greenhouse gas mitigation, the increase in global annual average temperature could reach 9°F [5°C] or more by the end of this century."[104]

The only hope for saving the planet from devastating rises in temperature lies, then, with mitigation. But here the news is not good. "Limiting human-induced warming to less than 2°C relative to the period 1861–1880 with a probability of >66% would require cumulative CO_2 emissions from all anthropogenic sources since 1870 to remain below about 2900 $GtCO_2$. . . . About 1900 $GtCO_2$ had already been emitted by 2011" (10). And despite the implementation of various mitigation strategies, "total anthro-

103. IPCC Fifth Assessment Report, 8 (hereafter cited in the text).

104. "Overview," *Climate Science Special Report:* Fourth National Climate Assessment (NCA4), vol. 2: Impacts, Risks and Adaptation in the United States, https://www.globalchange.gov/browse/reports/overview-fourth-national-climate-assessment-volume-ii-impacts-risks-and-adaptation/ (Washington: US Global Change Research Program, 2018), 11.

pogenic [greenhouse-gas] emissions have continued to increase over 1970 to 2010 with larger absolute increases between 2000 and 2010" (5); they are currently increasing exponentially at a rate of around 3%,[105] and even under the most unrealistically optimistic assumptions, by 2100, they will have increased by three thousand billion metric tons relative to 1870 levels.[106] It is apparent that global emissions have shifted inexorably in the direction of the IPCC's worst-case scenario; reversing that trend would require rapid and far-reaching reductions in CO_2 emissions—about a 45% decrease from 2010 levels by 2030, reaching "net zero" around 2050.[107] To put this differently: having just a 46% chance of keeping temperature rises at 2°C would require stabilizing carbon-equivalent greenhouse-gas concentrations at 450 parts per million, but "even an optimistic interpretation of the current framing of climate change implies that stabilization much below 650 ppmv CO_2e [parts per million by volume CO_2 equivalent] is improbable," and "even this level of stabilization assumes rapid success in curtailing deforestation, an early reversal of current trends in non-CO_2 greenhouse gas emissions and urgent decarbonization of the global energy system."[108]

What would this probable increase in global mean temperatures of 4°C look like? Kevin Anderson puts it like this. First, that mean temperature would equate to around 5°–6°C warming of global mean land surface temperature. Translated into local effects,

a 4°C world would likely see the hottest days in China being 6–8°C warmer than the hottest days experienced in recent heat waves that China has struggled to cope with; Central Europe would see heat waves much like the one in 2003, but with 8°C on top of the highest temperatures; during New York's summer heat waves the warmest

105. Kevin Anderson and Alice Bows, "Reframing the Climate Change Challenge in Light of Post-2000 Emission Trends," *Philosophical Transactions of the Royal Society A* 366 (2008), 3877.
106. Hamilton, *Requiem for a Species*, 21.
107. IPCC, Summary for Policymakers, *Global Warming of 1.5°C* (2018), 14.
108. Anderson and Bows, "Reframing the Climate Change Challenge," 3877.

days would be around 10–12°C hotter—all as a consequence of an average global warming of around 4°C. As it is, our infrastructures and our way of living are not attuned to these temperatures, with the very real prospect of dire repercussions for many—particularly for vulnerable, communities.[109]

In addition, however, a warming of 4°C would trigger a range of tipping points that would insert positive feedback into the climate system, leading to a cascading instability that would have potentially catastrophic consequences. Such a future would be "incompatible with any reasonable characterisation of an organised, equitable and civilised global community."[110]

VIII

How do I know this is true? I'm not a scientist, I haven't done original research, I have nothing more than my reading of the research—or, in almost all cases, of informed summaries of the research—to guide my judgment.[111]

What I "know" is that the scientific research on which I base my judgment is detailed, methodical, cumulative, constantly subjected to questioning, and grounded in an institution which is, as far as the science itself is concerned, dispassionate and structurally self-critical. The knowledge asserted by the denialist counterinstitutions is not based in detailed and methodical

109. Kevin Anderson, "Climate Change Going Beyond Dangerous—Brutal Numbers and Tenuous Hope," *Development Dialogue* 61, no. 1 (2012), 28.

110. Anderson, "Climate Change Going Beyond Dangerous," 29; cf. Mark New et al., "Four Degrees and Beyond: The Potential for a Global Temperature Increase of Four Degrees and its Implications," *Philosophical Transactions of the Royal Society A* 369 (2011), 6–19.

111. For two recent examples of such informed summaries, cf. K. Richardson et al., *Climate Change—Global Risks, Challenges and Decisions: Synthesis Report* (Copenhagen: Museum Tusculanum, 2009); and "Executive Summary," in *Climate Science Special Report: Fourth National Climate Assessment (NCA4)*, vol. 1, https://science2017.globalchange .gov/chapter/executive-summary/ (Washington: U.S. Global Change Research Program, 2017).

research, is in most cases demonstrably incoherent and has been repeatedly falsified, and is grounded in the particular interests of the fossil-fuel industries. Climate modeling doesn't provide me with a *truth* about the state of the natural world; it gives me a judgment of the probabilities as they can best be constructed by existing scientific procedure and on the basis of the assumptions and protocols that underpin it. More generally, my relative confidence is a function of the fact that I am an educated member of the knowledge class, with a commitment to the "culture of careful and critical discourse" that constitutes the prevailing ethos of that class;[112] and it is a function of the particular kind of concern that I feel.

Much of the responsibility for the wretched inadequacy and the belatedness of mitigation strategies lies with corporations, the media, and the political institutions which have permitted themselves to indulge a willful and dangerous ignorance that "balances" the degradation of the climate against the interests of the fossil economy. While pretending to take an even-handed approach, politicians have acted as the agents of the polluting industries that pay for their election campaigns. They have espoused voluntary programs and the semblance of action, while doing just enough to avoid public exposure. They have acted with reckless contempt for the science.[113] But indeed, there are powerful disincentives for all of us to believe in the reality of climate change, and there is ultimately little point in blaming individuals. It's a matter of a whole complex system, the fossil economy and the ways of life it has sustained, that gives everyone a stake in its continued survival and makes it almost impossible to grasp—to

---

112. Alvin Gouldner, *The Future of Intellectuals and the Rise of the New Class: A Frame of Reference, Theses, Conjectures, Arguments and an Historical Perspective on the Role of Intellectuals and Intelligentsia in the International Class Contest of the Modern Era* (New York: Oxford University Press, 1979), 27; and cf. my commentary in *Cultural Studies and Cultural Value* (Oxford: Clarendon Press, 1995), 114.

113. These lines paraphrase Clive Hamilton's denunciation of the Australian Howard Government in *Scorcher*, 14–15.

grasp emotionally as well as intellectually—the enormity of the damage being done to the planet.

And yet . . .

I have tried to keep this chapter as dispassionate as I could. But I'm not dispassionate. I'm angry that the world I live in may be destroyed by the greed and the blind stupidity of the business-people and the politicians and the compliant media who have been so deeply invested in the fossil economy that they have allowed themselves to turn their eyes away from the science that has patiently projected and explained the consequences of carbon pollution. I have children who should, if the planet survives, live another 50 years; I have grandchildren who, if the planet survives, should live another 80 or 90 years. I am desperately unhappy that they may not—that their planet, that my world, may no longer be habitable, or that if it is it will be overwhelmingly a place of misery. This book has argued that all knowledge, including knowledge of climate change that seems on the face of it amenable to proof and disproof and that has direct consequences for the survival of human and nonhuman life on earth, is formed within and according to the protocols of specific institutions of interpretation, and that while it is never in any absolute sense "relative," it is always, in principle and in practice and in both good and bad faith, contestable and conflicted. But knowledge is never simply a reflex function of institutions, and it is never simply detachable from social interest. It is always at once a way of representing the world and a form of social organization that carries our position in and toward the world. I declare my interest, and I declare my anger.

Coda:
Interpretation and Judgment

In the introduction to *The Critique of Judgment*, Kant distinguishes between two distinct powers of judgment that he calls "determining" (*bestimmend*) and "reflective" (*reflectirend*). Each is an aspect of the general role of judgment, which is to understand the relation of the particular to the universal. But whereas *determining* judgments look like what Kant had previously understood to be the sole function of judgment, that is, the subsumption of the particular under an antecedently given universal, *reflective* judgments have a new and somewhat anomalous role in his work. These are judgments that take place when "only the particular is given, for which the universal [*das Allgemeine*] is to be found."[1] They must generate their own laws, in a kind of bootstrapping operation that takes place in the absence of any pregiven framework.

---

1. Immanuel Kant, *Critique of the Power of Judgment*, ed. Paul Guyer, trans. Paul Guyer and Eric Matthews (Cambridge: Cambridge University Press, 2000), 66; hereafter cited in the text. I use the more familiar abbreviated title in my discussion. The German text I have consulted is *Kritik der Urtheilskraft, Kants Werke* V, Akademie Textausgabe (Berlin: de Gruyter, 1968), 179.

Kant includes three kinds of judgment in this category: judgments about whether an object is beautiful or sublime; teleological judgments that ascribe purposive functionality to natural things; and empirical scientific inquiry as it seeks to generalize its findings. Aesthetic judgments, which are subjective but have a normative validity, are evaluative, whereas teleological and scientific judgments are cognitive, and this division repeats *en abyme* the split between the single, cognitive mode of judgment posited in *The Critique of Pure Reason* and the modes of reflective judgment posited in *The Critique of Judgment.* More generally, it repeats and, in the same movement, undermines the deep division between cognitive and evaluative judgment that Kant's philosophy institutes and authorizes for all subsequent Western thought.

In the case of aesthetic judgment, there is in fact no general law under which the particular judgment can be subsumed other than the principle that underpins human subjectivity itself and that one can therefore "presuppose in everyone else" (97). Because aesthetic judgments are subjectively derived from feelings (of pleasure or displeasure) rather than from any objective property of the object, judgments that something is beautiful or sublime are not based on concepts, and yet they have a necessity which is that of "the assent of **all** to a judgment that is regarded as an example of a universal rule that one cannot produce" (121).[2]

Kant thus sets in play the paradox of the simultaneous impossibility and necessity of an a priori principle that would ground the universal validity of judgments of the beautiful and sublime (a principle that is "*necessarily* subjective" and yet "in effect, not subjective").[3] This a priori principle, he argues, is that of the op-

2. Sianne Ngai, following Stanley Cavell and pointing to the resonance of Kant's account of reflective judgment with her own account of the category of the "interesting," stresses the compulsory aspect of this need to seek assent: our "inescapably subjective feelings of pleasure or displeasure" are what we "cannot *not* share." Sianne Ngai, *Our Aesthetic Categories: Zany, Cute, Interesting* (Cambridge, MA: Harvard University Press, 2012), 117.

3. Barbara Herrnstein Smith, *Contingencies of Value: Alternative Perspectives for Critical Theory* (Cambridge, MA: Harvard University Press, 1988), 68.

eration of a "common sense" (122) which is equivalent to "the state of mind in the free play of the imagination and the understanding": a "subjective relation" that must nevertheless, as "common" [*gemein*], "be valid for everyone" (103) and must operate *as though* the judgment were objective (that is, it operates as a kind of simulacrum of cognition).

Now, making a judgment seems like a different activity from making an interpretation: it is perhaps more lawlike, less tentative. Yet, as we have seen, Kant's concept of reflective judgment includes both cognitive and evaluative acts—which is to say that it already has something of the breadth of reference that I have claimed for my use of the concept of interpretation. I spoke of interpretation as "a procedure . . . for imputing intention or pattern to an object or an event or a set of data by placing it within an ordered series," where the "ordered series" corresponds to the forms of generality (law, rule, principle) that Kant posits as a necessary component of the power of judgment. I want now to look back briefly over the four case studies that have made up the body of this book in order to think about how they work in relation to Kant's dichotomy of determining and reflective judgment.

The judicial determinations made in *District of Columbia v. Heller* are, of course, directly and literally *judgments*. On the face of it they would seem to conform to the principle that legal judgment works by applying the general normative principle that is articulated as law to the facts of a case. It is true that the judges on each side of the decision spend a lot of time seeking to explicate the particular facts that would elucidate the constitutional amendment: questions of grammar and semantics, questions of historical context, and so on. But the law, the general normative principle which is supported by these facts, is itself the primary object of interpretation here. Much of the judges' efforts goes into a meta-analysis of the hermeneutic principles by which the amendment is to be understood: How strictly and how literally should constitutional law be interpreted? What degree of determinacy should be imputed to its provisions? What are the relevant interpretive canons? Is constitutional interpretation similar or dissimilar to common-law interpretation? How does the letter of the law relate to developing legal doctrine? These questions belong to a higher level of generality than that of the Second Amendment, beyond which lie questions of the still more general normative principles by which this particular normative principle is to be understood: for example, the principle that popular sovereignty should take precedence over the sovereign state. Finally, the judgment that is enunciated in the majority decision involves the performative construction of a right. The work of interpretation, deferring to a text which its very activity creates as an interpretable object, constructs the universal that is supposed to preexist it.

The judgments made in *Heller* are reflective, then. So, in one sense, are the judgments made about *The Merchant of Venice*, which we can take to be aesthetic judgments to the extent that they concern questions of genre, of artistic pattern and balance, of the interplay of character and plot, and of thematically structured symbolism. But are they not also moral judgments, judgments of practical reason, and to that extent invoking "a determinate concept of a law" (169)? Moral judgments are extensively represented *within* the play: the choice of casket is made according to moral principles (the priority of risky gift over calculation) and in the exercise of moral freedom; the conflict between Antonio and Portia, on the one hand, and Shylock on the other counterposes behavior based in contractual obligation to behavior based in customary principles. More generally, the judgment that we make about Shylock is a general moral or political judgment grounded in what we may take to be the play's stereotype of the usurious Jew. Each theatrical interpretation acts out a moral stance—one of acceptance or of condemnation—toward that stereotype, and its "judgment" is at once determining, in relation to an implicitly invoked universal principle, and reflective, to the extent that that principle is never given in advance.

The aesthetic regimes of the sacred and of the museum that I discuss in chapter 3 contain a similar ambivalence that reflects the central role played by iconoclasm in each. Religion asserts a universal law, and iconoclasm proclaims that it acts in accordance with it; but the conflict over the icon undoes that relationship between practice and the law by making the latter subject to interpretation. In the case of the museum, the valorization of a formal beauty that stands outside time is undone by the temporality of endless self-supersession that constitutes the dynamic of the post-Romantic work of art. The question of whether, if we wish to take seriously the "ontological communion" between the image and what it represents, we can understand its conditions of possibility without relying on a quasi-theological regime of reading is an open one: I seek to answer it in the affirmative, as a question of reflective judgment, but theology, with its apparatus of timeless laws, is deeply embedded in any conception of presence.

Finally, the modality of scientific reason that informs the simulation modeling of climate systems brings into question some central ambiguities in Kant's account of science. In *The Critique of Pure Reason* and *Metaphysical Foundations of Natural Science*, Kant understands scientific reason as having an apodictic certainty grounded in the systematic rules of mathematics. Mathematics is the foundation of the metaphysics of nature that allows empirical data to be subsumed under general laws such as those of causality, and scientific reasoning thus involves judgments which are determining. In *The Critique of Judgment*, however, Kant complicates this picture by finding that these general laws have only a very general applicability, since

> there is such a manifold of forms in nature, as it were so many modifications of the universal transcendental concepts of nature that are left undetermined by those laws that the pure understanding gives *a priori*, since these pertain only to the possibility of a nature (as object of the senses) in general, that there must nevertheless also be laws for it which, as empirical, may indeed be contingent in accordance with the insight of **our** understanding, but which, if they are to be called laws (as is also required by the concept of a nature), must be regarded as necessary on a principle of the unity of the manifold, even if that principle is unknown to us. (66)

Understanding these more particular laws thus requires the exercise of reflective judgment which must discover a principle that it cannot find experientially: it "can only give itself such a transcendental principle as a law, and cannot derive it from anywhere else" (66), and it does so by forming the hypothesis of the purposiveness of nature—"a special *a priori* concept that has its origin strictly in the reflecting power of judgment" (68).

The simulation modeling of climate systems combines empirical observation with mathematical algorithms in a relation which is not hierarchical and in which mathematical parameterizations may take the place of observational data. Indeed, the peculiarity of computer modeling using vast data sets is that the traditional dialectic of hypothesis and observation, theory and experiment, deduction and induction seems to be replaced by an autopoietic operation in which the particular and the general seek each other out and, in a sense, construct each other. This is closer to Kant's account of reflective judgment, and it certainly lacks the subsumptive ordering of the particular and the universal that characterizes determining judgment.

In each of my case studies, then, even those areas that one might have expected to be closest to the model of determining judgment instead turn out to deploy procedures that are more like those of reflective judgment, to the extent that we might perhaps take reflective judgment as a *general* (but not exclusive) model of sense-making. Kant's complication of the work of judgment opens the way, I think, for the conception of interpretation I propose as "the complex of knowing, interpreting, judging, valuing, feeling, and consequentially acting which works as an inseparable whole in every act of making sense of things."

Methodologically, *The Critique of Judgment* marks a shift away from the individualism of Kant's earlier work, where judgment takes place in isolation (or rather, takes place *nowhere*, performed by a transcendental subject) rather than in company. In the later book, aesthetic judgment is understood to be "reflective" in the sense that, as Samuel Weber puts it, "it reflects an effort and a process of judgment itself—Kant calls this the judging subject—

rather than a cognition of the object," and this process is always and necessarily incomplete.[4] Inherent in it is the necessity of appealing from the reflective judgment to the "common sense" in which it will (or rather, *should*) receive its validation (173).[5] The subject that experiences itself in reflection recognizes itself as a historical and social being in the act of judging, where it experiences what others might be likely to experience too. This historicity of the subject which flows from the invocation of a communal standard of judgment is nevertheless still abstracted from any specific historical conditions of existence: the community to which the subject appeals is not internally differentiated by the relations of inclusion and exclusion that are formative of group existence.

Neither does my own model of the regime and the interpretive institution specify at any level of descriptive detail who occupies the position of the interpreting subject. I do, however, try to specify the positions themselves; that is, I seek to describe the institutional conditions of possibility of interpretation in particular domains of knowledge and value, the distinctive protocols of evidence and proof that they deploy, and the kinds of knowing or valuing or feeling subject that are appropriate to them, together with the modes of power and authority, of inclusion and exclusion, that they facilitate. My interest is in social conflict over interpreting and judging rather than in cognitive universals.

Kant's account of judgment, by contrast, is a model of Law: of the subsumption of particular instances under a general rule, or of the quest to find the as yet unknown rule that might cor-

4. Samuel Weber, "The Foundering of Aesthetics: Thoughts on the Current State of Comparative Literature," in *The Comparative Perspective on Literature: Approaches to Theory and Practice*, ed. Clayton Koelb and Susan Noakes (Ithaca: Cornell University Press, 1988), 65.

5. Kant distinguishes two ways of understanding *sensus communis*: (1) as "common sense," that is, healthy but uncultivated "vulgar" understanding (*der gemeine Menschenverstand*), and (2) his preferred interpretation, as "the idea of a communal sense [*die Idee eines gemeinschaftlichen Sinnes*], i.e., a faculty for judging that in its reflection takes account (*a priori*) of everyone else's way of representing in thought, in order as it were to hold its judgment up to human reason as a whole. . . ." (173).

respond to those instances. This model of a quasi-legal ordering that takes place in accordance with a hierarchy of authority is intimately bound up with the way we continue to understand knowing, interpreting, and judging, and in this book I have described a number of examples of it: the procedures of constitutional interpretation in *Heller*; the imposition of one interpretation of the law over another in the courtroom in *The Merchant of Venice*, as well as the evolution of contract law as it embodies and enables changes in behavior; the theological Law that motivates and justifies iconoclasm; and the scientific and mathematical laws that inform climate modeling. But in each of these cases the logic of a subsumptive ordering turns out to be problematic.

Without wanting to discount the validity, for certain domains, of the model of determining judgment, I take it that Kant's account of reflective judgment better describes the simultaneous necessity and impossibility of interpretation that underlies each of those successfully achieved interpretations that the book describes—an "impossibility" because no reading of general rules and the orderings they govern can ever acquire the lawlike authority it seeks. If there are laws, then—the question at the heart of Kafka's "The Problem of Our Laws"—it may be that they resemble the Law that is described in another parable of Kafka's: a Law that applies only to me; that will however never be available to me; and that stands as a figure of whatever resists knowledge, judgment, and interpretation.[6]

---

6. Franz Kafka, "Vor dem Gesetz," in *Sämtliche Erzählungen*, ed. Paul Raabe (Frankfurt am Main: Fischer, 1970), 131–32; "Before the Law," in *Franz Kafka: The Complete Short Stories*, ed. Nahum M. Glatzer (New York: Schocken, 1971), 3–4.

Index

Made in the USA
Coppell, TX
07 January 2022

71182145R00129